THE CAMPAIGNS FOR VICKSBURG, 1862–1863

The siege of Vicksburg. *Courtesy of the Library of Congress*

LEADERSHIP LESSONS

The Campaigns for Vicksburg 1862–1863

KEVIN J. DOUGHERTY

CASEMATE

Philadelphia & Newbury

Published in the United States of America and Great Britain in 2011 by
CASEMATE
908 Darby Road, Havertown, PA 19083
and
17 Cheap Street, Newbury, Berkshire, RG14 5DD

Copyright 2011 © Kevin J. Dougherty

ISBN 978-1-61200-003-9
Digital Edition: 978-1-61200-014-5

Cataloging-in-publication data is available from the Library of Congress
and the British Library.

10 9 8 7 6 5 4 3 2 1

Printed and bound in the United States of America.

For a complete list of Casemate titles please contact:

CASEMATE PUBLISHERS (US)
Telephone (610) 853-9131, Fax (610) 853-9146
E-mail: casemate@casematepublishing.com

CASEMATE PUBLISHERS (UK)
Telephone (01635) 231091, Fax (01635) 41619
E-mail: casemate-uk@casematepublishing.co.uk

Contents

Introduction   7

PART ONE: UNDERSTANDING VICKSBURG

Leadership During the Civil War   12
Vicksburg Campaign Overview   25

PART TWO: LEADERSHIP VIGNETTES

1 — The Mighty Mississippi: Winfield Scott and Strategic Vision   40
2 — The Battle of Corinth: Ulysses Grant and
Creating the Necessary Conditions   45
3 — Set Up to Fail: The Confederate Departmental
System and Strategic Organization   49
4 — The Wrong Man for the Job: John Pemberton
and the Peter Principle   53
5 — The Confederate Conflict: John Pemberton and
Poor Relations with Subordinates   58
6 — The Federal Team: Ulysses Grant and Positive
Relations with Subordinates   63
7 — Chickasaw Bayou: William Sherman and
Knowing When to Quit   68
8 — The Self-Made Man and the Reinvented Man:
The Raids of Forrest and Van Dorn   73
9 — Other Failed Attempts: Ulysses Grant and Perseverance   83
10 — A Close Call for the Federals: Charles Dana and
Dealing with Weakness   92
11 — Asymmetric Warfare: Zedekiah McDaniel,
Francis Ewing, and Innovation   96
12 — Running the Gauntlet: Ulysses Grant, David Porter,
and Unity of Effort   102
13 — Helping Run the Gauntlet: William Sherman and
Playing a Supporting Role   109

Contents *(continued)*

14 — The Battle of Port Gibson: John Bowen and
    Technical Competence   113
15 — "Cutting Loose": Ulysses Grant and Taking Risk   119
16 — Confederate Confusion: John Pemberton and
    Frame of Reference   126
17 — Grant Heads Northeast: Ulysses Grant and
    Clear Communication   131
18 — The Battle of Raymond: John Gregg and
    Understanding the Situation   137
19 — The Battle of Jackson: Joseph Johnston and Pessimism   141
20 — The Battle of Champion Hill: Ulysses Grant and
    Personal Presence   146
21 — Retreat from Champion Hill: Lloyd Tilghman and
    Personal Sacrifice   150
22 — Assault on Vicksburg: Thomas Higgins and
    Heroic Leadership   154
23 — Problem Removed: John McClernand and
    Destructive Ambition   158
24 — Siege Warfare: Henry Foster and Problem Solving   163
25 — The Federal Mine: John Logan and Initiative   168
26 — Surrender and Parole: Ulysses Grant and Pragmatism   173
27 — Little Help from Above: Jefferson Davis and
    Strategic Direction   177
28 — A Decisive Victory: Abraham Lincoln and Admitting
    When You're Wrong   182
29 — The Meridian Campaign: William Sherman and
    Creating Opportunity   187
30 — A Tragic Hero: John Pemberton and Selfless Service   193

    Conclusions about Leadership During
        the Vicksburg Campaign   197
    Appendix
        Vicksburg Campaign Order of Battle   203
    Bibliography   233

Introduction

LONG RELEGATED TO A SECONDARY POSITION BEHIND GETTYSBURG, Vicksburg has more recently earned consideration by many historians as the truly decisive battle of the Civil War. Indeed, Vicksburg is fascinating on many levels. The Federal campaign of maneuver that isolated the Confederates in the city was masterful. The Navy's contribution to the Federal victory was significant. The science of the fortifications and siege tactics are rich in detail. The human drama of Vicksburg's beleaguered civilian population is compelling. But perhaps more than any other factor, the key to the Federal victory at Vicksburg was simply better leadership. It is this aspect of the campaign that *Leadership Lessons from the Vicksburg Campaign* endeavors to explore.

The outcome of several Civil War battles can be easily explained by one side's superior leadership over the other. In the Shenandoah Valley, Major General Thomas "Stonewall" Jackson overcame a tremendous disparity in troop strength by outgeneraling a motley assortment of Federal commanders. At Chancellorsville, Major General Joseph Hooker lost his nerve in the face of General Robert E. Lee's audacious leadership. At Gettysburg, Colonel Joshua Chamberlain saved Little Round Top for the Federals by his strong leadership in crisis. In an opposite way, Major General William Rosecrans abandoned hope and fled the battlefield at Chickamauga in his moment of crisis. In the subject of this study, Vicksburg was decided as much if not more by the leadership differential between Major General Ulysses Grant and Lieutenant General John Pemberton as it was by the troops they led.

Grant's genius lay not in tactics so much as it did at the operational and strategic levels of war. He was able to conceptualize and to place events in a larger context. He understood the big picture and was able to articulate his intent to a team of competent subordinates and fellow commanders with whom he built an environment of cooperation and shared purpose. Vicksburg was a leadership triumph for Grant.

Pemberton, on the other hand, was more of a technician who was most comfortable dealing with known quantities in a sequential way. When faced with an ambiguous and uncertain situation, Pemberton became paralyzed. His impersonal and bureaucratic approach to leadership distanced him from his subordinates, who responded by being suspicious, uncooperative, and sometimes even hostile. Pemberton was a good man, but he found himself beyond his capabilities at Vicksburg. For him, the campaign was a leadership failure.

If Pemberton was going to be successful at Vicksburg, he would need clear guidance and support from President Jefferson Davis and nominal theater commander General Joseph Johnson. Both these leaders failed to provide Pemberton the direction he needed, thus the Confederate leadership failure at Vicksburg was not limited to Pemberton.

On the other hand, Grant benefited from strong senior leadership. General Winfield Scott had provided the Federals with a proper appreciation of the importance of the Mississippi River with his Anaconda Plan at the beginning of the war, and President Abraham Lincoln trusted, supported, and understood Grant. The Federal command hierarchy enjoyed the synergy and unity that the Confederates lacked.

Leadership Lessons from the Vicksburg Campaign explores the Vicksburg Campaign through this lens of leadership. Part One of the book is called Understanding Vicksburg. It contains sections on Leadership During the Civil War and a Campaign Overview. The first section familiarizes the reader with the challenges, characteristics, and styles associated with leadership during the Civil War in general. The second section outlines the Vicksburg Campaign by explaining the strategic significance of the Mississippi River and Vicksburg, detailing the opposing forces and the terrain, discussing the failed attempts to capture Vicksburg over the winter of 1862–1863, tracing the brilliant campaign of maneuver and logistics that allowed Grant to ultimately lay siege to the city, and concluding with the significance of the Federal victory. Part Two of the book consists of thirty Leadership Vignettes that span the actions of the most senior leaders down to those of individual soldiers. Each vignette focuses the Campaign Overview to the specific situation in order to provide the appropriate context, explains the action in the terms of leadership lessons learned, and concludes with a short, bulletized list of "take-aways" to crystallize the lessons for the reader. The section ends with a set of Conclusions about Leadership during the Vicksburg Campaign. The book also includes a campaign order of battle as an appendix and a comprehensive bibliography.

Leadership Lessons from the Vicksburg Campaign is intended to appeal to a variety of readers. Civil War historians will appreciate its detail in recounting the campaign. Students of the military art will be drawn to its emphasis on the importance of leadership in determining a battle's outcome. Leaders will find practical examples of positive and negative leadership in action in the vignettes. The Vicksburg Campaign was decided by more than just shot and shell, and *Leadership Lessons from the Vicksburg Campaign* offers the unique perspective of the campaign as a leadership laboratory.

Pemberton's headquarters, Vicksburg. *Courtesy of the Library of Congress*

Part One

Understanding Vicksburg

Leadership During the Civil War

LEADERSHIP IS THE PROCESS OF INFLUENCING OTHERS TO WORK TO-wards organizational goals; it provides purpose, direction, and motivation. In war, it is the most dynamic element of combat power. Civil War leaders at Vicksburg and elsewhere were shaped by their frame of reference and background, the military organizational structure, the rudimentary development of staffs and communications, and their own capabilities and limitations. The lessons they learned during the campaign are transferrable to a variety of leadership situations, both in battle and elsewhere.

FRAME OF REFERENCE AND BACKGROUND

Many Civil War generals were products of the United States Military Academy at West Point. Of the Civil War's sixty major battles, West Pointers commanded both sides in fifty-five of them. Even in the other five battles, a West Pointer commanded on one side or the other. All told, 151 Confederate and 294 Federal generals were West Point graduates. At Vicksburg, West Point was represented among others by Ulysses Grant (Class of 1843), James McPherson (Class of 1853), and William Sherman (Class of 1840) on the Federal side, and John Pemberton (Class of 1837), Joseph Johnston (Class of 1829), John Bowen (Class of 1853), and Carter Stevenson (Class of 1838) on the Confederate side.

Founded in 1802, West Point emerged as a premier institution under the superintendency of Sylvanus Thayer. Beginning in 1817, Thayer broadened and standardized the curriculum, established a system to measure class standing, organized classes around small sections, improved cadet discipline, created the office of commandant of cadets, and improved military training. He also used West Point to stimulate a systematic American study of war, which was largely based on the European theorist Antoine Henri de Jomini.

Jomini was a product of the Enlightenment, and he sought to interpret and explain the genius of Napoleon by finding natural laws that governed the art of war. In 1838, Jomini wrote the *Summary of the Art of War*, which was translated into English in 1854 by Major O. F. Winship and Lieutenant E. E. McLean. West Point's strongest advocate of Jominian thought was Dennis Hart Mahan, who joined the faculty in 1832 and became West Point's principal instructor of warfare. A staunch proponent of Napoleonic methods, Mahan immersed his students—such as Henry Halleck—in the influences of Jomini. In 1846, Halleck published *Elements of Military Art and Science*, a work which was the product of this exposure. Although it was never adopted as a West Point text, Halleck's book was probably the most widely read strategic treatise among American military officers. According to David Donald, the end result was that, "Every West Point general in the [Civil War] had been exposed to Jomini's ideas, either directly, by reading Jomini's writings or abridgments or expositions of them; or indirectly, by hearing them in the classroom or perusing the works of Jomini's American disciples." James Little agrees, claiming, "Many a Civil War general went into battle with a sword in one hand and Jomini's *Summary of the Art of War* in the other."

Jomini offered an almost geometrical approach to warfare, and among his most pervasive theories was his notion of "interior lines." For Jomini, the problem was to bring the maximum possible force to bear against an inferior enemy force at the decisive point. This condition could best be achieved by properly ordering one's lines of communication relative to the enemy's, so that the friendly force possessed interior lines. Interior lines allowed the friendly commander to move parts of his army more rapidly than could an enemy operating on exterior lines. In this way, the force operating on interior lines could defeat in detail an enemy operating on exterior lines.

One way to gain interior lines is by central position, placing one's army between segments of the enemy force and dealing with each force sequentially to prevent the enemy from massing. At Vicksburg, Grant took advantage of interior lines by positioning himself between the Confederate forces at Edwards and Jackson. James Arnold explains, "Grant believed he could deal with Jackson and return to fight Pemberton before that general realized what was afoot. It was an audacious plan of Napoleonic vision.... By virtue of careful logistical preparation followed by rapid marching, Grant had achieved the central position Napoleon cherished. Having interposed his army between the two Confederate wings, Grant intended to use the central position in Napoleonic style by defeating one wing and then countermarching to defeat the other before the two wings could cooperate." When General Joseph Johnston arrived at Jackson he found "the enemy's force between this place and General Pemberton, cutting off communication. I am too late." Grant's successful use of interior lines allowed him to neutralize Jackson and then turn west to focus on Vicksburg.

In addition to West Point, a variety of military schools throughout the nation provided trained officers for each side. One of the biggest was the Virginia Military Institute, which provided 1,781 of its 1,902 matriculates from 1839 to 1865 for service in the Confederate Army. Included in that number at Vicksburg was John Waddy (VMI Class of 1853), who had also served on Pemberton's staff in Charleston, South Carolina.

Not all Civil War generals, however, were products of a professional military education and background. The rapid expansion of both the Federal and Confederate Armies forced Presidents Abraham Lincoln and Jefferson Davis to appoint large numbers of generals. In 1861, Lincoln commissioned 126 generals and Davis 89. Sixty-five percent of those appointed by Lincoln and fifty percent of those appointed by Davis were professional soldiers. The others, forty-four Federal generals and forty-five Confederate ones, were often appointed for political reasons. While both presidents faced genuine problems involving shortages of suitable professional senior officers, the need to placate valuable constituencies, and the need to build national cohesion, many of the political appointees still proved disappointing on the battlefield. Major General Henry Halleck captured the opinion of many professional officers when he wrote of the nonprofessionals, "It seems but little better than murder to give important commands to such men . . ." At Vicksburg, Major General John McClernand was a political appointee who owed his position to his ability to secure for President Lincoln the loyalty of southern Illinois, a region with noteworthy Southern sympathies. Yet McClernand was politically ambitious and sought independence from Grant's authority, ultimately compelling Grant to relieve him. On the other hand, Grant received more reliable service from former politicians Brigadier Generals Francis Blair, Jr. and John Logan.

Many Civil War leaders, both from military professional and political backgrounds, were shaped by previous service in the Mexican War, a conflict which Herman Hattaway and Archer Jones consider "was in a real sense a dress rehearsal for the Civil War leadership." Some 194 Federal generals and 142 Confederate generals served in the Mexican War. What they carried forward from Mexico to the Civil War varied based on their specific experiences, but in many cases the influence was profound. As a young quartermaster in Mexico, Ulysses Grant had seen General Winfield Scott cut loose from his line of supply as he marched across the Valley of Mexico. At Vicksburg, Grant duplicated the same maneuver when he turned northeast after crossing the Mississippi River. Grant's Mexican War frame of reference served him very well at Vicksburg. Not all commanders leveraged their experience as adeptly.

MILITARY ORGANIZATIONAL STRUCTURE

One thing that experience in Mexico could not prepare Civil War generals for was the unprecedented size of the Federal and Confederate armies. In the Mexican War, Scott had commanded less than 13,000 men, the size of roughly a corps in the Civil War. At Vicksburg, Grant commanded over 44,000 effectives while Pemberton had over 43,000. While the aggregate numbers were about the same, Grant's army was more efficiently organized into corps, which improved his span of control.

Such corps stemmed from Napoleon's formal adoption of the *corps d'armee* system in 1800. These corps consisted of several divisions, elements of all arms, and a small staff. They were highly mobile, flexible, and able to operate independently. Following this same principle, Grant organized his maneuver force of ten divisions into three corps, reducing his requirement to coordinate with multiple subordinates. Corps in the Confederate Army were not authorized until September 18, 1862, and not actually formed until November 6. While General Robert E. Lee quickly organized his Army of Northern Virginia into corps, Pemberton's army remained organized only at the division level, leaving Pemberton to coordinate with five division commanders who were each responsible for their own relatively large units. At Vicksburg, Grant repeatedly was able to take advantage of the flexibility offered by the corps system, such as when he advanced on three parallel columns toward Raymond in order to facilitate foraging.

One organizational problem that plagued Civil War commanders was the absence of doctrine governing joint army-navy operations. Instead, responsible commanders were left to their own devices to work out arrangements. Obviously, this situation had more of an impact on Grant than Pemberton, because Pemberton had no significant naval assets with which to coordinate. The Mississippi River Squadron of Admiral David Porter was an important part of the Federal force, and Grant and Porter were able to achieve excellent unity of effort during the Vicksburg Campaign.

RUDIMENTARY DEVELOPMENT OF STAFFS
AND COMMUNICATIONS

Military commanders are assisted in controlling their units by staffs. General Winfield Scott had benefited greatly from a loose team of staff officers during the Mexican War, and in 1855, he formalized the asset by establishing a "general staff" and a "staff corps." The general staff consisted of a chief of staff, aides, an assistant adjutant general, and an assistant inspector general. The staff corps included engineering, ordnance, quartermaster, subsistence, medical, pay, signal, provost marshal, and artillery. Similar staff representation existed down to the regimental level, and, for the most part, Federal and Confederate staffs were organized along similar lines. Some improvements would be made by the time of the Civil War, but staff functions remained rudimentary by modern standards.

The staff maintained a very direct connection to the commander. The chief of staff and aides-de-camp were considered personal staff and would often depart when the commander was reassigned; these positions were often filled by relatives or close friends. For example, Grant's chief of staff was John Rawlins, who lived next door to Grant's sister Hannah in Galena, Illinois, and became good friends with Grant after he moved there.

This personal nature of the chief of staff position meant that commanders used their chiefs in a variety of ways. Grant used Rawlins as someone with whom he could carry on conversations in which various points of view were presented, without Rawlins advocating one course of the other. Grant could listen to this neutral presentation of conflicting proposals and then make his own decision. Even more important than his contributions to military decision making was the personal accountability and genuine concern that Rawlins provided Grant. Rawlins's father reportedly died an alcoholic, and Rawlins was well aware of the dangers of drink. He knew and understood Grant's weakness and, in the words of William McFeely, helped Grant "to keep . . . in command of himself." Rawlins's service to Grant in this capacity was never more apparent than when President Lincoln dispatched Charles Dana to Grant's headquarters to investigate complaints against Grant.

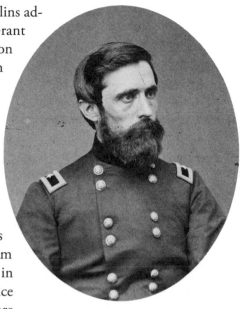

John Rawlins, Grant's chief of staff. *Courtesy of the Library of Congress*

Seldom, however, was the chief of staff used as the central coordinating staff authority, as the position is understood in today's army. Pemberton, who had much personal difficulty processing the fluid and uncertain situation he faced, would have greatly benefited from a chief of staff performing this function. Although a lieutenant general at Vicksburg, Pemberton had never before commanded a force of any size in battle. If any commander ever needed a strong chief of staff, it was Pemberton. Unfortunately, his staff suffered from the same lack of field experience that plagued their commander, and John Waddy—Pemberton's chief of staff—had little impact on the army's efficiency or synchronization.

While staffs helped commanders locally, the telegraph kept them in touch with headquarters in Washington, Richmond, and elsewhere. During most of the Civil War, the Federals enjoyed more reliable telegraphic communications than did the Confederates, but Grant's river lines of communication during the Vicksburg Campaign negated this usual advantage. Instead, Grant was forced to send messages by steamboat courier to Memphis, the nearest telegraph station upriver. This was a two-day trip and even then, Confederate guerrillas often had cut the lines running north from Memphis. Once Grant began operating south of Vicksburg, he essentially broke off communications with Washington. The aggressive Grant benefited from this independence when he made his decision to cut loose from his base of supplies, a decision he knew General-in-Chief Henry Halleck's "caution would lead him to disapprove." Grant also knew "the time it would take to communicate with Washington and get a reply would be so great that I could not be interfered with until it was demonstrated whether my plan was practicable." Free from the need to get permission, Grant used his lack of communications with Washington to act accordingly as he thought the situation required.

Until he withdrew behind his siege lines, Pemberton had access to excellent telegraphic communications but experienced mixed results. The telegraph alerted him of Major General William Sherman's Chickasaw Bayou expedition, allowing Pemberton to send reinforcements to the threatened area, but the telegraph also brought Pemberton conflicting instructions from President Davis and General Joe Johnston, which served to confuse Pemberton.

The nature of the terrain at Vicksburg generally made tactical communication by the signal flag system difficult, and both sides were forced to rely heavily on couriers, a means that was not completely reliable. Mounted staff officers or detailed soldiers would deliver messages from one headquarter to another, but the couriers were subject to becoming captured, lost, delayed, or killed. In addition, the messages could be misinterpreted, ignored, or made irrelevant by subsequent developments.

Both sides experienced difficulties with couriers. On May 13, 1863, one of the three couriers Johnston sent Pemberton with instructions to join him at Clinton was a spy, who promptly delivered the message to the Federals. On May 16, at the Battle of Champion Hill, Grant sent a message to McClernand to bring the two unengaged Federal columns to the battle. Instead of taking the three-mile cross-country route, the courier took the twelve-mile road route, delaying and weakening McClernand's contribution to the battle. On all battlefields, weaknesses in the courier system tended to compound other command errors and misjudgments, and Vicksburg proved no exception.

CAPABILITIES AND LIMITATIONS

Among the ways individual capabilities and limitations manifested themselves during the Vicksburg Campaign were the ability to prioritize, the leader's approach to the war, and interpersonal skills. In all these areas, the Federals held important advantages.

While both the Federals and the Confederates largely treated the Western Theater as a secondary effort, the Federals increased its priority once the war had reached a stalemate at the end of 1862. Federal forces in Kentucky were reinforced from Virginia, and the control of the Mississippi River—a component of Scott's original Anaconda Plan—was given renewed emphasis by increasing Grant's strength and initiating an expedition upriver from New Orleans. Additionally, Major General Henry Halleck, who had finally found his calling as President Lincoln's general-in-chief, had come from the Western Theater and brought to Washington a familiarity with the situation there.

One factor that made this additional emphasis possible for President Lincoln was the fact that his generalship in the West was much more capable than its Confederate counterpart. Grant and Sherman were the best generals the North had to offer, McPherson was a solid corps commander, and Logan and Crocker were effective at the division level. On the other hand, the Western Theater often became somewhat of a dumping ground for Confederate generals who could not meet General Robert E. Lee's exacting standards for the Army of Northern Virginia, or who had run afoul of President Davis or some other key Confederate official. William Loring had performed poorly in the campaign in western Virginia in 1861, and in October 1862, Lee advised the Secretary of War, "I have no position in this army for Genl. Loring." Pemberton had been relieved from his command at Charleston after having lost the confidence of South Carolina Governor Francis Pickens. Even erstwhile theater commander Joseph Johnston had been displaced from the Eastern Theater by President Davis, according to Michael Ballard, to get Johnston "far away from Virginia." The result was a significant Federal leadership advantage during the Vicksburg Campaign.

An important characteristic of the Federal generalship is that, much more so than the Confederate generalship, it grew and evolved during the war. Many Federal officers began the Civil War with a firm grounding in the limited war theory practiced by General Winfield Scott in the Mexican

War. Indeed Scott's time-consuming but low casualty-producing Anaconda Plan was a product of this approach to warfare. The strategy of conciliation argued that the South had been led into secession by a few fire-eaters and that, if treated generously and given time, the Confederate people would realize they had been duped and decide to return to the Union. To others, however, such a patient and deliberate strategy appeared to play into the Confederacy's hands by maintaining the status quo and making the self-declared Confederate independence more and more of the norm with each passing day. By the time of the Vicksburg Campaign, the strategy of conciliation had been largely displaced by a steady evolution toward total war.

Major General William Sherman gave an early indication that conciliation had fallen out of fashion in December 1862, at the small village of Wyatt, shortly before launching the Chickasaw Bayou operation. Retreating Confederates had burned the bridge over the Tallahatchie River, and Sherman rebuilt it using the boards and timbers of the houses of Wyatt. Several Southerners petitioned Sherman for US government vouchers covering the value of the materials taken from their houses. "Call upon the Southern Confederacy," Sherman answered. "You let them burn the old bridge, and I was forced to build another. To do this I was forced to use your houses, in exchange for which I give you the bridge. Take good care of it; do not force me to build another."

This is not to say that the Vicksburg Campaign was one of wanton Federal destruction. The most famous anecdote of leniency is Grant's treatment of Port Gibson, declaring according to local lore, the town to be "too pretty to burn." More characteristic, however, is Grant's next decision to cut loose from his line of supply and live off the bounty of Mississippi, resolving to supply his men "what rations of hard bread, coffee and salt we can, and make the country furnish the balance." An even stronger example is Sherman's raid on Meridian after the fall of Vicksburg, which in many ways was a practice run for his later March to the Sea.

The evolution toward total war is one part of what T. Harry Williams ascribes to the Federal superiority in achieving "a broad view of war." Williams argues, "The North developed at an early date an over-all plan of strategy, and it finally devised a unified command system for the entire military machine. The South was unable to accomplish either one of these objectives." The result was that, "Confederate strategy was almost wholly defensive and designed to guard the whole circumference of the country," rather than launching concentrated mass offensives. Certainly that is how Davis, Johnston, and Pemberton waged the Vicksburg Campaign.

Interpersonal skills also played an important part in leadership during the Vicksburg Campaign. Grant enjoyed excellent relations with all of his key subordinates except for McClernand, whose ambitious and self-serving personality eventually led to his removal. With his other subordinates, Grant's interpersonal skills achieved noteworthy results. A good example is Grant's naval counterpart, Admiral David Porter, who had a reputation for ambition that rivaled McClernand's and could be a parochial advocate of naval independence. In spite of these tendencies, Grant quickly won Porter's cooperation and confidence, and the army and navy enjoyed a harmonious relationship throughout the Vicksburg Campaign. Other Federal leaders, such as Sherman during Porter's "running of the gauntlet" past the Vicksburg batteries, also demonstrated excellent interpersonal skills by establishing a highly cooperative and synergistic organizational climate.

Pemberton, on the other hand, suffered from a mix of his own lack of interpersonal skills and resistance from some of his key subordinate commanders, who Christopher Gabel writes lacked, "any real respect for their commander and would prove to be less than supportive of him." Pemberton's bureaucratic approach to his duties and his introverted personality served to distance him from his subordinates and negatively affected his ability to lead. He suffered from particularly troublesome relations with Major General William Loring and Brigadier General Lloyd Tilghman, but even lower ranking soldiers took issue with Pemberton. One sergeant declared Pemberton, "the most insignificant 'puke' I ever saw and [he] will be very unpopular as soon as he is known."

BILLY YANK AND JOHNNY REB AT VICKSBURG

While the leader is an obviously important element of the leadership equation, the nature of the subordinates is also critical. The Federal and Confederate soldiers at Vicksburg brought with them their own capabilities and limitations with which their leaders would have to contend. Additionally, the common soldier had strongly developed ideas of what was required of a leader, as demonstrated by the Confederate sergeant who so defiantly sized up Pemberton. Generally speaking, Civil War soldiers had far greater expectations of independence and individuality than do their modern counterparts, and these demands would also impact leaders at Vicksburg. While Billy Yank and Johnny Reb had much in common, they also had subtle differences that would have to be accounted for by their leaders. Finally, leadership is not exclusively a function of positional hierarchy. Private soldiers at Vicksburg, such as Thomas Higgins, rose to challenges in specific situations, and their individual actions also comprise an important part of the leadership story at Vicksburg.

The Battle of First Manassas dispelled any notions that the war would be a short one, and both the Federal and Confederate governments began enlisting large numbers of soldiers. For the most part, both nations continued the American political philosophy that the chief responsibility for raising volunteers rested with the state rather than the central government. Thus the two war departments merely levied a requirement on each state to provide a certain number of volunteer regiments.

Most Civil War soldiers were between eighteen and thirty years of age, but the ranks also contained young boys and old men. Most came from rural areas and had little education. Few had ever been far from home, which must have made service in Mississippi somewhat of an adventure for the Federal soldiers from as far away as Massachusetts. Most of the men in Grant's army, however, were from western states like Illinois, Iowa, and Indiana. The western soldiers had reputations as proven fighters. Additionally, three regiments of black soldiers formed the African Brigade and fought well to help stave off the Confederate attack at Milliken's Bend.

Most of the Confederate soldiers at Vicksburg were from nearby Louisiana. Missouri, a slave state with considerable Confederate sympathies, remained in the Union and fought its own civil war within the Civil War. During the Vicksburg Campaign, Missouri units fought both as Federals and Confederates, and today, the Missouri State Memorial bears the unique distinction as being the only state memorial in the Vicksburg National Military Park dedicated to soldiers of both armies. It stands just south of the Stockade Redan on Confederate Avenue where two opposing Missouri regiments fought each other. The Vicksburg order of battle that is an appendix of this book records the organizations of the Federal and Confederate Armies.

Some Civil War soldiers were already in the US Army or a state militia when the war broke out. Most, however, were new volunteers. To meet the ever-increasing demand for soldiers, first the Confederacy and then the Union resorted to conscription.

The Federal Army had the advantage of being able to build on its prewar foundation, and some units at Vicksburg, like the Thirteenth US Infantry, consisted of regular soldiers. This unit participated in the ill-fated May 19 assault on the Confederate fortifications and was able to plant both the regiment and US colors on the Confederate works before the attack collapsed. Upon returning to friendly lines, regimental color bearer Sergeant Thomas Nelson counted four bullet holes in his clothes, eighteen holes in the regimental colors, and two pieces of canister and one Minie ball in the flagstaff. The US flag had fifty-six bullet holes in it. For its heroic deeds that day, the Thirteenth earned the motto "First at Vicksburg."

However, most of the soldiers at Vicksburg were from volunteer units, and after the Civil War and throughout the remainder of the 19th Century, a vigorous debate developed between those who favored building the US Army around volunteers or professional soldiers. Emory Upton, who had fought with Grant in Virginia, became the principal champion of a professional force while John Logan, who commanded the Third Division in McPherson's corps at Vicksburg, became the post-war champion of volunteers. Logan's division included the original volunteer regiment he had organized and commanded, the 31st Illinois. His experience convinced him of the value of volunteers, and after the war he argued that the US had, ". . . an exclusive military establishment to which are attached the essentials of a caste or class-distinction, and within the mechanism of which reside all of the possible dangers belonging to the military establishment of an absolute monarchy." He claimed that Regular Army officers could claim no better battlefield record in the Civil War than volunteers because of the "lamentable failure of so large a portion of them in actual battle." His *Volunteer Soldier of America* was published posthumously in 1887 and provided the intellectual support for those advocating the militia as the foundation of the US Army. Logan's ideas on officer education eventually manifested themselves in the National Defense Act of 1916, which created the Reserve Officer Training Corps (ROTC) program.

Amid this mix of background, organization, resources, and personal and systematic strengths and weaknesses, the stage was set for the Vicksburg Campaign, considered by many historians to be the Civil War's decisive action. The Federal victory at Vicksburg was not a foregone conclusion. The two armies were relatively equal in size, with the Confederates enjoying considerable advantages associated with the defense, the terrain, and a friendly population. In many ways, the campaign's outcome was as much as anything the product of superior Federal leadership.

Vicksburg Campaign Overview

THE MISSISSIPPI RIVER DOMINATED THE WESTERN THEATER OF THE Civil War. Not only was the river the main north-south artery in the interior of the United States, it also divided the Confederacy into two halves. Northern farmers in places like Illinois and Wisconsin had long relied on the Mississippi to get their goods to market. In fact, at the time of the Civil War, the Mississippi River was the single most important economic feature of the North American continent. With the outbreak of hostilities, Confederate forces closed the river to navigation, which threatened to strangle northern commercial interests. For the Confederacy, the agricultural produce of the relatively peaceful trans-Mississippi Confederacy was making a substantial contribution to the Confederate armies in Virginia and Tennessee. If the Federals could gain control of the Mississippi River, they would not only secure the free flow of their internal commerce, they would cut the Confederacy in two in a way that challenged its very identity as a nation.

Winfield Scott had recognized this importance of the Mississippi River in the opening stages of the war, and his original Anaconda Plan had envisioned an amphibious attack on New Orleans from the Gulf of Mexico that would serve as a springboard for securing the Mississippi and splitting the South in two. Although President Abraham Lincoln rejected Scott's plan as being too time consuming, various Federal operations at places like Columbus, Kentucky, and Island No. 10 had in fact gobbled up control of much of the river. A critical development occurred on April 25, 1862, when Admiral David Farragut captured New Orleans and then began working his way upriver. By November, the Confederates controlled only the stretch of river between Vicksburg, Mississippi, and Port Hudson, Louisiana. Still, that was enough to block Federal commerce and maintain a tenuous rail connection with the trans-Mississippi Confederacy. With his intuitive grasp of strategy, President Lincoln understood the situation and put it in perspective. "See what a lot of land these fellows hold, of which Vicksburg is the key! The war can never be brought to a close until that key is in our pocket . . . ," he told his civil and military leaders. "We can take all the northern ports of the Confederacy, and they can defy us from Vicksburg."

TERRAIN

What made Vicksburg so formidable as a defensive position was the terrain. About 300 miles downstream from Memphis, Tennessee, Vicksburg stood at a hairpin turn where the city dominated the river from a high bluff. The river channel there narrowed to one-quarter mile, and the current velocity was about six knots, making navigation treacherous. Under such geographic conditions, the Confederate guns at Vicksburg could threaten any river transport.

Foreboding terrain protected Vicksburg from the land approaches as well. To the north of Vicksburg was the Yazoo River Delta, which sprawled along the eastern bank of the Mississippi for some 140 miles. Forty miles wide in some places, the Delta was a patchwork of swamps and waterways that would bar the way of any large army attempting to move overland. What roads that did exist were made of dirt that quickly turned to mud in the heavy rains. On the western side of the Mississippi in Louisiana the land was just as flat and swampy, if not more so. Roads there would have to be corduroyed—reinforced by logs or planks laid side by side—to support military traffic. The Confederates had good reason to feel secure in their Vicksburg stronghold.

FEDERAL FORCES

Major General Ulysses Grant commanded the Army of the Tennessee. Ostensibly Grant controlled four corps, but most of his XVI Corps, led by Major General Stephen Hurlbut, remained in Memphis during the Vicksburg Campaign performing rear area missions. This situation left

Grant with three corps—some 44,000 effectives—to form his maneuver force during the campaign.

Two of Grant's corps commanders were capable and highly trusted. Major General William Sherman commanded the XV Corps and Major General James McPherson led the XVII Corps. Sherman was the more senior of the two and had greater experience, but McPherson was competent and already showing great promise. Grant's other corps commander, Major General John McClernand, was more of a problem. A prewar Democratic congressman, McClernand had used his political connections to persuade President Lincoln to allow him to raise the XVII Corps for what McClernand envisioned as an independent expedition to open the Mississippi. McClernand was ambitious and self-serving and would prove to be a continual irritation to Grant.

Where the Federals had a dramatic advantage over the Confederates was with their naval forces. Flag Officer David Porter commanded the Mississippi River Squadron, which consisted of some sixty combat vessels. About twenty or twenty-five of these were available at any one time for use in the Vicksburg Campaign. Of those that ultimately participated, thirteen were ironclads. Ironclads had been used during the Crimean War, but had not appeared in the United States until March 1862, with the duel between the USS *Monitor* and the CSS *Virginia*. Their thick iron plating and sloped sides made these vessels nearly impervious, even to direct fire from forts.

While the Mississippi River Squadron represented a powerful contribution to Grant's effort, Porter reported to the Navy Department in Washington rather than to Grant. Neither Grant nor Porter had the authority to act as a joint commander and direct the combined efforts of the army and the navy. Instead, Grant and Porter would have to cooperate with each other in order to achieve unity of effort.

CONFEDERATE FORCES

Commanding the Confederate far-flung Department of Mississippi and East Louisiana was Lieutenant General John Pemberton. Pemberton was responsible for not just the river defenses at Vicksburg and Port Hudson, but also the field forces confronting Grant in northern Mississippi. To handle these wide threats, Pemberton had over 43,000 effectives organized in five infantry divisions with no intermediate corps headquarters. Pemberton's division commanders were a mixed bag. Brigadier General John Bowen was Pemberton's most tactically proficient subordinate, but Pemberton also had to deal with the likes of Major General William Loring, who was antagonistic and showed little loyalty to or respect for his commander.

Pemberton also suffered from a paucity of naval support. By the time Grant began challenging Vicksburg, the "River Defense Fleet" had been reduced to possessing no ironclads and only a handful of gunboats. Instead, the best the Confederates could do to challenge Federal control of the Mississippi waterways was to respond asymmetrically with mines, "torpedoes" in the lexicon of the day, such as the one that would sink the USS *Cairo*. The Confederates did succeed in capturing two Federal ironclads in February 1863, but this brief triumph scarcely elevated the Confederate naval prowess.

The final reality conspiring against Pemberton was the Confederate departmental system. Under this arrangement, Pemberton's department ended at the Mississippi River. He had no control over Confederate forces on the other side, a situation which left an opening for Grant to exploit. Even more damaging to the Confederate effort was that Pemberton's superior, General Joseph Johnston, the erstwhile commander of the Western Theater, had no real authority to direct operations in his theater. The fact that Pemberton was allowed to report directly to President Davis rendered Johnston's position largely a nominal one, even if the cautious Johnston had been predisposed to try to influence the situation.

THE FIRST ATTEMPT

So with the disadvantage of terrain, a rough parity in troop strength, and a huge naval advantage, Grant opened his first attempt to wrest control of the Mississippi River in November 1862. His plan involved advances on two axes, which were to converge in the Vicksburg-Jackson region. Grant personally led 45,000 troops southward from near La Grange in western Tennessee while Sherman conducted a river-borne expedition from Memphis to the Yazoo River just above Vicksburg. Grant's column advanced methodically, rebuilding the Mississippi Central Railroad as it went. Pemberton seemed reluctant to give battle, but on December 20 he received a stroke of good fortune when Confederate cavalry under Brigadier General

Nathan Bedford Forrest and Major General Earl Van Dorn raided Grant's extended line of communications in several places. Forrest wrecked a good portion of the railroad from which Grant received his supplies, and Van Dorn destroyed the major Federal advanced depot at Holly Springs. These losses compelled Grant to call off the overland campaign and return to Tennessee. In the process though, Grant made conclusions about his ability to live off the Mississippi countryside that would be very influential later in the campaign.

Sherman's effort fared even worse than Grant's. Sherman had sailed down the Mississippi River to Chickasaw Bluffs, just north of Vicksburg. There, Sherman was supposed to seize Vicksburg while Grant distracted Pemberton. Grant's retreat after Holly Springs, however, allowed Pemberton to bolster his lines at Chickasaw Bluffs, terrain that already favored the defender and provided little room for offensive maneuver. On December 29, Sherman suffered a stiff repulse and, like Grant, was forced to withdraw.

While Sherman was in the process of returning north, McClernand reclaimed the troops he considered Sherman had "borrowed" from him and proceeded to lead an expedition up the Arkansas River that ultimately captured the Confederate fort at Arkansas Post on January 10, 1863. As McClernand planned further operations in the interior of Arkansas, Grant ordered him to return with his force to the Vicksburg area. McClernand, who disputed Grant's authority over him, reluctantly complied, and subsequent orders from Major General Henry Halleck compelled McClernand to bring his force under Grant's command. However, tensions continued between Grant and McClernand, and Grant would eventually find an opportunity to relieve his troublesome subordinate on June 18. For the time being, however, Grant decided that his newly united force would operate against Vicksburg by way of the river, not overland. On January 30, Grant established a headquarters at Young's Point, Louisiana, on the west bank of the Mississippi River, just ten miles above Vicksburg.

FAILED SCHEMES

Before tamed by the Army Corps of Engineers in the 20th Century, the Mississippi River would periodically flood, more or less inundating the entire floodplain. During these floods, only the tops of the levees remained above water, and many of the tributaries and abandoned channels that surrounded the river were rendered temporarily navigable. Such was the case in early 1863, when unusually heavy rains filled the floodplain with water and kept the river well above flood stage from mid-January until early April.

Although he was just a few miles north of Vicksburg, Grant still faced the problem of getting into a position from which he could assault what had become "the Gibraltar of the West." Grant had to get his army out of the floodplain and on to high ground on the Vicksburg side of the river. The saturated conditions effectively precluding any sort of direct approach across the lowlands, thus Grant explored ways to bypass the Vicksburg fortifications by water and then approach the city from dry land.

Thus from January through March 1863, Grant tried at least four separate plans to break through to Vicksburg. First was the Lake Providence scheme, in which his engineers tried to connect a series of creeks, old river channels, swamps, and bayous into a waterway capable of carrying vessels around Vicksburg to the south. Once that was accomplished, Grant intended to march his army down to the vessels, which would then ferry the soldiers across the river to the dry ground on the eastern shore. After weeks of arduous labor, the plan was abandoned. Next came the canal bypass scheme, in which Grant tried to dig a canal across the peninsula formed by the great bend in the river directly opposite Vicksburg. Grant hoped this action would change the course of the Mississippi so that its main channel would bypass Vicksburg. This effort also failed and gave way to the Steele's Bayou expedition. Similar to the Lake Providence scheme, this plan hoped to create a waterway through the Yazoo Delta. Confederate sharpshooters eventually convinced the Federal gunboats to turn back from the narrow passageway. Finally, Grant tried to create a waterway running from the Yazoo Pass at the northern end of the Delta, but like its predecessors, this scheme failed.

In spite of the failure of what he later called this "series of experiments," Grant remained optimistic. With perhaps some historical license in his *Memoirs*, Grant claimed that he never expected the schemes to work, but only undertook them to keep his men busy and to create the illusion of activity necessary to silence his critics. Fortuitously for Grant, the failures also created a certain amount of bewilderment in his opponent. The seemingly haphazard endeavors gave Pemberton the impression that Grant was operating everywhere, thus leaving him in a state of confusion when Grant finally attacked in earnest after the water levels began to drop in late March. Grant set aside his "bayou expeditions" and decided to outflank Vicksburg on foot.

THE APRIL CAMPAIGN

Grant's new strategy was to avoid a frontal assault on the Confederate defenses by marching his army down the west side of the Mississippi River to a point below Vicksburg. There, the troops would meet Porter's vessels that would ferry the men across the river. To accomplish this, the transports would have to run the gauntlet past the Vicksburg batteries. It was a daring move, but other vessels had made the run and Grant was willing to take the chance.

On March 31, Grant began his overland march with McClernand in the lead, followed by McPherson. Sherman's corps stayed behind to protect the base of operations above Vicksburg. To create a diversion, Grant sent a detachment commanded by Brigadier General Frederick Steele to Greenville, Mississippi, where the Federals then moved inland and operated along Deer Creek. The idea was to convince Pemberton that Grant had abandoned his campaign against Vicksburg in favor of operations upriver. In addition to this ruse, several Federal steamers returning north toward Memphis further strengthened Pemberton's perception that Grant was withdrawing.

The biggest diversion, however, was Colonel Benjamin Grierson's cavalry raid. On April 17, Grant sent Grierson and 1,700 men from La-Grange, Tennessee through the state of Mississippi on a generally diagonal route from northeast to southwest. Along the way, Grierson sent out small detachments in various directions. The haphazard pattern convinced Pemberton that the Federals were everywhere and left him in a quandary as to how to respond.

With these movements and diversions in motion, it was time to get the Federal river transports in place below Vicksburg. On the night of April 16–17, Porter ran the batteries at the fortress city with eight of his gunboats and three transports. More steamers made the dash five days later. With Porter's vessels south of Vicksburg, Grant now had the means to cross to the east bank of the Mississippi without facing the stiffest Confederate defenses. By the time Pemberton figured out what Grant was up to, it was too late.

GRAND GULF AND PORT GIBSON

As Grierson eluded Pemberton's feeble attempts to run him down, Grant launched another diversion. This time, Sherman conducted a demonstration at Snyder's Bluff north of Vicksburg to distract Pemberton from the Federals' main effort at Grand Gulf. Grand Gulf lay some thirty air miles south of Vicksburg at the first place below the city where the river met the bluffs. There, the Confederates had built two forts and established a formidable defense. Grant's plan was for Porter's ships to shell the Confederates into submission and then ferry McClernand's men across the river.

On April 28, eight Federal gunboats began a fierce bombardment that lasted five hours; however, they could not defeat the staunch defense of Brigadier General John Bowen's Confederates. Porter assessed Grand Gulf to be "the strongest place on the Mississippi," but the setback was only a momentary one for the Federals. Grant soon received information from a runaway slave that just twelve miles south of Grand Gulf there was an undefended crossing at Bruinsburg. Grant moved his men there and began crossing the Mississippi on April 30. By the end of the day, 22,000 Federals were on the Mississippi side of the river.

Poor intelligence and Grant's diversions had left Pemberton confused and unprepared for the Federal attack. The Confederates had just 8,000 troops in the Grand Gulf area, and Bowen rushed them to Port Gibson to meet McClernand's advance inland. The outmanned Bowen fought tenaciously, but McClernand—eventually reinforced by McPherson—forced the Confederates to withdraw. In the process, Pemberton had missed his opportunity to defeat Grant before the Federals were safely ensconced on high, dry ground on the eastern side of the river. The Confederates evacuated the outflanked fortress at Grand Gulf, and Porter promptly occupied it and began turning it into a Federal logistical base.

His foothold in Mississippi secure, Grant paused from May 3–9 to evaluate his options, bring his supply trains forward, and allow Sherman's corps to join the main body. The addition of Sherman's two divisions gave Grant 42,000 men, with more reinforcements and supplies arriving regularly. The Federals were well postured for their next move.

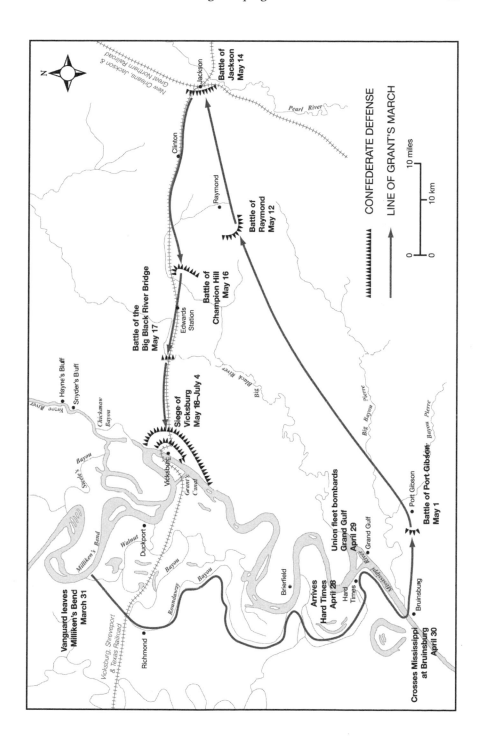

LOGISTICS

Grant's location afforded him plenty of options. He was squarely between Vicksburg and Port Hudson, Louisiana, and about forty miles west of Jackson. In addition to being Mississippi's capital, Jackson was the site of the convergence of four railroads. One of these, the Southern Railroad, was Vicksburg's main line of supply. If Grant could cut that link, he would make Vicksburg much more vulnerable to attack. However, if Grant marched toward Jackson, he would be exposing his own line of supply, and the early raids of Forrest and Van Dorn had made him well aware of the consequences of such a risk.

As Grant considered these circumstances, he received word that Major General Nathaniel Banks had begun operating on the Red River in Louisiana and would not be able to join him for an attack on Port Hudson for several days. With this new development, Grant "determined to move independently of Banks, cut loose from my base, destroy the rebel force in rear of Vicksburg or invest or capture the city." In a bit of exaggeration, Grant proposed to live off the land. In fact, he would also benefit from his newly established base at Grand Gulf and a steady stream of wagons to keep him supplied, but the point remains that Grant was taking some logistical risk in order to facilitate maneuver.

With this decision made, Grant set off in a northeastward direction, up the watershed between the Big Black and Bayou Pierre, with an objective of cutting the railroad link between Vicksburg and Jackson. The Federals advanced on a wide front, with McClernand's corps on the left, Sherman's coming up in the center, and McPherson's on the right. The multiple axes both facilitated foraging and kept Pemberton guessing.

RAYMOND AND JACKSON

As Grant cut a swath toward central Mississippi, Pemberton offered little resistance. Divided by instructions from President Davis to "hold both Vicksburg and Port Hudson" and from General Joe Johnston to strike Grant, Pemberton played it safe and consolidated his forces west of the Big Black to protect Vicksburg. Thus Pemberton kept two of his five divisions near the Vicksburg fortifications and used the other three to fortify and guard the Big Black River near Edwards. In the meantime, Davis ordered reinforcements to Jackson and told Johnston to take command personally in Mississippi.

For the time being, however, the forces in Jackson consisted only of a small brigade that Brigadier General John Gregg had recently brought from Port Hudson. Thinking he faced only a small detachment, Gregg marched out of Jackson and encountered an entire division of McPherson's corps at Raymond on May 12. Gregg fought valiantly but was simply outnumbered. After a battle characterized by uncoordinated attacks and counterattacks, Gregg withdrew to Jackson.

Gregg's tenacious resistance, as well as reports that Johnston was assembling an army in Jackson, convinced Grant to modify his plans. Rather than risk being caught between Pemberton and Johnston, Grant decided to shift his objective from the railroad and first deal with Johnston before then turning his attention to Pemberton. On May 13, Grant sent Sherman and McPherson on two separate axes toward Jackson while McClernand waited in reserve to prevent any advance by Pemberton. That same day, Johnston arrived in Jackson and, betraying his predetermined pessimism for the entire affair, declared, "I am too late." Behind a small screen from Gregg, Johnston withdrew to the north. On May 14, the Federals began their assault on Jackson.

Jackson could offer little in the way of resistance to Grant, and he took the city with less than 300 casualties. He then proceeded to neutralize anything of military value, leaving residents to nickname Jackson "Chimneyville," in allusion to the only structures left standing. With Johnston out of the picture and Jackson under control, Grant had Vicksburg isolated. He could now turn west and deal with Pemberton.

CHAMPION HILL

While Sherman remained in Jackson to finish the destruction of industrial and transportation assets, Grant sent McClernand and McPherson west. By this point, Pemberton was in an advanced state of bewilderment and shattered confidence. In a May 14 council of war, his subordinates convinced him to abandon his own inclination to fight Grant from prepared positions on the Big Black River and instead launch an offensive southward against Grant's line of communication. Having barely started this movement on May 15, Pemberton received orders from Johnston to march eastward and unite forces with him near Clinton on the railroad, about ten miles west of Jackson. Pursuant to this new order, Pemberton had just begun to countermarch on May 16 when Grant's forces surprised the Confederates in the vicinity of Champion Hill.

The Battle of Champion Hill proved to be the decisive engagement of the campaign. Grant's prebattle preparations had allowed him to converge from three directions with a force ratio advantage of three-to-two over the Confederates. Outgeneraled during a day of ferocious fighting, especially on the Confederate left, Pemberton was forced to order a general retreat, leaving Brigadier General Lloyd Tilghman to act as rearguard.

Pemberton withdrew the rest of his army to the east side of the Big Black where he waited for the rearguard to join him. While Pemberton lingered, McClernand struck the dejected Confederates on May 17. Pemberton escaped thanks to some well-placed infantry and artillery on the west bank of the Big Black and the burning of the railroad bridge across the river. The Confederates soon reached their considerable defenses at Vicksburg, and, with Grant close on his heels, Pemberton prepared to meet the Federal attack. He was safe for the time being, but his defeat at Champion Hill had cost him the ability to maneuver and given Grant the advantage of time.

In spite of this victory, Grant was frustrated that he had not been able to finish off Pemberton. Impetuously, Grant hurled two assaults against the Vicksburg fortifications, one on May 19 and a second on May 22. Both failed. Grant then decided to lay siege to Vicksburg, concluding that the trapped Confederates "could not last always." Grant also used McClernand's poor conduct during and after the May 22 assault to finally relieve the troublesome subordinate.

THE SIEGE

The siege phase of the campaign lasted six weeks, and the results were largely inevitable. Every day Grant's force became stronger, thanks to his robust logistical base that provided reinforcements and supplies. Pemberton, on the other hand, became steadily weaker, as both his army and the civilian population of Vicksburg consumed the finite provisions in the city. The only way for the Confederates to break the siege was either for the besieged force to attack outward to escape, or for an external force to come to their relief. Pemberton lacked the audacity and initiative necessary to attempt the former, and Johnston certainly lacked the offensive spirit to try to break through the Federal ring.

Using formalized European siege tactics, Grant dug fortifications facing the Confederate works and battered their strongpoints with siege batteries. Porter's vessels contributed to the siege both with fire from the river and by delivering supplies. Within the siege lines, the Federal troops dug approaches and exploded mines on June 25 and July 1, but undertook no general assaults after the failed effort on May 22.

As the siege dragged on, morale within Vicksburg deteriorated. Pemberton even received a letter signed "Many soldiers," that suggested surrender so the men would not have to desert. When Pemberton polled his generals to see if they thought a breakout was possible, they unanimously said no. Thus, on July 3, Pemberton opened negotiations with Grant.

Initially, Grant demanded unconditional surrender, but later agreed to terms that allowed the Confederates to give up their weapons and be paroled. On July 4, the Federals took control of Vicksburg, just one day after the failure of Pickett's Charge sealed the Federal victory at Gettysburg. Within a week, Banks captured the Confederate stronghold at Port Hudson, thus opening the length of the Mississippi River to Federal traffic. Summarizing the development, President Lincoln declared that the mighty Mississippi once again flowed "unvexed to the sea."

SIGNIFICANCE OF THE CAMPAIGN

Often overshadowed by the twin Federal victory at Gettysburg, Vicksburg is arguably the more decisive of the two battles. With the parole of Pemberton's army, the Confederacy lost critical manpower, and the Federals could now concentrate on the only remaining Confederate army in the west, the Army of Tennessee. In addition to facilitating their own commerce, by controlling the Mississippi the Federals bisected the Confederacy, leaving it with logistical and strategic problems as well as damaging the Confederacy's sense of nationhood. Perhaps the most important legacy of Vicksburg is that the victory propelled Grant to such renown that he was made commanding general of all U.S. forces in 1864. In this new position, Grant brought a new approach to the Federal war effort that would ultimately result in total victory.

Chickasaw Bayou battlefield. *Courtesy of the Library of Congress*

Part Two

Leadership Vignettes

THE MIGHTY MISSISSIPPI
Winfield Scott and Strategic Vision

Years of growing sectional tension over the issue of slavery and its expansion erupted on April 12, 1861, with the Confederate bombardment of the Federal garrison at Fort Sumter, South Carolina. Ultimately, eleven states seceded from the Union, leaving President Abraham Lincoln with a divided country and a desperate need for a military strategy.

WINFIELD SCOTT REMAINS ONE OF THE TRULY GREAT FIGURES IN American military history. A hero of the War of 1812 and the Mexican War, Scott was still on active duty at the outbreak of the Civil War and continued to enjoy an amazing reputation. John Eisenhower notes, "Winfield Scott was the man on whom all others in the Lincoln administration depended, the 'old soldier,' the repository of knowledge and understanding of military matters." Thus, once war became inevitable, President Lincoln turned to Scott to produce a strategy to defeat the Confederacy. In this capacity, it was Scott who first articulated how important control of the Mississippi River would be to determining the outcome of the Civil War. Like Scott, all strategic leaders must be able to formulate a strategic vision and a plan to fulfill that vision.

Scott's approach was to avoid a bloody war by mobilizing an army so big and powerful that the Confederacy would negotiate a return to the Union without a fight. In the meantime, he envisioned seizing the entire line of the Mississippi and Ohio Rivers in order to split the Confederate states east of the Mississippi from those in the west. At the same time, he would impose a naval blockade of the Confederate coast. The plan became known as the "Anaconda Plan," because, like the big snake, it would squeeze the Confederacy into submission.

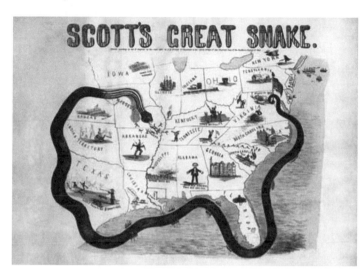

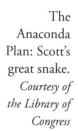

The Anaconda Plan: Scott's great snake. *Courtesy of the Library of Congress*

Part of Scott's plan for gaining control of the Mississippi involved a decisive battle at New Orleans. He told President Lincoln the Federals must "fight a battle at New Orleans and win it, and thus end the war." On April 25, 1862, Scott's desire was accomplished when Admiral David Farragut conducted a daring run past the two forts that were supposed to safeguard New Orleans and captured the city.

New Orleans was indeed a great achievement for the Union, placing one of the South's premier cities and the mouth of the Mississippi under Federal control. Still, New Orleans was a limited victory in that the strategic momentum was soon lost. The problem was that the Federals did not have a detailed plan in place for what to do next.

As Farragut pondered this situation, one obvious target was the Confederate bastion at Vicksburg, about 400 miles above the Crescent City. Using a plan similar to what had worked for him at New Orleans, Farragut attempted to subdue the city in May, but this time his bombardment was unsuccessful. Then, fearing the receding waters of the Mississippi might strand his oceangoing warships in the summer months, Farragut reluctantly decided to withdraw. He left six gunboats below Vicksburg and returned to New Orleans. Historian Rowena Reed laments Farragut's delay and half-hearted attempt at Vicksburg writing, "Had the Federal expedition moved upriver in force immediately after the fall of New Orleans, without allowing the enemy time to recover from the initial confusion of defeat, the entire Mississippi would have been in Union control by the summer of 1862."

Farragut made another attempt on June 28, running a three-mile gauntlet of Confederate fire at Vicksburg and eventually linking up with Flag Officer Charles Davis's Mississippi River Flotilla above the city on July 1. Farragut ran past the forts again on the night of July 21–22, but was attacked in a wild running battle by the Confederate ironclad *Arkansas*. Two days later Farragut returned to New Orleans, leaving two gunboats at Baton Rouge to deter the *Arkansas* from venturing south.

Farragut understood the problem. He reported to the Navy Department, "The Department will perceive from this report that the forts can be passed, and we have done it, and can do it again, as often as may be required of us. It will not, however, be an easy matter for us to do more than silence the batteries for a time, as long as the enemy has a large force behind the hills to prevent our landing and holding the place." To do so would require a cooperating army force of some 12,000–15,000 men, according to Farragut's estimation. In fact, the Federals would not be able to wrest Vicksburg from Confederate control until some 43,000 men commanded by Major General Ulysses Grant, with the help of a powerful fleet commanded by Admiral David Porter, did so on July 4, 1863, after a lengthy campaign of maneuver and siege.

LEADERSHIP LESSONS

Strategic leaders provide their organization with a "vision" which helps focus effort and map progress toward a desired future. The vision is both an image of a future state and a process the organization will use to guide future development. It provides direction, purpose, and identity. A vision also requires an implementing strategy or plan to ensure its attainment.

Scott's vision for the Federal war effort was based on his adherence to the limited war theory. In limited war, the minimum amount of force necessary is used to compel a political solution. Scott had practiced limited war successfully in the Mexican War, where a large part of his conduct involved restrained treatment of the Mexican population and maneuver rather than costly fighting. Scott hoped to replicate this vision in the Civil War.

Scott understood that the desired end state was a reunified United States. He felt that long-term destruction of the Confederate infrastructure or demoralization of the Confederate people would not be in the national interest in the postwar era. Thus, he developed a plan that sought to avoid large-scale fighting. Scott argued that his plan "will thus cut off the luxuries to which the people are accustomed; and when they feel the pressure, not having been exasperated by attacks made on them within their respective States, the Union spirit will assert itself; those who are on the fence will descend on the Union side, and I will guarantee that in one year from this time all difficulties will be settled." If, on the other hand, Lincoln chose to invade the South, Scott predicted, "I will guarantee that at the end of a year you will be further from a settlement than you are now."

Scott's plan was strategically sound, and by the end of the war, the Union had implemented it in full. However, it simply would not pass political muster in 1861. The public and the Lincoln Administration had no stomach for such a time-consuming strategy. The cry then was for an immediate, all-out assault on the Confederate army, not a long, drawn-out strategy of exhaustion. Scott's Anaconda Plan, as the Union's main effort, was rejected.

Strategic leaders must recognize that they operate in a complex web of overlapping and sometimes competing constituencies. While Scott's Anaconda Plan may have made perfect sense to a military unprepared for war and in need of time to mobilize and train the masses of recruits rushing to its ranks, it simply was not sensitive to the needs of the Lincoln Administration or the American public who demanded action.

This is not to say that strategic plans must always align themselves with the whims of every constituency. On the contrary, strategic leaders must use their own expertise to develop what they consider to be an appropriate plan. In the process, however, they must use highly developed interpersonal skills to build consensus and communicate their vision.

Scott lacked these abilities, especially when interacting with politicians. His experience in the Mexican War was plagued by what he considered political interference and intrigue generated by President James Polk, and by the time of the Civil War, Scott likely had little energy for the demands of consensus building. Nicknamed, "Old Fuss and Feathers," Scott was never known for his interpersonal skills, and his failure to effectively communicate his Anaconda Plan or accommodate President Lincoln's situation led to the plan's rejection.

Informally, however, the Federal *de facto* war effort took on many of the characteristics of the Anaconda Plan, to include the capture of New Orleans. Perhaps because of this informal nature of the planning, the victory at New Orleans was not exploited effectively. Part of the problem was that Farragut's New Orleans operation violated the dictum that every plan must also include "branches and sequels." Branches are options built into the basic plan. They add flexibility to plans by anticipating situations that could alter the basic plan as a result of enemy action, availability of friendly capabilities or resources, or even a change in weather. Related to the branch is the sequel. A sequel is a subsequent operation based on possible outcomes—victory, defeat, or stalemate—of the current operation. The reason the Federals were unable to capitalize on Farragut's victory at New Orleans was because there was no planned sequel.

The leadership lessons learned from Scott's Anaconda Plan include the importance of not just developing, but also communicating, a strategic vision. Scott had a vision and developed a plan to implement it. However, he did not communicate that vision in a way that ensured its adoption. This communication failure rested in Scott's lack of interpersonal skills and his failure to address the needs of constituencies other than the military. With the rejection of the Anaconda Plan, the Federals largely abandoned detailed strategic planning and therefore had no sequel ready to execute after the capture of New Orleans. If Scott had been more willing to accommodate President Lincoln and planned an aggressive sequel after the capture of New Orleans, Federal control of the Mississippi River could have been accelerated.

Takeaways:
- *Strategic leaders must develop a strategic vision and a plan to fulfill that vision.*
- *They must remain sensitive to the fact that they interact with a multitude of constituencies.*
- *They use interpersonal skills to build consensus and communicate their vision.*
- *All plans must have branches and sequels.*

TWO

THE BATTLE OF CORINTH
Ulysses Grant and Creating the Necessary Conditions

Railroads played a key role in the Civil War, and railroad junctions like the one at Corinth, Mississippi, were of strategic value to both the Federals and the Confederates. Before Ulysses Grant could turn his attention to Vicksburg, he had to have Corinth firmly in his control.

WHILE LEADERS MUST BE VIGILANT FOR UNFORESEEN OPPORTUNITIES to seize the day, more often victory comes only after much time and energy has been expended to accomplish the prerequisites required for decisive action. Leaders need to create the conditions necessary for success. Such work is often frustrating, time-consuming, and unglamorous, but it is also essential. Before he began his Vicksburg campaign, Ulysses Grant accomplished such a piece of preliminary conditions-setting by gaining control of the strategically located Corinth, Mississippi.

At the outbreak of the Civil War, Corinth was a fairly nondescript town with a population of some 1,200. What separated it from any of the hundreds of other similar-sized towns throughout the Confederate west was the railroad. At Corinth, the east-west Memphis and Charleston Railroad, which President Davis considered the "vertebrae of the Confederacy," met with the north-south Mobile and Ohio line. The importance of this junction gave Corinth the nickname, "the crossroads of the Confederacy."

Control of Corinth meant control of railroads from Columbus, Mississippi and Memphis, Tennessee, as well as those running south into Mississippi and eastward to connect with Nashville and Chattanooga, Tennessee. Many Federal military and political leaders believed that if the

Union could occupy two points in the South, the rebellion would collapse. Obviously, one point was Richmond. The other was Corinth. Grant recognized its significance, calling this modest town "the great strategic position at the West between the Tennessee and Mississippi rivers and between Nashville and Vicksburg." It was all-important enough to cause Corinth to play a pivotal role in facilitating the launching of the decisive Vicksburg campaign.

Confederate forces under General Pierre Goustave Toutant Beauregard had withdrawn to Corinth after the Battle of Shiloh and later evacuated to Tupelo. On May 30, 1862, Major General Henry Halleck cautiously occupied Corinth and found Beauregard gone. There was little promise of action until July 11, 1862, when President Lincoln ordered Halleck to Washington to serve as General-in-Chief.

Assuming Halleck's command largely by default, Grant inherited a widely scattered army that lacked the centralized striking force he wanted. Even more problematic were Confederate forces in Mississippi under Major Generals Earl Van Dorn and Sterling Price, which threatened Grant's communications with Federal forces in Tennessee and represented possible reinforcements to Confederate forces there. Grant resolved to act, attacking Price at Iuka on September 19, but the Federal pincer movement failed to close, and Price escaped. Price and Van Dorn then joined forces near Ripley, southwest of Corinth, on September 28, and Grant ordered most of his army back to Corinth, a position now made even more crucial to the Federals because of the combined threat posed by Van Dorn and Price.

Still, Grant's army was relatively scattered and Van Dorn considered the Federal force at Corinth, led by Major General William Rosecrans, to be isolated enough to be a vulnerable target. Van Dorn planned to defeat Rosecrans, seize the railroad junction at Corinth, and use it to support a campaign into western Tennessee. It was not a particularly well thought-out plan, and after two days of fighting on October 3–4, Van Dorn was forced to withdraw.

Rosecrans now had an opportunity to cut off the Confederate retreat, and Grant had high hopes for such a vigorous pursuit, but instead Rosecrans told his men to get some rest and be ready to go after Van Dorn in the morning. Major Generals Edward O. C. Ord and Stephen Hurlbut did attempt a pursuit, but without Rosecrans to press the Confederates from the southeast, the trap could not be closed. When Rosecrans finally got moving on October 5, he advanced only eight miles and went into camp.

The second battle of Corinth was over. It had been a costly affair for both sides, with the Federals suffering 3,090 casualties and the Confederates 4,467. While Grant was disappointed Van Dorn had not been destroyed, securing Corinth was still a major victory for the Federals.

With Corinth safely in Federal hands, Van Dorn and Price could no longer reinforce Confederate forces in Tennessee. Grant was now free to concern himself with greater ventures, explaining, "The battle relieved me from any further anxiety for the safety of the territory within my jurisdiction, and soon after receiving reinforcements I suggested to the general-in-chief a forward movement against Vicksburg." The railroad had made Corinth worth fighting for, but, having won it, Grant was ready to move on. Grant now held significant portions of the Mobile and Ohio, Mississippi Central, and Memphis and Charleston railroads, but he wanted to get out of the business of guarding railroads and depots and go on the offensive. "By moving against the enemy into his unsubdued, or not yet captured, territory, driving their army before us," Grant reasoned, "these lines would nearly hold themselves; thus affording a large force for field operations." The object of these "field operations" was to be Vicksburg.

LEADERSHIP LESSONS

Complex projects require a series of activities. Some of these activities must be performed sequentially, while others can be performed in parallel with other activities. For example, in the construction of a house, the drywall must be hung and finished before the interior can be painted. However, other activities such as installation of plumbing and electric wiring can be done simultaneously. This collection of sequential and parallel activities forms a network.

The Critical Path Method (CPM) is one way of modeling this network. It estimates the time required to complete each task and uses those estimates to assist with overall project management. While useful, CPM is not sensitive to time variations. Another model, the Program Evaluation and Review Technique (PERT), is superior in its allowance for randomness in activity completion times. It was developed in the late 1950s to facilitate work on the US Department of the Navy's Polaris submarine project. The PERT model and similar techniques allow planners to sequence tasks to minimize delays and make efficient use of time.

In addition to modeling the various activities and events associated with a complex project, today's military planners think in terms of decisive operations and shaping operations. Decisive operations directly accomplish the assigned task through a conclusive outcome. Shaping operations create and preserve the conditions for the success of the decisive operation. Seizing Vicksburg was the decisive operation for Grant, but gaining control of Corinth created the conditions necessary for this larger goal. Like Grant, leaders need to consider both shaping and decisive operations. What infrastructure must be built? What personnel must be trained? What contacts must be made? What capabilities must be developed? What must I do today to make possible the bigger goal I have for tomorrow? Most "overnight sensations" have usually spent a lot of time "paying their dues." The hard work of preparation often is not fun or showy, and in many cases the rewards are delayed. Leaders must maintain the broad perspective and expend the energy necessary to create the conditions required for ultimate success. This is exactly what Grant did at Corinth.

Takeaways:
- *Leaders need to create the conditions necessary for success.*
- *Complex projects are made up of some activities that must be performed sequentially and some that can be performed in parallel with other activities. Leaders must determine the correct order to keep the project moving forward efficiently.*
- *Leaders need to consider both shaping and decisive operations.*
- *Leaders must maintain the broad perspective required to expend the energy necessary to create the conditions required for ultimate success.*

— THREE —

SET UP TO FAIL
The Confederate Departmental System and Strategic Organization

President Jefferson Davis faced many challenges in building a nation amidst the emergencies of war. The Confederacy had a vast amount of territory that needed to be somehow organized militarily, but the South's strong adherence to the principle of states' rights impeded efforts to form an efficient, centralized command system. Instead, Davis created a "departmental system" that in many ways hampered cooperation and efficiency.

AS IF PEMBERTON'S LEADERSHIP CHALLENGE AT VICKSBURG WAS NOT already big enough, two flaws in the Confederate command structure would complicate matters even more. First, the western boundary of Pemberton's department rested upon the Mississippi River, the largest high-speed avenue of approach in North America, and Pemberton had no authority over forces on the far shore. Second, Pemberton was authorized to report directly to Richmond, bypassing his nominal theater commander General Joseph Johnston, and when catastrophe loomed in 1863, the easily offended Johnston attempted to distance himself from Pemberton's situation. These problems were the result of what historian Thomas Connelly calls President Davis's "legalistic" departmental system, an ineffective effort to organize the defense of the Confederacy.

At the outset of the Civil War, the Confederacy developed a defensive strategy that viewed all territory as important. This emphasis on territory led President Davis to organize the Confederacy into departments and districts largely based on state lines and geographical features. The result was a system that may have been appropriate for peacetime administration, but was very unsuited for the fluidity of war.

Each department was commanded by an officer of appropriate rank, and most operational decisions were left to these departmental commanders. Theoretically, this arrangement would allow the Confederate government to focus on only the most important strategic decisions. In reality, the departmental commanders tended to operate in isolation from each other with only little interdepartmental cooperation.

The prevalence of the departmental system had strategic implications, in many ways becoming an end unto itself. In some cases, such as at Vicksburg, preservation of autonomous departmental organization came at the expense of broader coordination. Each department had its own area to protect, and departmental commanders could not help but think their own self-interest might suffer if they lent assistance to another threatened department.

By delegating authority and resources to the department commanders from the outset, President Davis left himself very little ability to later influence the situation. He was also reluctant to go against the judgment of a local commander in whom he had entrusted so much authority. Therefore, the system was based on a tremendous reliance on the departmental commanders—some of whom warranted such trust while others did not. For this reason, much of the military history of the Confederacy is biographical, being highly influenced by the personalities of men like Generals Robert E. Lee, Braxton Bragg, and Joseph Johnston. Unfortunately, the Confederacy's tendency to assign its best generals to the Eastern Theater left the Western Theater with many second and third tier departmental commanders.

Because President Davis and his War Department were reluctant to order cooperation, the departmental system served to preclude any effective means of strategic direction. In November 1862, General Samuel Cooper, the Confederate Army's Adjutant General, began bombarding the Department of the Trans-Mississippi commander, Lieutenant General Theophilus Holmes, with requests such as, "Can you send troops from your command—say 10,000—to operate either opposite to Vicksburg or to cross the river?" Holmes parried each request, complaining that to comply would threaten Arkansas. Eventually, Cooper acquiesced, telling Holmes, "You must exercise your judgment in the matter." President Davis resumed the dialogue later in December, writing Holmes that it was "unquestionably best" that Holmes reinforce his neighbor department east of the Mississippi River, but Davis stopped short of ordering Holmes to do so.

Lieutenant General Edmund Kirby Smith superseded Holmes in February 1863, and on May 9 Pemberton advised his new counterpart, "You can contribute materially to the defense of Vicksburg and the navigation of the Mississippi River by a movement upon the line of communications of the enemy on the western side of the river. . . . To break this would render a most important service." Finally, Major General John Walker's Texas Division began operating on the east side of the Mississippi and attacked Milliken's Bend on June 7. Even then, support from the Trans-Mississippi was grudging. Smith's independent-minded subordinate, Major General Richard Taylor, who commanded the District of Western Louisiana, preferred to use Walker against New Orleans but was overruled by Smith. Still, Taylor complained in his memoirs that, "Remonstrances were to no avail. I was informed that all the Confederate authorities in the east were urgent for some effort on our part in behalf of Vicksburg, and that public opinion would condemn us if we did not try to do something." He insisted, "That to go two hundred miles and more away from the proper theatre of action in search of an indefinite something is hard; but orders are orders." Such was the state of cooperation between the departments less than a month before Vicksburg fell.

LEADERSHIP LESSONS

Bill Creech writes that organization "more than anything determines the overall health and vitality of the system." He argues that, "how you choose to organize can either

Richard Taylor.
Courtesy of the Library of Congress

make you or break you" because organization either "serves or squashes the human spirit." The Confederate departmental system was an example of what Creech calls a "centocracy," a centralized, functionalized bureaucracy held together by managership.

Instead, Creech advocates a decentralized approach to organization. Where the structure of centralism is based on functions, decentralism is based on teams. Where supervisory focus in centralism is concerned with inputs, decentralism centers on outputs. Where the work-accomplishment mindset in centralism is on each person's job, decentralism measures results by the team product.

During the Vicksburg Campaign, the Confederate departmental system's emphasis on the function of defending autonomous departments inhibited teamwork and unity of effort. Thus Holmes focused on his function as departmental commander of securing the Trans-Mississippi rather than seeing himself as a part of the Confederate Army team. Under the departmental system, the various department commanders focused on the input of their department to the system rather than the results of the system. Therefore, the fact that their department was secure was more important to them than the fact that the Confederacy was secure. The commanders in the departmental system emphasized their own jobs rather than the team product, which explains the reluctance to send reinforcements or act in concert with other departments.

Leaders must organize their subordinate agencies in a way that facilitates cooperation and synergy. Excessively hierarchical and bureaucratic structures often result in "stovepipes," in which the various departments act independently of each other and tend to further their own interests rather than larger organizational ones. The Confederate departmental system is an example of the dangers of such an organization.

Takeaways:
- *Leaders must organize for success.*
- *The organization must be structured to produce results (outputs) rather than focusing on inputs.*
- *Organizations must foster, not inhibit, teamwork and cooperation.*

— FOUR —

THE WRONG MAN FOR THE JOB
John Pemberton and the Peter Principle

Responsibility for the defense of Vicksburg rested on Lieutenant General John Pemberton. His inexplicably meteoric rise to this position left him unprepared for the immense responsibilities it entailed.

THE CONFEDERATE VICTORY AT FIRST MANASSAS DISPELLED MOST hopes of a short war, and both the Federal and Confederate sides began building large armies based on both volunteer and conscripted soldiers. The result was armies the size never before seen in the United States. In the Mexican War, Winfield Scott's entire army was less than 13,000 men. By Civil War standards, such a force would barely comprise a corps. At First Manassas, Irvin McDowell commanded 35,000 men. George Mc-Clellan moved 121,500 men to Fort Monroe, Virginia, for his Peninsula campaign. Robert E. Lee led some 70,000 men into Pennsylvania for his Gettysburg campaign. Grant attacked Lee with 119,000 at the Wilderness. Providing senior leadership for such large numbers of men would stress both the Confederate and Federal governments. As casualties took their toll, junior officers were often promoted before they were ready, many reaching their "highest level of incompetence" as predicted by Laurence Peter's "Peter Principle." Sadly for the Confederate cause, John Pemberton fell into that category. As such, he reminds leaders to not only be aware of their own limitations, but to select subordinates for promotion based more on their potential than past performance.

Pemberton was a captain in the US Army before he tendered his letter of resignation on April 24, 1861. A Pennsylvanian, his decision to join the

Confederacy is usually attributed to the fact that his wife was a Virginian. In support of this theory is the fact that Pemberton waited until after Virginia had seceded to make his decision.

Upon reporting to Richmond, Pemberton was nominated by Virginia Governor John Letcher to be a lieutenant colonel of volunteer state troops. He was assigned to the command of General Joseph Johnston, who tasked him to supervise an instructional camp near Norfolk. In a bit of irony based on the bitter debate Johnston and Pemberton would carry on following the Vicksburg Campaign, Johnston's advocacy is often considered to be a significant reason for Pemberton's rapid rise in rank.

On May 8, Pemberton became a lieutenant colonel of artillery in the Provisional Army of Virginia. On June 15, he was designated a major in the Confederate States Army. Just two days later, Pemberton bypassed the intermediate ranks of lieutenant colonel and colonel and was promoted to brigadier general. Pemberton's biographer, Michael Ballard, concludes, "There is no clear answer to why Pemberton moved up in rank so quickly."

Pemberton remained in the Norfolk area until November, when President Davis reorganized the coasts of South Carolina, Georgia, and north Florida into a single department and named General Robert E. Lee as its commander. Responding to South Carolina Governor Francis Pickens' complaint that Lee lacked brigadier generals, President Davis dispatched Pemberton to Charleston on November 29. On January 14, 1862, he was promoted to major general, and in March he was given command of the Department of South Carolina and Georgia. His principal mission in this capacity was to ensure the defense of Charleston, and he therefore learned little of maneuvering a force in the field, the skill he would need at Vicksburg.

Pemberton's stay in Charleston was marked by conflict with Pickens, and on August 28 Pemberton was informed that he was being replaced as commander by General Pierre G.T. Beauregard. Beauregard assumed command on September 24, and Pemberton departed for a brief stay in Virginia. On October 1, he was informed he would assume command of "the state of Mississippi and that part of Louisiana east of the Mississippi River," where he arrived on October 9. On October 13, he was promoted to lieutenant general.

Pemberton's elevation to such an advanced position of responsibility was puzzling to many. By all accounts he was an honest and good man, but he certainly had demonstrated no qualifications for high-level command, particularly not of a field army. He was unprepared for the demands of the Vicksburg Campaign, and the Confederacy suffered for it. Pemberton shows the dangers of promoting individuals beyond their abilities.

LEADERSHIP LESSONS

One of the key responsibilities of senior leaders is to develop subordinate leaders. Picking the right people for the right jobs is essential to the success of an organization. Pemberton was neither properly prepared for the responsibilities he was given nor was there anything in his background that would equip him for the situation in Vicksburg. In fact, his developmental experiences actually ran contrary to the current demands.

The "skills approach" to leadership argues that effective leadership depends on technical, human, and conceptual skills. Technical skills involve having knowledge about and being proficient in a specific type of work or activity. Pemberton's technical skills involved military administration and bureaucracy as well as artillery and defense of a static location. Human skill is having knowledge about and being able to work with people. Pemberton was deficient in this category, as illustrated by his difficult relationship with Governor Pickens in South Carolina. Conceptual skills are abilities to work with ideas, abstractions, and concepts. Again, Pemberton had little of this characteristic. He was comfortable with a fixed set of factors, including mission, intelligence, and geography. The much more demanding and ambiguous concepts associated with maneuvering a large force in the field were foreign to him.

Level of Leadership   Relative Percentage of Skills Required

	Technical	Human or personal	Conceptual
Top/Strategic	Low	High	High
Middle/Organizational	Medium	High	Medium
Low/Direct	High	High	Low

Different levels of leadership require different combinations of skills. Low leadership levels require high competencies in the areas of technical and human skills, but less of a need for conceptual skills. Middle levels retain the high requirement for human skills while technical demands are lowered and conceptual demands are raised to medium levels. Top leadership positions place a premium on human and conceptual skills but a low priority on technical skills.

Pemberton's skill set was not conducive for high-level leadership. His strength lay in technical skills, the characteristic needed at lower rather than higher levels. His weaknesses were in the human and conceptual dimensions, which were what the situation at Vicksburg most required. In the absence of those necessary skills, Pemberton focused on his technical skills, which were inappropriate for the fluid situation he then faced. John Maxwell notes that, "When people aren't where they do things well, things don't turn out well." That is exactly what happened to Pemberton at Vicksburg.

Maxwell also highlights the responsibility of the leader to put people in situations where they can maximize their effectiveness. Because higher levels of leadership require different skills, leaders should not select subordinates for promotion based primarily on *performance* at lower levels. Instead, promotion should be more heavily based on the *potential* to serve in positions of greater responsibility. This focus on potential requires leaders to be very aware of subordinates' human and conceptual skills, rather than the often more obvious technical skills.

Many contemporary and modern-day observers remain puzzled by President Davis's high level of confidence in Pemberton. It certainly was not justified by any demonstrated potential for high command he had displayed. The result was that Pemberton was elevated to a situation beyond his capabilities. To be sure, he did not rise to the challenge, but equally certain, Davis should have never relied on Pemberton to do so. As Ballard concludes, "Fate and Jefferson Davis had misused a general who could have contributed valuable service to the Confederacy in an administrative capacity. Because he was given the wrong commands, both Pemberton and the Confederacy suffered."

Takeaways:
- *Leaders must equip and select subordinates for positions of increased responsibility.*
- *Promotion should be based primarily on potential, rather than performance.*
- *Top leadership positions place a premium on human and conceptual skills and a lower priority on technical skills.*
- *Beware of the Peter Principle.*

FIVE

THE CONFEDERATE CONFLICT
John Pemberton and Poor
Relations with Subordinates

While generals like Robert E. Lee and Stonewall Jackson were idolized by their men, John Pemberton did not endear himself to his subordinates. His relationship with William Loring, one of his division commanders, was especially strained.

JOHN PEMBERTON DID NOT HAVE A LEADERSHIP STYLE THAT FOSTERED positive relations with either the rank and file soldiers in his command or with his key subordinate commanders. He chose to command from afar, a technique that simply did not allow his men to get to know him. Without the information needed to make informed opinions, many men relied on rumor and camp gossip to size up their commander. General Bruce Clarke, who commanded the US Army, Europe in the early 1960s, felt that soldiers have a reasonable expectation "to be kept oriented and told the 'reason why'." Pemberton refused to meet this need, and the result was a general unpopularity with the men in his command. Indeed, Michael Ballard opines that Pemberton's "own personality would work against his ability to lead men in combat" in the Civil War.

Pemberton approached his duties in bureaucratic fashion, providing sound organizing and systematizing functions, but little contribution to battlefield leadership and military science. According to Ballard, Pemberton "indicated that he viewed his job as that of an administrator, not a combat general." Lieutenant General E. M. Flanagan, a distinguished paratrooper and frequent commentator on leadership in the Army throughout the 1980s and 1990s, argued passionately against such a limited approach to leadership. How a leader, Flanagan wondered, "can know and properly lead and be responsible for his outfit from the desk in his office escapes me."

Pemberton's remote leadership style stood in sharp contrast to the "management by wandering around" (MBWA) technique advocated by Tom Peters and successfully used by Hewlett Packard in the 1980s. Management by wandering around involves "making the rounds" in order to improve connectivity and communication in the organization. The leader sees for himself what is happening throughout the organization and in the process gets firsthand information from informal channels, has an opportunity to share his vision and communicate his perspective, and is able to forge a bond with subordinates. The subordinates get access to the leader and are able to directly voice their concerns, ask questions about rumors, and make suggestions. Within the military, commanders practice a form of MBWA through "battlefield circulation." While the staff is controlling the battle from the headquarters, the commander travels throughout his battlespace to gather his own information and form his own conclusions. He meets with subordinates, checks on the progress of actions and orders, and gets a perspective that cannot be obtained from a remote location. Pemberton failed to practice these personal techniques of interacting with his command. The sergeant who declared Pemberton an "insignificant puke" no doubt spoke to many others who were equally put off by his inaccessibility and detachment.

Pemberton fared equally poorly with his key subordinate commanders, especially Major General William Loring. Pemberton certainly had no prize in Loring, who had been sent west after quarrelling with Major General Stonewall Jackson during the Romney campaign. In Mississippi, Loring continued his argumentative behavior and contributed materially to the deterioration of the command climate under Pemberton.

Poor relations between Pemberton and Loring had emerged during the successful repulse of Grant's Yazoo Pass expedition, in which Loring continuously asked for more weapons and troops. Pemberton replied that the limited space of Fort Pemberton, Loring's defensive position, prohibited the effective employment of additional men, even if they had been available. Loring disagreed and openly criticized Pemberton.

In the ensuing feud, Loring was also able to co-opt Brigadier General

Lloyd Tilghman, a one-time friend of Pemberton's. That relationship had soured after Tilghman was arrested as a result of his men having burned some tents during the retreat from Abbeville. A court of inquiry later cleared Tilghman of any wrongdoing, and Pemberton had approved the court's decision, but the incident still had left hard feelings between the two men. It also gave Loring a common ally in his grudge with Pemberton.

The gap between Pemberton and these two subordinates widened over a series of confused communications after Grant crossed the Mississippi River. Pemberton sent Loring, then in Jackson, an urgent order on May 1 to have several designated detachments "proceed at once," and the message ended, "When can you move?" Befuddled, Loring replied, "Your telegram . . . does not say where we are to go." A reply instructed Loring to move to Port Gibson "via Vicksburg." For his part, Tilghman was ordered to move from Edwards Depot to Port Gibson, but then a subsequent telegram told him to send his men ahead but to personally wait for Loring. In the meantime, Loring had been told to pick up Tilghman and his brigade before proceeding to Port Gibson.

While neither Loring nor Tilghman had reputations for alacrity, this barrage of vague and unclear orders caused them to hesitate even more than usual. Knowing speed was essential, but not understanding that the messages from his own headquarters had contributed to the confusion, Pemberton became angry and ordered Loring to "obey . . . instructions at once" and told Tilghman that his commands were "peremptory, and will be obeyed at once."

While Pemberton's mood was directly influenced by the current need for urgency, he was predisposed to respond angrily by residual frustration stemming from Loring's earlier actions in Jackson. There Loring had issued departmental orders for northern Mississippi in his own name. When informed Loring had overstepped his authority, Pemberton sharply clarified "I command the department from [Vicksburg]. All orders [are] to be issued in my name."

By the time of the decisive Battle of Champion Hill, relations between Pemberton and his subordinates had become dysfunctional. Pemberton and Loring quarreled on the eve of the battle, May 15, as Loring claimed that certain information had not been given him the previous night. Pemberton insisted it had and that Loring knew it. An observer later understatedly recalled, "Their manner was warm." On the morning of May 16, as the battle opened in earnest, Loring and Tilghman were overheard saying "harsh, ill-natured things" about Pemberton and ridiculing his plans and orders.

Amid this strained command climate, when Pemberton called on Loring to provide reinforcements to the beleaguered Confederate left, Loring refused. John Bowen was left to shore up the flank himself, and after Bowen's initial success, Loring still ignored Pemberton's orders to join in the counterattack. It was not until 5 p.m., when the Confederates had already lost the battle, that Loring arrived in the Champion Hill area. By then the rest of the Rebel army was in full retreat and, finding himself cut off, Loring marched his division away and circled around the Union forces to join the army of Joe Johnston.

Pemberton lamented in his official report, "Had the movement in support of the left been promptly made when first ordered, it is not improbable that I might have maintained my position, and it is possible the enemy might have been driven back, though his vastly superior and constantly increasing numbers would have rendered it necessary to save my communications with Vicksburg." Pemberton's conclusion about Grant's superior numbers is not completely accurate. The fact is that Grant made better use of his men than Pemberton did, and at least part of the reason for Pemberton's failure was his adversarial relationship with Loring. It was an ineffective relationship that had been brewing long before it reached catastrophic conditions at Champion Hill.

LEADERSHIP LESSONS

Part of Pemberton's leadership failure can be attributed to a phenomenon demonstrated in the "Illumination Studies" conducted between 1924 and 1927 at AT&T's Western Electric Hawthorne plant in Cicero, Illinois. Operating under the hypothesis that greater illumination would yield higher rates of productivity, researchers studied two groups of workers operating in different lighting conditions. Surprisingly, productivity increased even when light levels were reduced. Psychologists have drawn different conclusions from the experiment, and it is not without its critics, but a commonly accepted explanation is that productivity increased not because of the lighting but because the researchers closely interacted with the workers in a positive way. Previously, managers had not shown any interest in the workers on a personal level. This "Hawthorne Effect" suggests that leaders need to interact interpersonally with their subordinates in order to optimize performance. Pemberton's bureaucratic approach to leadership did not meet this need of his men.

Leaders must nurture positive relationships with subordinates long before such times of crisis. To be sure, Pemberton had a troublesome lieutenant in Loring, and he did not have the luxury of simply getting rid of him like Stonewall Jackson had done earlier in the war. Pemberton had to play the cards that had been dealt him. Still, Loring's disposition for being uncooperative was well known, and Pemberton should have adjusted his leadership style to accommodate Loring's idiosyncrasies. He could have done this by improving his communications with Loring, but Pemberton's characteristic inflexibility and hands-off leadership style prohibited this from happening. The result was an uncooperative and disloyal subordinate who not only dragged his heels in a way that hindered mission accomplishment but also spread his discontent to other members of the command. To be sure, Loring ended up acting petty and unprofessional and may be the real villain in the story, but Pemberton, as the leader, is the one responsible for the success or failure of the organization. It was his job to foster a relationship with his subordinates that was going to best benefit the organization.

Takeaways:
- *You can manage things, but you must lead people.*
- *Leaders must actively nurture relationships in the organization.*
- *An unsupportive subordinate cannot be allowed to poison an organization.*
- *In many cases, especially with subordinates, perceptions are reality.*

SIX

THE FEDERAL TEAM
Ulysses Grant and Positive
Relations with Subordinates

*Ulysses Grant and William Sherman developed a relationship that
made them one of the Civil War's most effective command teams.
Sherman's loyalty to Grant was complete, and Grant returned it with
unmitigated trust. Grant also developed an effective relationship as a
mentor to James McPherson. This relationship helped the younger
McPherson grow and develop.*

WHILE PEMBERTON SUFFERED FROM NOT HAVING AN EFFECTIVE
relationship with his subordinates, Ulysses Grant enjoyed great support
and assistance from his. Both Major Generals John McPherson and
William Sherman were exemplary subordinates, and Grant developed
unique and appropriate relationships with each. Tamara Smith notes that
"McPherson adopted Grant as his mentor," and Charles Bracelen Flood
calls the relationship between Grant and Sherman, "the friendship that
won the Civil War."

Grant identified McPherson as an up-and-coming officer during the
campaign for Forts Henry and Donelson in early 1862, and McPherson
was promoted to brigadier general. As if to signify there would be some
special relationship between Grant and McPherson, Grant's wife sowed the
new stars on his uniform.

After performing well as military superintendent of railroads in the
District of West Tennessee, McPherson asked Grant to place him in more
active service, and Grant responded by placing him in charge of an impro-
vised division and dispatching him to reinforce Corinth. Pleased by

McPherson's handling of this responsibility, Grant recommended McPherson be given a regular command, noting that "I would feel more strengthened today if I could place McPherson in command of a Division than I would to receive a whole brigade of new levies." Indeed, Tamara Smith notes that McPherson's promotion was in part the result of Grant's "faith in his potential." Grant had identified a promising subordinate and ushered him into a position of responsibility. For his part, McPherson increasingly relied on Grant's "judgment and executive ability." The two were quickly forging a mentor-protégé relationship.

When McPherson was promoted to major general, Grant gave him command of the XVII Corps and regularly assigned him important tasks such as covering the rear of the army in its retreat after Van Dorn's raid on Holly Springs, and during the following spring, digging the Lake Providence canal. McPherson did these duties well. In fact his canal project was the only one of Grant's bypass schemes to result in the conditions Grant wanted. Later, McPherson won a critical victory at Raymond and used his engineering background to good effect during the siege of Vicksburg. When Pemberton surrendered, Grant rewarded McPherson by having his corps occupy the city as the unit most responsible for the victory. McPherson recommended Grant parole the captured Confederate soldiers, and once the terms were settled, Grant gave him command of the city, naming it the "District of Vicksburg." Mentorship involves developing a less experienced leader so that he can take on greater responsibilities in the future, and Grant certainly achieved this end with McPherson.

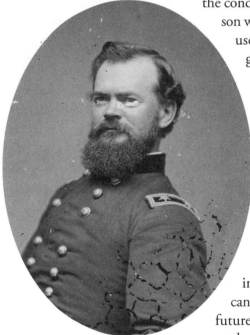

James McPherson.
Courtesy of the Library of Congress

Grant also had a positive relationship with Sherman, with the two men enjoying a mutual bond of friendship forged by respect and loyalty in good times and bad. Sherman once explained, "Grant stood by me when I was crazy, and I stood by him when he was drunk; and now, sir, we stand by each other always." Sherman was referring to accusations that he had "acted insane" while in command of the Department of the Cumberland in Louisville, Kentucky. He ultimately was forced to take a leave of absence, but recovered to cooperate with Grant in a supporting role at Forts Henry and Donelson. The pair continued their partnership at Shiloh where the Confederate surprise attack on the first day of the battle led many to accuse Grant of being drunk (reviving rumors that had risen after Donelson). Grant had stood by Sherman when Sherman was under attack, and now Sherman did the same for Grant. Leaders must create an environment where this type of support is possible.

Sherman represented the true characteristics of a loyal subordinate. He was unswervingly devoted to Grant, but he was certainly not a "yes man." As the Federal Army suffered one setback after another before the ultimately successful crossing of the Mississippi River at Bruinsburg, Sherman strongly recommended that Grant take most of the army back to Memphis, Tennessee and move south by some new route. Sherman outlined his plan in a conversation with Grant and then sent a detailed seven-point memorandum to Grant's chief of staff John Rawlins. But he also made it clear that Grant was the commander and that Sherman was prepared to follow any direction in which Grant chose to lead. Sherman closed his memo saying, "I make these suggestions, with the request that General Grant will read them and give them, as I know he will, a share of his thoughts. I should prefer that he should not answer this letter, but merely give it as much or as little weight as it deserves. Whatever plan of action he may adopt will receive from me the same zealous cooperation and energetic support as though conceived by myself."

LEADERSHIP LESSONS

Grant's relationship with McPherson and Sherman models two important aspects of a leader's interaction with his subordinates. With the younger McPherson, Grant took on the role of mentor. With the more seasoned Sherman, Grant could rely on thoughtful recommendations, even if they were contrary to Grant's own intuition.

Mentorship is "the voluntary developmental relationship that exists between a person of greater experience and a person of lesser experience that is characterized by mutual trust and respect." The relationship between Grant and McPherson certainly fits this definition. Grant identified McPherson's potential early and established a relationship that facilitated both his personal and professional development. Mentorship helps organizations maintain a highly competent set of leaders, and the Army of the Tennessee certainly reaped this benefit thanks to Grant's mentorship of McPherson.

Seniors need to create conditions in which their subordinates feel comfortable generating ideas, even if they may be new and different. Sherman's recommendation was expressed in a way completely consistent with General Colin Powell's understanding of loyalty. Powell tells his subordinates, "When we are debating an issue, loyalty means giving me your honest

Grant's headquarters, Vicksburg. *Courtesy of the Library of Congress*

opinion, whether you think I'll like it or not. Disagreement, at this state, stimulates me. But once a decision is made, the debate ends. From that point on, loyalty means executing the decision as if it were your own." Good leaders know that "yes men" are of little value so they welcome opinions and recommendations that are contrary to their own as they work through the decision-making process. Once the decision is made, however, loyalty demands teamwork and compliance in executing the decided upon course of action. Grant allowed Sherman to work in that kind of environment, and Sherman responded as a loyal subordinate.

Grant recognized unique qualities in both McPherson and Sherman, and he used them accordingly. When the task required relentless energy and risk taking, Grant knew he could rely on Sherman. When the task called for a more methodical, practical approach, Grant called on McPherson. With both men, Grant established a positive relationship that let each grow and excel.

Takeaways:
• *Leaders mentor promising subordinates to help them grow personally and professionally.*
• *Loyalty must go up, down, and laterally in the organization.*
• *Respectful, thoughtful dissent as an issue is being debated does not equal disloyalty any more than sycophantic agreement equals loyalty.*
• *Subordinates must execute the leader's ultimate decision as if it were their own.*

— SEVEN —

CHICKASAW BAYOU
William Sherman and Knowing When to Quit

While the Vicksburg Campaign ended as a great Federal victory, it began much more inauspiciously. The ill-fated Chickasaw Bayou expedition was one of several preliminary failures.

GRANT'S FIRST ATTEMPT TO WREST CONTROL OF THE MISSISSIPPI River took place in November 1862 and involved a two-pronged attack. He personally led over 40,000 troops southward from near La Grange in western Tennessee while Sherman with 32,000 more conducted a riverborne expedition from Memphis to the Yazoo River just above Vicksburg. Ultimately the two axes were to converge in the Vicksburg-Jackson region. Grant's column, however, was forced to turn back when Confederate cavalry raids threatened his lines of communications. Earl Van Dorn had slipped behind Grant's army in Mississippi while Nathan Bedford Forrest had begun ripping up his railroad and telegraph lines in western Tennessee. With Sherman left on his own his effort fared even worse than Grant's and demonstrated that a good leader must know when to quit.

On December 20, the same day that Major General Van Dorn's cavalry struck and captured Grant's advance supply base at Holly Springs, the lead elements of Sherman's force boarded transports at Memphis and headed south toward Vicksburg. On December 24, Sherman's full flotilla of seven gunboats and 59 transports arrived at Milliken's Bend, Louisiana and tied up for the night.

On Christmas Day, Sherman's men departed Milliken's Bend, ascending the Yazoo River in order to turn the flank of Vicksburg's main defenses.

Landing sites were limited, and the only real option was to land at the plantations that lined the riverbank near Chickasaw Bayou. Such a location put Sherman some three miles away from the line of bluffs that constituted his immediate objective. Between the landing site and the bluffs lay numerous swamps and bayous. In fact, Sherman had landed on what was virtually an island.

Grant's operation had been designed to distract Pemberton from Sherman's attack, but when Grant retreated after Holly Springs, Pemberton was able to bolster his lines at Chickasaw Bluffs. The Confederates were still outnumbered, but the terrain was such that the defenders had a significant advantage. The impending battlefield lay north of Vicksburg in front of the Walnut Hills, where the Confederates had established a strong defensive line. Natural water barriers and man-made abatis further strengthened the defenses.

When the Federals came ashore on December 26–27, they soon received fire from Confederates posted in the woods bounding Chickasaw Bayou. After a brief firefight, both sides withdrew and bivouacked for the night. The fighting escalated on December 27 and 28, and the Confederates brought several thousand additional troops on line. The climactic day of the battle was December 29.

That day Sherman began his attack at 7:30 a.m. with an artillery barrage. Confederate guns responded, and the two sides dueled for several hours without inflicting much damage. At 11:00 Sherman began deploying his men for battle, hoping to break through the Confederate center and then either move on to Vicksburg or turn north and capture the Confederate forts near Snyder's Bluff. Sherman knew the long odds he was up against, but he stoically resolved, "We will lose 5,000 men before we take Vicksburg, and may as well lose them here as anywhere else." Colonel John DeCourcy, whose men were to cross the Chickasaw Bayou and attack the base of Walnut Hills, saw things a little more personally and lamented, "My poor brigade!"

Events would indicate that DeCourcy was right to be pessimistic. Two Federal brigades attacked, only to be forced back across Chickasaw Bayou. Then Confederates under Brigadier General Stephen Lee counterattacked, capturing 21 officers, 311 enlisted men, four battleflags, and 500 stands of arms. Elsewhere, Federals advanced against the Confederate position atop an old Indian Mound, only to have five assaults repulsed, with 14 Federals killed and 43 wounded in the process.

The repulse of Sherman's men at Chickasaw Bayou as depicted
in the January 31, 1863 *Harper's Weekly.*

Realizing the Walnut Hills position was too strong to attack, the Federals withdrew and suffered through a long night of cold, hard rain. In order not to disclose the locations, fires were not permitted and the men, especially the wounded, suffered horribly. One soldier recalled, "The rain did not stop until morning—the storm raging with unbroken fury, and when daylight at last dawned upon the pitiful scene we found ourselves in a swamp… stiff blue and teeth rattling, scarcely able to walk, and many totally unable to speak!"

The next morning, Sherman inspected his lines and "was forced to the conclusion that we could not break the enemy's center without being too crippled to act with any vigor afterward." He consulted with Admiral David Porter to determine if any "new combinations" might present another opportunity, and for a time considered loading a force on gunboats and attacking the Confederate batteries at night. Unfavorable moon conditions precluded this operation, and Sherman was "forced to the conclusion that it was not only prudent but proper that I should move my command to some other point." On January 1, 1863, Sherman loaded his men on transports and withdrew from the Vicksburg area. The expedition had cost him 1,776 casualties, including 208 killed. The Confederates had lost just 57 killed and 130 wounded.

LEADERSHIP LESSONS

Throughout the war commanders on both sides would continue to press attacks long after defeat was obvious. The six failed assaults Major General Ambrose Burnside hurled at General Robert E. Lee's entrenched forces at Fredericksburg is a good example. Leaders must be able to assess the situation in an analytical fashion and avoid the temptation to "throw good money after bad." They must be able to address the dissonance that occurs when the results of a much-anticipated course of action do not meet expectations. They must not, in spite of evidence that the plan is flawed, continue the same pattern of behavior and hope for different results. Leaders must realize that "change will not occur without change."

To achieve this perspective, leaders must be able to recognize and discount what economists call "sunk costs" or unrecoverable past expenses. Generally speaking, these sunk costs should not be considered when determining whether to continue with a project or abandon it. Consider for example, a woman who has rented a beach house for a week, and halfway through the vacation it begins to rain with no let-up in sight. The woman has to decide whether to stay at the beach, in spite of the bad weather, for the rest of the week or pack up and go home. She may be tempted to stay based on the fact that she has already paid for the house. In actuality, that expense is a sunk cost that cannot be recovered whether she stays or goes and therefore should not be considered in her calculations. If the idea of walking away from the already spent money so gnaws at the woman that she feels compelled to stay, she should remember she is actually forfeiting the opportunity to spend the rest of the week doing something less hindered by the weather. In spite of such logic, sunk costs are often considered for emotional reasons and encouraged by such adages as "Finish what you started" and "Don't be a quitter."

But successful leaders know the difference between persevering through adversity to complete a project that shows promise and unimaginatively clinging to dead ends. Developing the skill of knowing when to cut losses enables leaders to regroup and have the resources necessary to succeed at a later date. This long-range perspective is important. As Sherman bemoaned his losses to Porter, the admiral was able to take the long-range view. "Only seventeen hundred men! Pshaw!," he chided. "That is nothing; simply an episode in war. You'll lose seventeen thousand before the war is over, and think nothing of it. We'll have Vicksburg yet before we die. Steward, bring some punch." Porter was right. The Federals may have lost a battle that day, but they went on to win the war. Leaders need to make hard decisions about isolated failures in order to remain competitive for greater future successes.

Takeaways:
- *Leaders avoid throwing good money after bad. They know when to quit one course of action and try something else.*
- *Do not let sunk costs tie you to an unproductive course of action.*
- *When faced with a setback, maintain a long-range view.*

EIGHT

THE SELF-MADE MAN AND
THE REINVENTED MAN
The Raids of Forrest and Van Dorn

The Confederate cavalrymen that so upset the Federals' first drive on Vicksburg are interesting case studies of individual responses to leadership opportunities. Brigadier General Nathan Bedford Forrest represents the self-made man who, without any formal military training, rose to greatness. On the other hand, Major General Earl Van Dorn represents a man who entered a leadership position with impressive credentials, failed to live up to expectations in one position, and later found his niche in another.

EARL VAN DORN GRADUATED FROM WEST POINT 52ND IN THE 56-man class of 1842. In spite of his lackluster performance as a cadet, he proved himself a capable junior officer, seeing a significant amount of Indian fighting on the frontier as well as service in the Mexican and Seminole Wars. He resigned from the US Army on January 31, 1861, and soon succeeded Jefferson Davis as Mississippi's state major general. On March 16, Van Dorn was commissioned a colonel in the Confederate Army and placed in command of Forts Jackson and St. Philip below New Orleans. On April 11, he became commander of the Department of Texas, and on April 20 he captured the Union vessel *Star of the West* at Galveston.

This celebrated event helped garner Van Dorn promotion to brigadier general on June 5 and to major general on September 19, leading to command of a division in Virginia. Douglas Southall Freeman describes Van Dorn as "a man of some reputation, whose arrival in Virginia had been chronicled with some applause." However, Van Dorn did not stay in

Virginia long. Frustrated by the long-running feud between Major General Sterling Price and Brigadier General Ben McCulloch, President Davis created a new Military District of the Trans-Mississippi and sent Van Dorn, his friend and fellow Mississippian, to command it in January 1862.

In his new capacity, Van Dorn developed a plan to join forces with Price, who had recently been forced out of Missouri into Arkansas, and strike the overextended lines of Federal forces commanded by Brigadier General Samuel Curtis. On March 7, Van Dorn launched Price on his main attack against Curtis's left rear at Elkhorn Tavern while McCulloch and Brigadier General Albert Pike launched diversionary and secondary attacks. Van Dorn's intention was to envelop Curtis around the south end of Pea Ridge at Leetown. It was a poorly planned attack made more difficult by the cold weather, an exhausting 55-mile march, and the fact that Van Dorn himself was sick and had to direct the battle from an ambulance. Curtis had also anticipated Van Dorn's attack and repositioned his forces to deliver a devastating fire across McCulloch's flank. The armies battled fiercely at Leetown, and the day ended with Price holding Elkhorn Tavern while the Confederates were in general disarray.

Van Dorn resolved to attack again the next day, but by then, Curtis had contracted his lines and was well prepared in the fields south of Pea Ridge. On March 8, he launched a furious counterattack that drove Van Dorn from the field. The Confederates then retreated from Arkansas, surrendering the initiative there to the Federals. The debacle demonstrated what Michael Ballard describes as "all the weaknesses that made [Van Dorn] an inept commander of a large army." According to Ballard, Van Dorn sprouted "grandiose plans based on unrealistic means," rendering him "a reckless battlefield commander." Even Van Dorn's apologist Harvey Ford admits that "Van Dorn's defeat can basically be attributed to poor judgment."

With this ignoble defeat behind him, Van Dorn crossed the Mississippi River to support Beauregard's army during the aftermath of Shiloh, and became commander of the District of Mississippi. There he was strategically located, along with Sterling Price, to both threaten Federal operations in Mississippi and reinforce General Braxton Bragg in Tennessee. First Van Dorn launched Price against the Federals commanded by Major General William Rosecrans at Iuka on September 19, only to have Price forced to withdraw after inconclusive fighting. Still Grant's army was relatively scattered, and Van Dorn considered Rosecrans' force at Corinth isolated enough to be a vulnerable target. Accordingly, Van Dorn planned to defeat Rosecrans, seize the railroad junction at Corinth, and use it to support a campaign into western Tennessee. It was not a particularly well thought-out plan, as events would demonstrate.

On the morning of October 3, Van Dorn struck. Rosecrans had greatly improved the already formidable defenses the Confederates had vacated when they abandoned Corinth in June, and the Federal fortifications now consisted of successive outer and inner entrenchments. The sweeping arc of the outer defenses stretched the Federals thin, but this initial line served its purpose even if it only delayed the attackers. After a day of hard fighting, the Federals withdrew to their inner defenses just before dark. Now Rosecrans was at his strongest defense line consisting of Batteries Robinette, Williams, Phillips, Tannrath, and Lothrop, in the College Hill area, just a few hundred yards outside Corinth. These batteries were connected by breastworks and in some cases protected by abatis—trees that were felled and sharpened to create an obstacle for the enemy.

Corporal Charles Wright of the 81st Ohio considered the College Hill line "a splendid place to make the fight." It was indeed an advantageous situation for the Federals. While the Confederates had been sapping their strength fighting through Rosecrans' defense in depth, Rosecrans was receiving a steady stream of reinforcements and improving his ability to mutually support his forces in his now contracted line. Even Van Dorn noted this, observing, "The line of attack was a long one, and as it approached the interior defenses of the enemy that line must necessarily become contracted."

The next day Van Dorn continued his attack, opening up with a predawn bombardment that amounted to "a real display of fireworks" according to one Federal. Many of the Confederate shells landed long, however, exploding in Corinth itself and killing civilians and one wounded Federal soldier who was in the Tishomingo Hotel. Price launched an initial charge at about 10:00 a.m. that showed promise when the Confederates found a weak point in the Federal line and penetrated into Corinth, where house-to-house fighting ensued. Rosecrans himself seemed to have thought the day was lost and began issuing panicky orders to burn various stockpiles of supplies.

But Rosecrans need not have worried. In a pitched battle in front of Battery Robinette, the Federal line rallied and pushed back Brigadier General Dabney Maurey's division of Van Dorn's army. The Confederates had thrown all they had at the Federals, who had reserves that the Confederates did not. Van Dorn had reached his culminating point and he knew it. To continue the attack risked complete destruction, and that afternoon he began marching away from the battlefield. To Grant's chagrin, Rosecrans delayed pursuit until October 5 and then advanced only eight miles and went into camp.

The second battle of Corinth was over. It had been a costly affair for both sides. Federal casualties were 3,090 and the Confederates suffered 4,467. While Grant was disappointed Van Dorn had not been destroyed, securing Corinth was still a major victory for the Federals that allowed Grant to launch his Vicksburg Campaign.

Confederate dead in front of the critical Battery Robinette at Corinth.
Courtesy of the Library of Congress

At Corinth, Van Dorn revealed several of the same failings that caused his undoing at Pea Ridge. Once again his plans demanded more of his men than he could reasonably expect, and he underestimated the scope of the task and the strength of the enemy. Van Dorn was called before a court of inquiry but exonerated at the trial. Nonetheless, Corinth settled once and for all that Van Dorn was not suited for high command.

The defeat at Corinth weighed heavily on him. Van Dorn was subjected to criticism not just within military circles but from the citizens, press, and public officials of his native Mississippi. Senator James Phelan opined that public sentiment was so soundly against Van Dorn that even "an acquittal by a court-martial of angels would not relieve him of the charge." Phelan then recommended that President Davis remove Van Dorn from Mississippi since its citizens harbored such complaints against him.

Such sentiment deeply affected Van Dorn, who complained to his wife,

I am weary, weary. I sigh for rest of mind and body. If I could retire from the army and join you and my dear children I should be happy. . . . Command is worse than a subordinate position. Indeed, if my death would give pain to no one I should court it. I have seen enough of life and feel its emptiness and its vanity. I am not ambitious and yet I have labored and have won position. Position has brought misfortune, criticism, falsehood, slander and all the vile things belonging to the human heart upon me. I have struggled for others and they have abused me.

This is the same Van Dorn who upon assuming command of the District of the Trans-Mississippi had confidently written his wife, "I am now in for it, to make a reputation and serve my country conspicuously or fail. I must not, shall not, do the latter. I must have St. Louis—then Huzza!" The transformation was stark and the fall from glory precipitous.

While Van Dorn was still mired in criticism and melancholy, Robert Hartje writes that he was yet "indefatigable as he struggled to put a strong force in the field," and his exertions won him admiration among several of his fellow officers. While his fellow Mississippians disparaged him, Van Dorn, drawing perhaps on his notable pre-war service on the frontier and his success at Galveston early in the Civil War, retained a certain loyalty from the Texas troops. Stinging from Mississippi's rebuke, Van Dorn declared, "I am a Texan," and Colonel T.N. Waul reciprocated, declaring that as far as he and his regiment of Texans were concerned, "Time and conduct have confirmed our appreciation of your merits as a soldier and a gentleman."

Indeed the Texans considered Van Dorn their champion. Lieutenant Colonel John Griffith of the 6th Texas Cavalry wrote Pemberton, suggesting, "If you will fit up a cavalry expedition, comprising three or four thousand men, and give us Major-General Earl Van Dorn, than whom no braver man lives, to command us, we will penetrate the rear of the enemy, capture Holly Springs, Memphis, and other points, and perhaps force [Grant] to retreat from Coffeeville." Pemberton saw promise in the plan, and on December 12 he ordered Van Dorn to take command of all the cavalry in the vicinity of Grenada, Mississippi and launch a raid against Grant's communications. For Van Dorn, the new assignment offered a chance to restore his reputation, and he made the most of it.

Pemberton assigned Van Dorn a force of some 2,500 Texans, Missourians, Tennesseans, and Mississippians. Much of the force had previously operated in and around Holly Springs so they were familiar with the territory, but in order to maintain surprise, Van Dorn kept the details of the operation a secret. On December 18, the force left Grenada with orders to ignore any Federal scouts or skirmishers, and keep pressing forward. By December 19, Van Dorn was at Ripley, well behind Federal lines, and he finally briefed his officers on his plan of attack. He sent scouts forward to Holly Springs and found that the Federals were in no state of heightened security. In fact, the soldiers were planning a ball for the next evening.

Van Dorn wanted to strike rapidly and maintain control of his force. He ordered the Mississippians to attack the fairgrounds, the Missourians the depot, and the Texans the town square. He detailed pickets to guard the periphery and warn of the approach of Federal reinforcements.

Grant finally got the belated news that a large Confederate cavalry force was in his rear, but was unable to dispatch anything more than a half-hearted and token pursuit. The Federals were still hopelessly unprepared when Van Dorn struck just after dawn on December 20. The Confederate attack scattered the Federals in Holly Springs, creating a scene one reporter described as "Yankees running, tents burning, torches flaming, Confederates shouting, guns popping, sabers clanking, abolitionists begging for mercy, Rebels shouting exultantly, women *en dishabille* clapping their hands, frantic with joy, crying 'kill them'."

By 8:00 a.m. Van Dorn had secured Holly Springs, along with 1,500 Federal prisoners, and he ordered his men to hold their positions. Until 4:00 p.m. the Confederates proceeded to destroy an estimated million and a half dollars' worth of supplies and gather as much booty as they could carry. Van Dorn then withdrew north, destroying as much of the Memphis and Charleston Railroad as he could before returning to Grenada on December 28.

In addition to Van Dorn's success at Holly Springs, Brigadier General Nathan Bedford Forrest conducted a raid against the important rail junction at Jackson, Tennessee on December 20. Unlike Van Dorn, who entered the Civil War with a considerable record of service in the "Old Army," Forrest had no formal military training and had risen from austere circumstances.

Nathan Bedford Forrest.
Courtesy of the Library of Congress

Born in the backwoods of Tennessee, Forrest moved with his family to northern Mississippi when he was thirteen. Just as the family was beginning to carve a homestead out of the wilderness, Forrest's father died, leaving him in charge of the family. Before leaving Tennessee, Forrest had attended school for only three months. He was to have little time for additional education now. Forrest worked hard on the family farm during the day and would often spend his evenings sewing clothes for his younger brothers. Thanks to Forrest's efforts, the family reached a state of pioneer prosperity it had never before experienced. Along the way, he grew to be a young man of impressive physical strength as well as an excellent marksman and rider.

In 1841, Forrest joined a volunteer militia company at Holly Springs with the intention of helping protect the Republic of Texas from a threat-ened invasion from Mexico. Most of the company disbanded in New Orleans due to a lack of transportation. Forrest and a few others continued to Houston, only to learn that the threat had subsided, and they returned to Mississippi. While Forrest missed this chance at combat, he certainly had his share of gun and knife fights in rough and tumble frontier Mississippi.

Forrest continued to succeed economically, first in a limited mercantile and livestock trading business partnership with his uncle in Hernando, Mississippi, and then as a real estate dealer and slave trader in Memphis. Forrest advanced socially as well, becoming an alderman on the Memphis City Council in 1858. At the outbreak of the Civil War, he had a 42-acre farm seven miles north of Memphis.

When Tennessee seceded, Forrest, along with his fifteen-year-old son, William, and youngest brother, Jeffrey, enlisted as privates in Captain Josiah White's Tennessee Mounted Rifles. Forrest's solid reputation in Memphis soon led several noteworthy citizens to petition Governor Isham Harris to offer Forrest a commission, and Forrest was then made a lieu-tenant colonel and authorized to raise a battalion of mounted rangers. Forrest used his private funds to obtain the arms and equipment he needed. He also proved to be an effective recruiter. By October 1861, he com-manded a force of about 650 men.

On December 15, Forrest began crossing the Tennessee River with the lead elements of a force of some 2,100. He headed west and brushed aside the Federal cavalry at Lexington on December 18. The Federals mounted a defense northeast of Jackson that seemingly repulsed a Confederate attack. In actuality, this action merely served as a feint while Forrest's men destroyed railroad tracks north and south of the town. When this work was completed, Forrest withdrew from the Jackson area to attack Trenton and Humboldt.

Trenton was an important stop on the Mobile and Ohio Railroad. Forrest attacked Federals there commanded by Colonel Adolph Englemann on December 20, 1862. After a brief fight in the depot area, the Federals withdrew toward Jackson, leaving Forrest free to ransack the courthouse and destroy military supplies in the town. It was also during this part of the raid that Forrest captured his famous Model 1840 United States Dragoon pattern "wrist-breaker" saber.

With the Federals pinned behind their fortifications in Jackson, Forrest was free to move toward Humboldt to continue his campaign. As he advanced, he was aided by Van Dorn's attack on Bolivar on December 23 which distracted the Federals from Forrest. Nonetheless, Forrest was forced to fight a brisk skirmish at Parker's Crossroads on December 31. In danger of being trapped by two Federal columns, he was said to have ordered his men to "charge them both ways."

By January 3, 1863, Forrest and his men were back in Columbia, Tennessee. Grant concluded, "Forrest got on our line of railroad between Jackson, Mississippi and Columbus, Kentucky, doing much damage . . . It was more than two weeks before rations or forage could be issued from stores." The raids of Van Dorn and Forrest left Grant in serious danger and forced him to withdraw back to La Grange, Tennessee, abandoning his effort to support Major General William Sherman's Chickasaw Bluff operation. They also illustrate the different paths individuals can take to leadership positions. For Van Dorn, Holly Springs was the result of failure and recovery. For Forrest, the raid on Jackson was the result of a steady climb up from a modest beginning. Indeed, Winston Groom describes Forrest's raid in terms that almost serve as an allegory for Forrest's steady evolution as a military leader. Groom says Forrest began the raid with "mostly green recruits, riding jaded horses and armed with shot guns and squirrel rifles." By the end of the operation, Forrest's command "was mounted admirably, well armed, and larger in strength than it was in the beginning."

LESSONS LEARNED

It is probably more correct to describe someone as a "developing leader" than to forthrightly declare someone to have arrived as a "full-fledged leader." Leaders' personal skills and situations change. They gain new responsibilities and shed old ones. New technologies emerge. Subordinates transfer in and out. Missions expand and contract. The result of this fluidity is that leaders are in a constant state of growth, development, and adaptation. Managers may be able to achieve a degree of steady state operations, but the world of a leader is very fluid.

Thus leader development often follows a circuitous path. Some like Van Dorn experience success and failure until they find the right leadership situation for their particular strengths and weaknesses. The key for leaders on this journey is to not give in to discouragement, but instead to critically review each experience, learn new skills, and be ready when an opportunity presents itself.

For others, leadership development is a longer, steadier process. Like Forrest, they may have to overcome some disadvantages such as a lack of formal education and replace it with the education that comes from on-the-job training. For those who like to debate whether leaders are born or made, Forrest illustrates that the answer is "some of both." To be sure, Forrest was naturally endowed with physical prowess that served him well as a close-quarters combat leader. Just as certainly, he developed his own cavalry tactics that recognized the proper use of mounted soldiers in the Civil War environment. Forrest's climb from fatherless boy to millionaire and from private to lieutenant general certainly can serve as inspiration for many aspiring leaders.

Takeaways:
- *Leader development follows different paths for different leaders.*
- *Leaders need to find their niche.*
- *Leaders must be able to weather storms.*
- *Everyone has the opportunity to become a leader.*

NINE

OTHER FAILED ATTEMPTS
Ulysses Grant and Perseverance

---

*Desperate to find an approach to Vicksburg, Grant was willing to try
most anything. While his preliminary attempts failed, they had the
unforeseen result of creating confusion in the Confederate command
once the campaign began in earnest.*

AFTER THE FAILURE OF THE CHICKASAW BAYOU EXPEDITION, GRANT
faced a difficult situation that required him to assess the future of his campaign. The winter of 1862–63 was particularly rainy, and the Mississippi
River and its tributaries soon rose to flood stage. With Grant's men huddled in miserable camps atop the levees within Milliken's Bend, one course
would have been to withdraw the army to the drier ground upriver at
Memphis. Instead, Grant launched a series of five expeditions designed to
turn the strong Confederate defenses. All five attempts failed, but they
show the persistence possessed by the Union commander. A man of lesser
determination might have succumbed to defeatism and quit. Instead,
Grant pressed on and demonstrated the determination and perseverance
required of a good leader.

The soggy conditions at Milliken's Bend not only plagued Grant's men;
they also increased the vulnerability of his still mixed reputation. The *New
York Times* complained that Grant "remains stuck in the mud of Northern
Mississippi, his army for weeks of no use to him or to anybody else." Grant
knew that inaction, or worse, a withdrawal north, would be interpreted as
defeat. Instead, he decided "to go forward to a decisive victory."

Grant had already recognized the difficulties the wet ground and the
strong Confederate defenses presented for an attack on Vicksburg from

the north. As early as January 18, 1863, he had realized "our troops must get below the city to be used effectively." However getting below the city presented its own set of challenges, and thus Grant wanted to investigate all his options.

Thus from January through March, Grant tried four separate plans to break through to Vicksburg. None of them succeeded.

The first effort was called "Grant's Canal." After capturing New Orleans, Admiral David Farragut made several attempts in the summer of 1862 to continue up the Mississippi River and capture Vicksburg. During that time frame, Brigadier General Thomas Williams began his own effort to dig a canal through the neck of De Soto Point, where the river makes a hairpin turn in front of Vicksburg. Williams hoped to divert the river south of the city, leaving Vicksburg high, dry, and irrelevant. Williams was unsuccessful in his effort.

From his headquarters at Young's Point, Grant could see the remnants of this earlier failure. While he did not think much of the idea, Major General Halleck advised him, "Direct your attention to the canal proposed across the point. The president attaches much importance to this." Pursuant to this admonition, Grant assigned Major General William Sherman responsibility for renewing the work when Sherman arrived at Young's Point on January 23, 1863.

Sherman described the remnants of Williams' project as being "no bigger than a plantation ditch," but he was nonetheless ordered to expand it into a canal 6 to 6 ½ feet deep, 60 feet wide, and 1 ½ miles long so as to accommodate Federal ironclads. Grant's chief engineer, Captain Frederick Prime, made some modifications to the design of the old canal, relocating the entry point to take advantage of the current, and then, using black labor and his XV Corps, Sherman began to dig.

The wet, damp weather made working conditions miserable, but Sherman's men began showing progress. Initially armed only with wheelbarrows and shovels, by February 19 soldiers had begun using steam pumps to draw the water out. When heavy rains played havoc with the pumps, Sherman brought two steam dredges from the Ohio River in early March to contribute to the effort. While such machinery paid off, the day after Grant reported to Washington that the "canal is near completion," disaster struck. The river broke through the temporary dam holding it back, and, instead of scouring out the canal as expected, it overflowed the banks, and flooded the surrounding area. To make matters worse, the Confederates realized what Grant was up to and positioned several big guns at the canal's exit, ready to destroy any vessels that should try to use it if Grant ever finished the project.

When the waters finally subsided enough for the Federals to resume work, they were met by a flurry of Confederate fire from across the river. Grant had had enough. On March 27, he ordered work on the canal to be halted.

Even as his men were digging the De Soto Point Canal, Grant was exploring other options. He ordered his engineers to study the possibility of opening a 200-mile route from the Mississippi River into the Red River near Port Hudson, Louisiana, some 250 miles by river below Vicksburg. Key to this strategy was Lake Providence, about forty miles north of Vicksburg in Louisiana. The lake had at one time been a bend in the Mississippi, but the river had changed course and the lake was now about a mile inland. If Grant could reconnect the lake and the river, he figured Porter's gunboats might be able to work their way through a series of south-ward-flowing waterways that winded their way to the Red River. From there, they could enter the Mississippi below Vicksburg. Grant thought this project would involve less than a quarter of the work required by the De Soto canal.

The route through Lake Providence would allow Grant to join forces with Major General Nathaniel Banks against Port Hudson and then the pair could move on to Vicksburg. Grant assigned Major General James McPherson, commander of the XVII Corps and a man of considerable engineering experience to the task. Upon reconnoitering the area, McPherson learned the Mississippi River was eight feet higher than the flat land behind the levee at Ashton, Arkansas. He concluded that the levee should be breached at Ashton in order to flood the area all the way to Bayou Macon, just over two miles west of Ashton. From there Bayou Macon flows into the Tenas River which flows into the Black River which flows into the Red River, giving Grant access to the Mississippi.

At first McPherson made great progress, breaching the levee at Ashton on March 4 and the one at Lake Providence on March 17. He was so pleased with the results that on March 23 he wrote Grant that "any

Cutting levees at Lake Providence from the March 21, 1863 *Harper's Weekly.*

steamboat that runs on the river can be taken in." A week later, however, McPherson began encountering problems in a cypress swamp west of Lake Providence. Because the swamp was only three and a half feet deep at its shallowest point, McPherson was confident he could dredge it out. First, however, he would need to cut about a dozen virgin cypress trees below the waterline, and to do this, he needed an underwater sawing machine that was being shipped from Memphis. Before it arrived, however, Grant lost interest in the Lake Providence Expedition, thinking he had found a better route at Yazoo Pass.

Yazoo Pass is six miles south of Helena, Arkansas, some 320 river miles north of Vicksburg. Until a levee was built in 1856, Yazoo Pass was used by small boats as the shortest and safest route between Yazoo City and Memphis. It ran from the Mississippi River through Moon Lake eastward to the Coldwater River. The Coldwater flows southeast to the Tallahatchie River which flows south to Greenwood, Mississippi where it joins the Yalobusha to form the Yazoo River. The Yazoo runs southwest to the Mississippi River and past the high ground north of Vicksburg.

Grant sent Lieutenant Colonel James Wilson to investigate the feasibility of reopening the Yazoo Pass, and on February 2 Wilson reached the levee that blocks the Pass from entering the Mississippi. The next day, Wilson and his men exploded fifty pounds of black powder and blasted a hole in the levee, which quickly filled with rushing water. Grant excitedly reported the development to Halleck on February 6, and the next day asked Porter to support a joint operation via the Yazoo Pass.

Porter agreed and provided six light-draft tinclads, two ironclads, two rams, and a mortar boat to protect thirteen transports. On February 7, Brigadier General Leonard Ross's division of 4,500 soldiers embarked on the Yazoo Pass Expedition. They quickly encountered huge trees the Confederates had felled to block the channel. Wilson complained that "for miles there was an entanglement so thick the troops could cross it from bank to bank." While some obstacles could be hauled away by ropes, others presented serious problems. The transports had been designed for regular river operations and their high, fragile superstructures and towering smoke-stacks were knocked down and swept away by overhanging branches. By the second day, Porter reported, "The vessels were so torn to pieces that no more harm could be done to them—they had hulls and engines left and that had to suffice." Against such odds it took the fleet four days to go just forty miles.

The painfully slow advance gave the Confederates plenty of time to prepare, and Major General William Loring and his force of 1,500 were ready and waiting at Fort Pemberton, built at the junction of the Tal-lahatchie and Yazoo Rivers. The fort was hastily constructed from cotton bales and dirt, but the defenders had narrowed the channel by sinking old ships. The fort was partially hidden by a bend so that approaching vessels would not know its location until it was too late. Once trapped, the surrounding ground was too swampy to allow Federal foot soldiers to maneuver.

The approach to Fort Pemberton was so narrow that the Federals could not bring to bear more than two gunboats attacking at one time, thus negating much of their firepower advantage. On March 11, 13, and 16, the Federals engaged Fort Pemberton, but could not force a passage. On March 21, elements of Brigadier General Isaac Quinby's division arrived to reinforce Ross, and when Quinby arrived, he assumed command. Although Grant professed "a great deal of confidence" in Quinby, he realized that the delays in the Yazoo Pass Expedition had given the Confederates time to strongly fortify. He ordered a withdrawal which began on the night on April 4, marking the end of a third failure.

In the meantime, however, Porter had been looking for an alternative route, and on March 13, he headed up the Yazoo River to investigate Steele's Bayou. This waterway ran north and eventually joined Black Bayou and then Deer Creek. Deer Creek continued north and had a branch called Rolling Fork which turned east and connected with the Sunflower River. The Sunflower headed back south and ultimately entered the Yazoo. It was a journey of 200 miles through five different waterways to end up just twenty miles north of the starting point, but in the process the route by-passed the Chickasaw Bluffs and Haynes' Bluff defenses north of Vicksburg to carry attacking troops to the city's rear.

Porter reported the results of his reconnaissance to Grant who was intrigued by the larger possibilities, and also saw it as a means of relieving Ross's floundering Yazoo Pass Expedition. Grant authorized Porter's plan, and on March 14, the admiral headed up the Yazoo with five ironclads and four tugs. Each tug towed a scow with a 13-inch mortar. On March 16, Grant ordered Sherman and a force of 10,000 men to begin moving in support of Porter.

Sherman was skeptical of the plan and he moved ahead of his soldiers aboard a tug to see things for himself. He caught up with Porter at Hill's Plantation, and together the commanders reconnoitered three miles up Deer Creek. Sherman did not think the ground was dry enough to support his marching troops, and he told Grant so. Porter, however, remained optimistic, and the plan went forward.

Soon Porter found himself in trouble. The Deer Creek channel progressively narrowed, and became choked with willows that fouled Porter's paddle wheels. The advance slowed to about a half mile per hour. Soon the Confederates learned of Porter's presence, and Lieutenant Colonel Sam Ferguson sent forward a detachment of cavalry to obstruct Deer Creek by felling trees. Ferguson then boarded a steamer with his infantry and artillery and reached the mouth of Rolling Fork Creek by the afternoon of March 19.

The next day, the Confederates opened fire on a forward position Porter had established on an Indian mound at the confluence of Deer and Rolling Fork Creeks. Although the Federals checked Ferguson's initial attack, Rebel reinforcements under the command of Brigadier General Winfield Scott Featherston soon arrived, and the Confederates attacked en masse.

Porter had already sent a request to Sherman to come to his aid, but his advance had been slowed by the rough terrain. On the night of March 20, Porter sent Sherman another note imploring him to "Hurry up for Heaven's sake. I never knew how helpless an ironclad could be steaming around through the woods without an army to back her." In danger of being trapped by obstacles to his rear and advancing Confederates to his front, Porter had no choice but to beat a hasty retreat. Desperate to free himself from the worsening situation, Porter released the rudders from his gunboats and allowed them to drift downstream, bouncing off the trees on the creek banks as they went.

In spite of this lack of control, Porter's vessels made good time in their withdrawal until one of the ironclads accidentally rammed and sank a coal barge, effectively blocking the exodus at a point just two and three quarters miles south of Rolling Fork. Ferguson's men had rushed forward and established a position on the Indian mound from which they began shelling the Federal flotilla at 6:00 a.m. on March 21. However, the Confederate shells were ineffective against the ironclads' protective plate, and Ferguson was forced to launch an infantry attack. Unfortunately for Ferguson, Featherston withdrew his men rather than joining in the attack and the Federals were able to hang on until 4:00 p.m. when Colonel Giles Smith arrived with the advance elements of Sherman's relief column. When Sherman personally arrived, he surveyed Porter's predicament and concluded, "I doubt if [Porter] was ever more glad to meet a friend than he was to meet me."

With the odds now evened and more of Sherman's men on the way, the Federals were able to stave off the Confederate attack and began clearing obstacles from the creek. By March 24, all of Sherman's men and the last of Porter's gunboats were safely back at Hill's Plantation. From there, Porter received an order from Grant on March 26 telling him to return to Young's Point. Steele's Bayou would prove to be the closest call and the last of Grant's bayou expeditions.

In spite of these abortive efforts, Grant never lost his optimism, and apparently his soldiers had also come to appreciate their commander's perseverance. In fact, a story began to circulate around the campfires of a Confederate general's interrogation of a Federal soldier captured in the Yazoo Delta:

"What in the thunder did Grant expect to do in there?" asked the general.

"Take Vicksburg," the prisoner calmly replied.

"Well, hasn't the old fool tried ditching and flanking five times already?" demanded the Confederate after adding Chickasaw Bayou to the four recent failures.

"Yes," admitted the soldier, "but he has 37 more plans in his pocket, and one of them will get there now you bet."

Such an optimistic attitude, however, was not shared by many in the Lincoln administration and in the Northern press. Grant's reputation was still weak from the surprise he suffered on the first day at Shiloh, and three months of no progress in the Mississippi swamps had done nothing to silence his critics. Papers like the *Cincinnati Gazette* claimed Grant had "botched the whole campaign," and calls for his removal began to increase. Grant withstood the attacks stoically. In his *Memoirs* he wrote, "Because I would not divulge my ultimate plans to visitors, they pronounced me idle, incompetent and unfit to command men in an emergency, and clamored for my removal." Yet he "took no steps to answer these complaints, but continued to do my duty, as I understood it, to the best of my ability." Grant's hold on his command was tenuous at best, but the failures and criticism had not dimmed his perspective or commitment.

Grant later claimed that he never expected the schemes to work, but only undertook them to keep his men busy and to create the illusion of activity necessary to silence his critics. J.F.C. Fuller agrees, writing, "All [the efforts] were extremely difficult, entailed immense labor on the part of the army and the fleet; and although all failed in their object, they undoubtedly formed admirable training for Grant's army, hardening and disciplining the men, in fact turning them into salted soldiers."

In addition to honing the mettle of his men, Grant's persistence also created a certain amount of bewilderment in his opponent Pemberton. The seemingly haphazard endeavors gave Pemberton the impression Grant was operating everywhere and left him in a state of confusion when Grant finally attacked in earnest after the water levels began to drop in late March. This development proved to be a fortuitous byproduct of Grant's refusal to give up.

LEADERSHIP LESSONS

Grant's successful application of perseverance should be distinguished from blind and unimaginative repetition of failed practices. The effective leader must know when to persist and when to cut his losses, just as Sherman did at the Chickasaw Bayou. Perseverance means continuing to move toward the ultimate goal, not just continuing unproductive activity. Leaders must keep their eye on the prize, but not become obsessed with a single course of action. The difference is a continuous assessment of the situation and the agility to respond. As James Arnold notes, Grant "accepted war's uncertainty by flexibly adjusting to new circumstances while maintaining a determined focus on the main chance." In the process, he modeled the leadership trait of perseverance.

Takeaways:
- *Leaders persevere, but persevering requires flexibility rather than blind adherence to an unproductive plan.*
- *Consider the message sent by inaction.*
- *You won't know unless you try. Investigate all options.*
- *Don't let criticism sway you from doing your duty.*

A CLOSE CALL FOR THE FEDERALS
Charles Dana and Dealing with Weakness

---

*The Western Theater of the Civil War was a long way from the eastern
capitals. With little apparent progress being made around Vicksburg,
President Abraham Lincoln dispatched Charles Dana to Mississippi
to check on what exactly Grant was up to.*

WHILE HISTORY HAS CONFIRMED GRANT'S PLACE AS THE HERO OF
Vicksburg, his position was much more tenuous as the campaign was un-
folding. Four months had brought little tangible progress toward capturing
the Confederate stronghold, and setbacks had been numerous. Rumors
persisted of Grant's drinking. Major General John McClernand, still chaf-
ing in his subordinate position, was doing his best to undermine Grant by
sending critical reports through his political allies in Washington. All these
variables put President Lincoln in the awkward position of risking an awful
lot on Grant, and he had to do something to determine if this trust was
warranted.

To help clear up the uncertainty, early in the spring of 1863, Secretary
of War Edwin Stanton dispatched his aide Charles Dana, the former man-
aging editor of Horace Greeley's *New York Tribune*, to Grant's headquarters.
Dana would be acting not as a journalist, but as a "special commissioner"
ostensibly appointed by Stanton to investigate the conduct of paymasters.
In fact, Dana would act as the Secretary of War's eyes and ears to determine
whether or not the negative reports about Grant were true. Dana even had
a secret code by which he could send his messages to the War Department
without fear of compromise. Stanton would then report Dana's findings
to Lincoln.

Dana was an interesting combination of intellectual and outdoorsman, and was well qualified for the important job Stanton had laid before him. He was a patriot and a strong supporter of Lincoln, and had wanted to join the military, but poor eyesight had prevented him from doing so. Although unable to serve as a soldier, Dana still wanted to help the Union cause. He knew both Lincoln and Stanton, and had met Grant in Memphis the previous year. Dana's initial impression had been that Grant was "a man of simple manners, straightforward, cordial, and unpretending." Dana certainly carried with him no predisposition to find fault with Grant, but he did not consider himself a champion of the general either. Dana was a neutral observer whose loyalties lay with his country and the Lincoln administration, and who took his duty seriously, knowing that the very state of the Union was in the balance.

Charles Dana. *Courtesy of the Library of Congress*

If Dana represented the detached investigator, and McClernand and others represented the political intriguers, Grant was also blessed with two strong allies in his camp. These were his chief of staff John Rawlins and his inspector general Lieutenant Colonel James Harrison Wilson. Both men were well aware of Grant's weakness but also appreciated his superior generalship. When Wilson first reported for duty at Grant's headquarters, Rawlins took him aside and explained the situation. "I'm glad you've come," explained Rawlins. "You're an Illinois man and so am I. I need you here. Now I want you to know what kind of man we are serving. He's a . . . Drunkard, and he's surrounded by a set of . . . Scalawags who pander to his weakness. Now for all of that, he is a good man, and a nice man, and I want you to help me in an offensive alliance against the . . . sons-of-bitches." With Dana's pending arrival, Rawlins and Wilson agreed on a strategy. As Wilson recalled, "It was finally decided that [Dana] was to have access to everything, favorable and unfavorable, official or personal. . . . With plenty of enemies about to bring him both truth and exaggerations, the worst tactics would be to arouse his suspicions by attempted conceal-ment. A wise decision and fully endorsed by Grant."

In such an open environment, it was only a matter of time before Dana would encounter Grant's weakness. The inevitable occurred as Dana accompanied Grant on a reconnaissance trip up the Yazoo River aboard Admiral David Porter's flagboat *Blackhawk*. As Dana later wrote, "Grant wound up going on board a steamer . . . and getting so stupidly drunk as the immortal nature of man would allow; but the next day he came out fresh as a rose, without any trace of the spree he had just passed through. So it was on two or three occasions of the sort and when it was all over, no outsider would have suspected such things had been."

Dana now had a choice. He could report the incident to Stanton, the very thing he had been dispatched to do, or he could keep quiet. If he did the former, Grant's career would likely be over. If Dana kept quiet, he would be violating his instructions from Stanton.

As a journalist, Dana's instinct must have been to report this sensa-tional story, but instead he decided to keep quiet. He had come to consider Grant "an uncommon fellow—the most modest, most disinterested, and the most honest man I ever knew, with a temper that nothing could disturb, and a judgment that was judicial in its comprehensiveness and wisdom." In Dana's mind, these qualities and Grant's importance to the Federal cause overshadowed his drinking problem.

LEADERSHIP LESSONS

Dana is often lauded as being among a handful of individuals who perhaps changed the course of the war. The argument goes that if Dana had given Stanton a negative report about Grant, the man who ultimately led the Federal Army to victory would have been relieved. To be sure, leaders must avoid a "zero-defects" mentality where a single shortfall is perceived as being career-ending. Instead, leaders must know when to underwrite the mistakes of deserving subordinates so that learning and growth can continue. Dana did just that.

However, leaders are also responsible for the actions of their subordinates. Particularly if the leader has firsthand knowledge of a subordinate's weakness, especially a critical one such as substance abuse, the leader must take action to protect the organization, its members, and its investors. The leader also has a responsibility to the subordinate. The leader cannot become a good-intentioned enabler to the subordinate's poor behavior. In some cases, the leader may even have legal responsibilities to report what she knows to the authorities. When the leader chooses to underwrite a subordinate's weakness, the leader then assumes the responsibility of ensuring those weaknesses do not cause damage. The leader must put in place some sort of check and balance system to meet that responsibility.

In Dana's case that check and balance was Rawlins. Dana would later witness Grant in another bout of binge drinking. This time he waited until the campaign ended to report the incident to Stanton, but Dana let the secretary know that, when necessary, Rawlins could control Grant's drinking. Dana did not turn a blind eye to Grant's problem or enable his destructive behavior. Instead he weighed the whole man, and, comfortable that a check and balance was in place, did not let one weakness ruin a general that was giving the Federals what they needed most—battlefield victories.

Takeaways:
- *No one is perfect. Leaders must weigh the whole person.*
- *Leaders may underwrite subordinate weakness but only with the utmost care and precaution. Underwriting does not mean enabling and cannot be extralegal.*
- *Leaders need someone to hold them accountable.*

ELEVEN

ASYMMETRIC WARFARE
Zedekiah McDaniel, Francis Ewing, and Innovation

The USS Cairo *was one of several Federal ironclads that patrolled Mississippi's inland waterways. Enterprising Confederates found a novel way to sink it.*

THE FEDERAL FLEET ON THE MISSISSIPPI RIVER, UNDER THE CAPABLE command of Admiral David Porter, was a decisive factor in Grant's success at Vicksburg. The Confederacy's limited industrial capacity left the defenders of Vicksburg woefully outmatched by the Federal Navy, including its powerful ironclads. Instead of confronting the threat conventionally, imaginative Confederates like Zedekiah McDaniel and Francis Ewing devised an innovative solution to help mitigate the disparity.

As early as 1822, naval theorists had begun proposing that wooden ships be replaced with iron ones, and the French had employed ironclads during the Crimean War. Still, the new technology attracted little attention in America, and on the eve of the Civil War, the tradition-bound United States Navy still relied on wooden ships.

The Confederates were the first to recognize the potential of ironclads in the Civil War. With few traditional resources at his disposal, Secretary of the Navy Stephen Mallory argued, "I regard the possession of an iron-armored ship as a matter of the first necessity . . . If we . . . follow their [the U.S. Navy's] . . . example and build wooden ships, we shall have to construct several at one time; for one or two ships would fall easy prey to her comparatively numerous steam frigates. But inequality of numbers may be compensated by invulnerability; and thus not only does economy but naval success dictate the wisdom and expediency of fighting with iron against wood."

When the Federals abandoned Gosport Navy Yard in Norfolk on April 20, 1861, they burned and scuttled the *Merrimack,* a 350-ton, 40-gun US steam frigate, in hopes of rendering it useless to the Confederates. In spite of this, Confederate engineers were able to raise the ship's hulk and found it to be in good shape, except for the upper works which had been destroyed by the fire.

With Mallory's urging, naval constructor John Luke Porter and Lieutenant John Mercer Brooke converted the *Merrimack* into an ironclad that was rechristened the CSS *Virginia.* Having learned of the Confederates' efforts to build an

David Dixon Porter, Rear Admiral.
Courtesy of the Library of Congress

ironclad, the Federals, led by Swedish-American inventor John Ericsson, began a similar project. Overcoming a three-month Confederate headstart, Ericsson built the *Monitor* in less than 100 days, and rushed it south just in time to prevent the *Virginia* from single-handedly destroying the Federal fleet. On March 9, 1862 the two strange-looking monsters battled to a tactical draw and ushered in a new era in naval warfare. Both the Federals and the Confederates soon embarked on ambitious programs to build or buy ironclads.

By the time of the Vicksburg Campaign, Porter had thirteen ironclads in his fleet. Among these was the USS *Cairo* whose casemate was protected by two and a half inches of armor fixed over timbers two feet thick. Rounded corners with railroad rails provided additional protection, and the octagonal pilothouse was covered by one and a half inches of iron over timbers. Such protection allowed Porter to attack the fortified Confederate batteries head-on, taking advantage of the location of the ironclads' thickest armor. As a result, many engagements were within 100 yards of an enemy fortification, with the ironclad blasting the position with grape and exploding shell in an attempt to break down the earthen parapet of the fort and disable its guns.

A variety of problems associated with funding and resources hamstrung Confederate efforts to build an ironclad fleet to rival that of the Federals. Indeed at Vicksburg, the greatest potential threat to the Federal Navy was from its own vessels falling into Confederate hands, an event which occurred in February 1863 when the Confederates captured the ram *Queen of the West* and the ironclad *Indianola* as they attempted to run downstream past the Vicksburg batteries. The *Queen of the West* served the Confederates until it was destroyed in action on the Atchafalaya River, and the Confederates foolishly scuttled the *Indianola* to prevent its recapture by what proved to be only an elaborate Federal ruse. With these losses, the Confederates at Vicksburg were forced to develop an innovative solution to contest the Federal Navy.

Lieutenant Isaac Brown had valiantly challenged the initial Federal naval blockade of Vicksburg with the ironclad *Arkansas* until August 6, 1862 when the vessel was destroyed to prevent capture. Without the *Arkansas*, Brown was in a quandary as to how to guard the Yazoo River until he was approached by Acting Masters Zedekiah McDaniel and Francis Ewing who told him of their experiments with naval mines.

Brigadier General Gabriel Rains had earlier pioneered the use of land mines by burying artillery shells along the roads and beach when the Confederates evacuated Yorktown, Virginia in May 1862. Both Federal and Confederate commanders criticized this "barbaric" method of warfare, and Rains was assigned to the river defenses where the use of his torpedoes was "clearly admissible." Matthew Maury, founder of the Confederacy's Submarine Battery Service, was also instrumental in experimenting with torpedoes and invented the electric version. Maury helped develop torpedo defenses for the James River, and Rains was instrumental in planning the torpedo defenses of Mobile Bay and Charleston Harbor. While Brown did not fully understand the technology behind this new weapon, he was willing to give it a try. He gave McDaniel and Ewing permission to develop their plan.

The two men built their torpedoes by filling five-gallon glass demi-johns with black powder and placing an artillery friction primer into the necks of the containers. The friction primer was in the form of a short tube, and in its top there was an explosive compound. Inserted into the compound was a roughened wire which protruded out of the top and connected to an external trigger line that joined pairs of demijohns. The design was such that when an unsuspecting enemy boat hit the trigger line, it would pull it tight and in the process provide the hard tug needed to start the explosive sequence. Ideally, the torpedo would explode toward the

The USS Signal. *Courtesy of the Library of Congress*

ironclad's rear or under the surface, locations which were both essentially unarmored. A creative system of floats, weighted pulleys, and adjustment lines kept the torpedoes hidden just below the surface of the water.

McDaniel and Ewing's innovation saw action on December 12 when a five-vessel Federal flotilla consisting of the *Marmora, Signal, Queen of the West, Pittsburgh*, and *Cairo* was patrolling the Yazoo. The day before, the *Marmora* and the *Signal* had seen numerous scows and floats that indicated torpedoes. One had exploded near the *Signal*, and the *Marmora* had successfully detonated another at a safe distance by rifle fire. As a precaution, the *Pittsburgh* and *Cairo*, both ironclads, were added to the force to provide extra support on the December 12 operation.

As the tinclad *Marmora* led the patrol, its sailors observed floating blocks of wood that served to hold McDaniel and Ewing's demijohns in place. Mistaking these buoys for torpedoes, the sailors began trying to safely detonate them with small arms fire. Unaware of the true situation, Commander Thomas Selfridge thought the *Marmora* had come under Confederate attack from the shore, and he ordered his ironclad *Cairo* ahead to provide support.

Because he was under orders not to run his vessels among torpedoes, Selfridge instead directed small boats be lowered to search for the devices. An ensign found and cut a line, most likely a trigger line, and when he did, a glass demijohn popped to the surface and revealed an adjustment line connecting it to the shore. Selfridge ordered this line cut.

In the midst of this excitement, the *Cairo* had drifted dangerously close to shore. When Selfridge belatedly saw what had happened, he ordered the engines reversed and called for the *Marmora* to get under way. Wary of the torpedoes he had just seen, the *Marmora's* lieutenant hesitated, which frustrated Selfridge. He repeated his order to the *Marmora* and then impetuously ordered the *Cairo* to push ahead.

Almost immediately, the *Cairo* was rocked by two explosions in quick succession, apparently having run into a trigger line that exploded one torpedo under the port bow and the linked torpedo just off the port quarter. Although the crew escaped with their lives, a fourteen-year-old crewman remembered that water "rushed in like Niagara." In just twelve minutes, the *Cairo* sank with only her smokestacks and flagstaff visible above the water. It was the first naval vessel in history to be sunk by a mine.

LEADERSHIP LESSONS

The sinking of the *Cairo* is an excellent example of asymmetric warfare. In asymmetric warfare, the weaker of two dissimilar opponents adopts new techniques to exploit the dissimilarity. The Federal Navy on the Mississippi reflected the latest technology while, by the time of the Vicksburg Campaign, the Confederate conventional naval threat there had all but ceased to exist. Symmetrically, the Confederates did not have a chance.

Sun Tzu, one of the classic military theorists whose popularity extends beyond the military to such realms as business, sports, and politics, was an early advocate of asymmetry. His writings include such advice as "as flowing water avoids the

heights and hastens to the lowlands, so an army avoids strength and strikes weakness," and "when confronted with an enemy one should offer a bait to lure him; feign disorder and strike him," and "when I have won a victory, I do not repeat my tactics but respond to circumstances in an infinite variety of ways." The mismatch of naval resources left the Confederate defenders of Vicksburg no choice but to use asymmetric tactics, but leaders in all situations must exercise the same innovative thinking in a variety of problem-solving situations. They must carefully weigh their strengths and weaknesses, and arrive at a solution that creates an advantage that, on the surface, is not apparent.

> ### *Takeaways:*
> • *Exploit strengths and avoid weaknesses.*
> • *Think asymmetrically, especially in disadvantageous situations.*
> • *Be innovative in problem solving.*
> • *Figure out what the competition expects, and then consider doing something different.*

— TWELVE —

RUNNING THE GAUNTLET
Ulysses Grant, David Porter,
and Unity of Effort

Vicksburg was a "joint" operation, meaning that it was an operation involving two or more military services. In this case, the joint forces were Grant's land force and Porter's naval force.

DURING THE TIME OF THE CIVIL WAR, THE PLANNING AND EXECUTION of joint operations were totally dependent on ad hoc actions by the responsible commanders. There were no formal command arrangements or doctrine to facilitate such coordination in the modern sense. Instead, successful joint operations were largely the result of improvisation and the personal actions of the commanders involved. Key to the difference between success and failure was the commanders' ability to achieve the military principle of unity of effort.

Unity of effort focuses on cooperation rather than command. Accordingly, it is distinct from the traditional military principle of unity of *command* which requires that "all forces operate under a single commander with the requisite authority to direct all forces employed in pursuit of a common purpose." Unity of *effort*, on the other hand, "requires coordination and cooperation among all forces toward a commonly recognized objective, although they are not necessarily part of the same command structure." Unity of effort was what joint operations during the Civil War required. To get it, effective communication, personal relationship skills, consensus building, and shared purpose would all be required.

Grant had some positive experience in this regard in his operations against Forts Henry and Donelson on the Tennessee and Cumberland

Rivers respectively, in early 1862. Grant's naval counterpart for this campaign was Captain Andrew Hull Foote, who Secretary of the Navy Gideon Welles had instructed to cooperate with the army without putting himself in a subordinate position. As a strong temperance man from New England, Foote presented a contrast to Grant, the Midwesterner known for being a binge drinker. In spite of their different backgrounds, the pair established an excellent working relationship.

Grant first proposed his operation against the two Confederate forts to his senior, Major General Henry Halleck, in January, but Halleck rejected the plan. In fact, Grant reported that he was "cut short as if my plan was preposterous." Although deeply disappointed, Grant still believed in the concept, and he shared it with Foote who agreed the idea was a good one. Both Grant and Foote hated inactivity, and together the two commanders cabled Halleck on January 28 and asked permission to operate against Fort Henry. Foote specifically assured Halleck that a naval force of four ironclads was sufficient. With Foote's endorsement, Halleck changed his mind and approved the plan.

Grant and Foote proceeded to work closely together to arrange for transportation and prepare for the landing of the troops. The operation was a huge success, with the Confederates surrendering after a fierce bombardment from Foote's gunboats and then Grant's soldiers arriving after the surrender to occupy the fort. They then cooperated in the even greater victory at Fort Donelson. Neither commander showed any undue concern over who got credit for success. Instead, through shared purpose, cooperation, and effective communication, the two achieved unity of effort.

Grant built on this experience at Vicksburg, but, in Porter, he had a much more volatile counterpart than he had in Foote. This admiral had an ambitious and self-seeking personality that led one fellow officer to opine, "Porter would assassinate the reputation of anyone in his way."

Porter had experience in joint operations at New Orleans, but his conduct there offered no assurance of his ability to work cooperatively. Always concerned with gaining glory and recognition for himself, throughout the attack's preparations Porter sent disloyal communications to the Navy Department, undermining his commander and foster brother Admiral David Farragut. Even after the victory, Porter became entangled in a squabble with army commander Major General Benjamin Butler over who had made the decisive contribution to the battle. Given Porter's brash temperament, it would be up to Grant to set the tone for cooperative effort at Vicksburg.

Grant knew a joint force was essential to success. After Farragut's victory at New Orleans, the admiral had made two unsuccessful naval attempts to capture Vicksburg. Farragut wrote to the Navy Department, "The Department will perceive from this report that the forts can be passed, and we have done it, and can do it again, as often as may be required of us. It will not, however, be an easy matter for us to do more than silence the batteries for a time, as long as the enemy has a large force behind the hills to prevent our landing and holding the place." To do so would require a cooperating army force of some 12,000 to 15,000 men according to Farragut's estimation.

Grant understood from the very beginning that capturing Vicksburg would require both land and naval forces. He explained, "I had had in contemplation the whole winter the movement by land to a point below Vicksburg from which to operate—my recollection was that Admiral Porter was the first one to whom I mentioned it. The cooperation of the Navy was absolutely essential to the success (even to the contemplation) of such an enterprise." In evaluating how this planned cooperation eventually transpired, Grant wrote that "The navy under Porter was all it could be, during the entire campaign. . . . The most perfect harmony reigned between the two arms of the service. There never was a request made, that I am aware of, either of the flag-officer or any of his subordinates, that was not promptly complied with."

One of the most important services provided by Porter and the navy was to run supplies and transports past the Confederate batteries to a position south of Vicksburg. The first passage occurred on the night of April 16 and consisted of twelve vessels—seven ironclads, a ram, a tug, and three transports. In addition to operating under the cover of darkness, Porter took other precautions such as venting exhausts into paddle-wheel housings to muffle the noise, and removing all animals from onboard to help maintain silence. Some crews had stacked grain sacks and cotton and hay bales on the decks to provide protection for people and vulnerable parts of the vessels. Others had lashed coal barges to the sides of their vessels to absorb enemy fire. Designated teams stood ready with cotton wads to patch any shell holes before they could fill with water. In the event a ship was disabled, captains had been instructed to stagger the column formation so they could easily pass a slowed vessel.

The tug *Rumsey* configured to run the Vicksburg batteries as depicted in the May 30, 1863 *Harper's Weekly.*

In contrast to these detailed Federal preparations, many of the Confederate defenders had relaxed their guard. Thinking Grant had withdrawn to Memphis, Pemberton was preparing to send an 8,000 man infantry division to reinforce General Braxton Bragg in Tennessee where he appeared harder pressed. On April 16, the *Vicksburg Whig* had concluded that Grant's men were demoralized and his gunboats damaged, leaving "no immediate threat here." In fact, that very night many officers and citizens gathered at the hillside home of Major William Watts for an elegant ball. Pemberton was at his headquarters in Jackson.

This Confederate confidence was shattered when Confederate pickets patrolling the river in skiffs saw the shadows of Porter's approaching fleet. The pickets set fire to several buildings on De Soto Point across the river while Confederates on the east bank ignited barrels of pitch. The river was soon illuminated, clearly revealing the targets for the Rebel batteries. Recalling the fire that soon erupted, one Federal captain reported, "It was as if hell itself were loose that night on the Mississippi River."

The entire passage took two and a half hours with most of Porter's vessels sustaining several hits before they reached safety at New Carthage, Louisiana. Nonetheless, the fleet fared remarkably well. Some forty-seven shots had struck the ironclads without doing significant damage, and only one transport was lost. Fifteen crewmen had been wounded and one was killed.

On April 20, Grant ordered the remainder of his army to move to New Carthage. Additional supplies would be necessary, so on April 22 Porter ran the Vicksburg batteries a second time. This passage consisted of six transports and twelve barges. Because their regular civilian crews were fearful of the danger, volunteers from infantry regiments served as crewmembers. The volunteers were offered thirty-day furloughs if they survived, and competition for the positions was so fierce men were willing to pay hard cash for the opportunity.

As with the first passage, crews fortified their vessels with various protections and prepared to deal with damages. Likewise, alert Confederates spotted the movement and illuminated the river. This time the Confederate fire took a heavier toll. Six barges were lost and the steamer *Tigress*, which Grant had formerly used as a headquarters ship, was struck thirty-five times and sank. The damage was sufficient that Grant prohibited future attempts to run the batteries. Nonetheless, by now he had what he needed below Vicksburg. With seven transports and fifteen or sixteen barges, Grant had a sufficient flotilla to carry his men across the Mississippi River.

The Confederate defense had placed a great deal of confidence in not just the Vicksburg batteries but in Pemberton's assumed expertise from Charleston in using artillery against ships. The two Federal passages demonstrated that these expectations were misplaced. One problem was there were simply too few guns to cover the large stretch of river, and the artillery had of necessity been widely dispersed. Moreover, the guns could not depress sufficiently to hit the vessels that hugged the eastern shoreline, a problem exacerbated by the thick parapets that protected the gunners.

During the first passage, the *Tuscumbia* and the *Forest Queen* had collided, leaving the pair helplessly vulnerable directly below the Confederate artillery. However, frustrated gunners found that if they depressed their barrels sufficiently to hit the targets, the shot literally rolled out of the muzzle before the gun could be fired. During the second passage, Federal pilots purposely hugged the eastern shore to take advantage of this situation. Confederate efforts were also hamstrung by the fact that the windless conditions on April 22 failed to disperse the heavy smoke from the guns, obscuring the targets. During both passages, the Confederate gunners exhibited poor fire discipline. Rather than engaging all vessels, the Confederates concentrated on the damaged ones, allowing others to slip by. For example, on the night of April 22, the Confederates fired 391 shots, but aside from barges, only managed to sink the *Tigress*.

These Confederate shortcomings aside, the key to the successful passage of Grant's army south of Vicksburg was the cooperative effort of the army and the navy. Grant had reached out to Porter, recognizing that the navy's support was critical to success. Porter, who undoubtedly realized from Farragut's earlier attempt that the navy needed the army as well, reciprocated by doing what Grant needed done, in spite of the operation's uncertainty and danger. Together, the pair achieved the unity of effort necessary to accomplish the mission.

LEADERSHIP LESSONS

James MacGregor Burns distinguished two types of leadership: transactional and transformational. The bulk of traditional leadership models are transactional ones in which the focus is on the exchanges that occur between leaders and their followers. A typical exchange under this leadership arrangement is a teacher who gives a student a grade based on a certain level of demonstrated knowledge on a test.

On the other hand, transformational leadership is a process in which an individual engages with others and forms a connection that raises the level of motivation, commitment, and morality in both the leader and the followers. The transformational leader is keenly aware of and responsive to the needs and motives of his/her followers and tries to help them achieve their fullest potential.

As organizational structures become increasingly horizontal and leadership becomes increasingly transformational, the ability to achieve unity of effort is critical. Grant built this cooperative environment by early and frequent communication with Porter. He used his excellent personal relationship skills to disarm the ambitious admiral and allow them to form a partnership built on the shared purpose of capturing Vicksburg.

> ***Takeaways:***
> • *Even in cases where there is no hierarchal command relationship, leaders must establish unity of effort.*
> • *Communicate early and use personal relationship skills to establish trust and break down barriers.*
> • *Build consensus based on shared purpose. Find a common denominator.*

THIRTEEN

HELPING RUN THE GAUNTLET
William Sherman and
Playing a Supporting Role

In spite of all the preparations and precautions, Admiral David Porter's running the gauntlet was still a hazardous affair. With the ominous Confederate batteries on the Vicksburg bluffs poised to deliver deadly fire, many Federal vessels would no doubt be hit. While it would be up to Porter and the navy to make the treacherous passage, Major General William Sherman was ready to assist in whatever way possible.

IN PREPARATION FOR PORTER'S RUN, GRANT HAD ACQUIRED VARIOUS yawls and barges from St. Louis and Chicago to be used as ferries once the army got below Vicksburg. Sherman had ordered his men to haul four of these vessels across the swamps and into the Mississippi River below Vicksburg. There they were "manned with soldiers, ready to pick up any of the disabled wrecks as they passed by." On the night of the passage, Sherman positioned himself on one of these yawls well off shore, ready to support the operation.

The first passage was conducted on April 16, 1863, and it went remarkably well. Many ships were hit but only one was lost, and only one Federal was killed. Grant ordered another passage the night of April 26, which again was successful. On this passage Grant's headquarters steamer *Tigress* was hit and sunk. Grant personally was not on board, and Sherman and his men were close at hand in a yawl to help the stranded sailors ashore.

The destination of Porter's run was New Carthage, Louisiana, on the west bank of the Mississippi about twenty miles below Vicksburg. There

Sherman greeted each vessel as it arrived. When Porter's flagship reached the location, Sherman went aboard and welcomed the admiral by saying, "You are more at home here than you were in the ditches grounding on willow trees," a reference to the ill-fated Steele's Bayou expedition in which Sherman's infantry had to help rescue Porter from Confederate obstructions and sniper fire. Sherman had obviously embraced the spirit of joint cooperation and unity of effort that Grant had instilled in his command.

After the safe passage of Porter's fleet, Sherman and his corps returned to Milliken's Bend where they would be ready to strike Vicksburg's upriver defenses if the Confederates got careless. To further confound Pemberton, Grant also initiated a series of feints, the most notable being Colonel Benjamin Grierson's cavalry raid through Mississippi. Grant also intimated to Sherman that a feint near Chickasaw Bluffs, the site of Sherman's earlier repulse, might also be useful. Grant knew the delicacy of this suggestion, telling Sherman, "The effect of a heavy demonstration in that direction would be good as far as the enemy are concerned, but I am loath to order it, because it would be hard to make our own troops understand that only a demonstration was intended and our people at home would characterize it as a repulse. I therefore leave it to you whether to make such a demonstration."

For Sherman, such matters as what the newspapers thought were of little concern. The feint would help the army and Grant, and that was enough for Sherman. He wrote Grant, "I will make as strong a demonstration as possible." He began his move on April 29 with ten regiments loaded on Porter's transports.

It seems odd that Sherman, by far Grant's most trusted subordinate, would be allocated supporting roles of assisting Porter's passage and conducting feints while the troublesome Major General John McClernand spearheaded the army's march down the west side of the Mississippi. The day Sherman began his feint was the day Porter shelled Grand Gulf in hopes of paving the way for McClernand to cross the river there. When the Grand Gulf defenses proved too strong, Grant continued his march southward, and Porter ferried McClernand across the river at undefended Bruinsburg on April 30. On May 1, McClernand initiated the Battle of Port Gibson, a few miles north, with reinforcements from Major General

James McPherson soon arriving. Missing all this action, Sherman was hurrying his corps south to join Grant. Outflanked by the Federal forces moving inland, the Confederates evacuated Grand Gulf on May 3, and Sherman crossed there from Hard Times on May 6 and 7. Only then did he assume the center position in Grant's march toward Edwards on May 11.

Grant offers no explanation in his *Memoirs* as to why he relegated Sherman to a supporting role in these early stages of the spring campaign. Perhaps Grant felt more comfortable with the trusted Sherman operating independently, and preferred a plan where he could more closely supervise the ambitious McClernand and the capable but young McPherson. Regardless of Grant's reasoning, Sherman never questioned his supporting role. Instead, he pursued it with enthusiasm and purpose, content that he was making the contribution that his commander required of him.

LEADERSHIP LESSONS

With very few exceptions, even the most senior leaders are themselves part of a larger organization and are responsible to an even more senior leader. Leaders must be able to understand their role in serving the needs of the larger organization. John Maxwell's observation that "everyone is part of a team," applies to leaders as well. Maxwell has identified "17 Indisputable Laws of Teamwork," and Sherman's actions illustrate several. Maxwell's "law of the big picture" states that "the goal is more important than the role." For Sherman, the big picture was Federal victory, not individual glory. He was willing to do whatever he could to contribute to Grant's plan. Maxwell also argues that "as the challenge escalates, the need for teamwork elevates." Again, Sherman understood this. Vicksburg was a Confederate stronghold that had thus far withstood repeated Federal advances. One early failure occurred when Admiral David Farragut had pushed upriver from New Orleans without army support. Sherman knew a team effort was required, and he supported Porter as the navy undertook the dangerous task of running the gauntlet. Finally, Sherman epitomizes Maxwell's "law of countability" which holds that "teammates must be able to count on each other when it counts." Although Grant felt he would benefit from Sherman conducting a feint toward Chickasaw Bluff, he did not order Sherman to undertake the awkward task. As it turned out, he didn't need to. He could count on Sherman to realize the value of the move and to do it, even without an order, because of Sherman's sense of team-work.

Takeaways:
- *Even leaders must know how to follow.*
- *Leaders always find a way to contribute to the organization, regardless of the role.*
- *The demands for teamwork increase with seniority and complexity.*

— FOURTEEN —

THE BATTLE OF PORT GIBSON
John Bowen and Technical Competence

Having passed below Vicksburg, Grant still had to cross the Mississippi River and secure a foothold. The Battle of Port Gibson left Grant safely on high ground on the eastern side of the river.

WHILE ADMIRAL DAVID PORTER WAS RUNNING THE GAUNTLET, Grant's army was marching down the western side of the Mississippi River toward New Carthage. Grant considered crossing the river at Warrenton, about ten miles south of Vicksburg, before ultimately deciding to cross at Grand Gulf. On April 26, he ordered Major General John McClernand to march his corps south to Hard Times, which lay slightly upriver from Grand Gulf on the opposite shore.

Grand Gulf stood about thirty air miles south of Vicksburg where the river-bluff interface afforded a strong defensive position. Brigadier General John Bowen, an 1853 graduate of West Point, commanded the Confederate forces there. Bowen was Pemberton's best combat general, leading Michael Ballard to speculate that, "Had Pemberton had a few more Bowens to send into the field, the Vicksburg campaign might have turned out differently." Bowen certainly had a reputation as a fighter, having been wounded at Shiloh and having fought a stiff rear-guard action that saved Major General Earl Van Dorn's army at Corinth. Bowen had little patience with incompetent subordinates or superiors, and he no doubt found Pemberton's indecision frustrating.

Admiral David Farragut had burned Grand Gulf in 1862, and Bowen had built two fortified batteries, approximately 1,000 yards apart, on either side of the town's ruins. Fort Cobun lay on the upstream side and downstream was Fort Wade. Fort Cobun was built by cutting a notch into the face of the bluff forty feet above river level, and piling the spoil to form a parapet forty feet thick. Its defenses included one 8-inch Dahlgren, one 30-pounder Parrott, and two-32 pounder rifles. Fort Wade was about twenty feet above river level and approximately 300 yards back from the river. It had one 100-pounder Blakely rifle, one 8-inch Dahlgren, and two 32-pounders. Several more field pieces stood between the forts. Some of Bowen's infantry manned a line of rifle pits that connected the forts, but most were behind the crests of the hills.

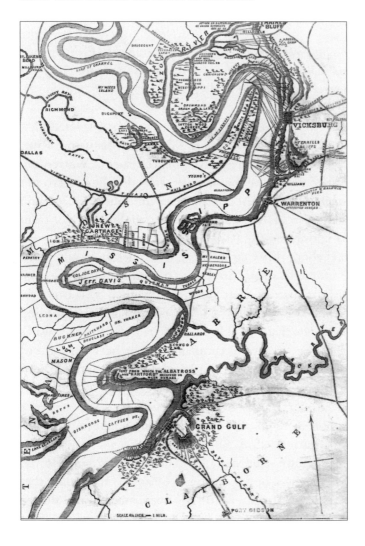

Map of Vicksburg and Grand Gulf from the May 23, 1863 *Harper's Weekly.*

By April 27 McClernand was at Hard Times, and McPherson was closing rapidly. Sherman was still opposite Vicksburg, and this dispersal of Federal troops kept Pemberton guessing. Grant further confused Pemberton by having Sherman send a strong force back up the Yazoo to create a diversion around Hayne's Bluff.

Grant had a truly joint plan for Grand Gulf. Porter and the navy would silence the Confederate batteries, followed by rapid landings by McClernand's corps to seize the fortifications and secure a foothold for the rest of the army. On April 29, Porter's ironclads opened fire on Grand Gulf. They were able to neutralize Fort Wade, but Fort Cobun remained active. At 1:00 p.m., Porter called off the bombardment, declaring, "Grand Gulf is the strongest place on the Mississippi."

Undeterred, Grant decided to outflank Grand Gulf by moving south to Bruinsburg, where he had learned from a runaway slave that there was an unguarded landing site. Bruinsburg was roughly halfway between Grand Gulf and Rodney, and early on the morning of April 30, McClernand's corps boarded Porter's ironclads and transports and steamed downstream. They conducted an unopposed landing of over 17,000 men, making Bruinsburg the largest amphibious operation in American history until the Allied invasion of Normandy in World War II.

Even with the successful crossing, Grant could still not feel safe. The bluff line that represented high, dry ground was about a mile inland from the Bruinsburg landings, and if the Confederates could establish defensive positions at the bluffs before Grant reached them, the Federals would be faced with a situation similar to the Chickasaw Bayou disaster. Such a potential crisis never developed, however, because Pemberton was confused by all the diversions and conflicting reports. He completely misread Grant's intentions, leaving Christopher Gabel to conclude, "Thus, the Battle of Bruinsburg, potentially the most important engagement of the Vicksburg campaign, never took place."

Instead, Grant advanced unopposed on the Rodney and Bruinsburg Roads toward Port Gibson until he eventually met Confederate outposts after midnight on May 1. The opposing forces clashed for about three hours, and then the Confederates fell back and the Federals renewed their advance on Rodney Road at dawn. In subsequent fighting, the Confederates established new defensive positions at different times during the day,

John Bowen.
Courtesy of the Library of Congress

but they could not stop the Federal advance.

Michael Ballard describes Bowen as "a taskmaster who always had his men prepared," and, true to form, Bowen was now as prepared as he could have been under the circumstances. Two days before the attack on Grand Gulf, he had recognized the danger of a Federal landing downstream and dispatched his engineers "on a reconnaissance selecting a line of battle south of Port Gibson." His intention was to use the dense ground in front of Port Gibson to delay Grant long enough for Pemberton to mount a meaningful counterattack. Grant recalled, "The country in this part of Mississippi stands on edge, as it were, the roads running along ridges except when they occasionally pass from one ridge to another. Where there are no clearings the sides of the hills are covered with a very heavy growth of timber and with undergrowth, and the ravines are filled with vines and canebrakes, almost impenetrable."

This thick vegetation and loess hills would serve to restrict the Federal advance to the roads, compounding the effect of Bowen's much smaller force. With this slight advantage, Bowen held on until about 5:30 p.m. when he realized that further resistance would mean sacrificing his entire command. He ordered a general retreat, but for twelve hours, with less than 7,000 Confederates, he had held back a Federal force that had swollen to 24,000. James Arnold credits Bowen with having fought "a masterful offensive-defensive delaying action," and even Grant conceded that Bowen's plan was "very bold" and "well carried out."

Nonetheless, Bowen's skillful effort was largely for naught. Rather than using the time Bowen and his men had dearly bought, Pemberton remained confused. He had sent three infantry brigades in fruitless pursuit of Colonel Grierson's diversionary cavalry raid, making them unavailable as reinforcements against the Federals' main thrust. In spite of Bowen's early warning of the Federal landing at Bruinsburg, Pemberton merely moved his headquarters from Jackson to Vicksburg rather than coming to Port Gibson to personally direct operations. Other than belatedly dispatching two brigades from Brigadier General Carter Stevenson's division to reinforce Bowen, Pemberton had little positive influence on the battle. Much too late Pemberton realized, as he reported to President Davis, "Enemy's success in passing our batteries has completely changed character of defense."

Bowen was forced to abandon more than just Port Gibson. With his position turned, Grand Gulf was also untenable, and he ordered a withdrawal from that location on the night of May 7. The victory at Port Gibson had secured Grant's position on Mississippi soil, and the evacuation of Grand Gulf provided him a supply base he could use to support future operations.

LEADERSHIP LESSONS

Bowen is a good example of what the US Army describes as the "be, know, and do" requirements of a leader. A leader must "be" a person of certain qualities that he possesses all the time. While leadership comes more naturally to some people than it does to others, all leaders develop their skills as a result of experience, study, and positions of increased responsibility. Bowen was this kind of leader. He was a West Point graduate who had been shaped by practical experience at Shiloh, Corinth, and elsewhere. It was too late for Bowen to develop into a leader when Grant forced his passage of Vicksburg. Bowen already had to be one.

Next a leader must "know" how to respond to a certain situation. He must have the prerequisite skills to fulfill his leadership responsibilities. As Major General William Cohen notes, to be a leader you must "know your stuff." Again, Bowen's actions demonstrate a remarkable ability to assess the situation and develop a course of action. He promptly identified the Federal threat (long before Pemberton did), and the dispatch of his engineers to reconnoiter the area in front of Port Gibson showed both excellent presence of mind and technical knowledge of defensive operations. He understood the big picture and the need to buy time for Pemberton to formulate a coordinated counterattack.

Finally, Bowen was able to "do." At the end of the day, leadership is about action. There are many people who possess great skill. There are still others who can develop detailed plans that account for every possible contingency. However, if the leader stops short of putting these skills and these plans into action, nothing will be accomplished. Bowen acted. He succeeded in delaying a much larger force with little help from his commander. It is unfortunate for the Confederate cause that Pemberton did not make better use of Bowen's contribution, but that in no way diminishes Bowen's skillful delay of Grant's approach to Port Gibson.

Takeaways:
- *Leaders must "be, know, and do."*
- *Leaders must correctly assess the situation.*
- *Leaders must make the best of the resources available.*
- *Leaders must be realistic about what can be done under the circumstances.*

— FIFTEEN —

"CUTTING LOOSE"
Ulysses Grant and Taking Risk

After crossing the Mississippi River, Grant "cut loose" from his base of supplies and headed northeast. It was a critical decision that allowed him to isolate Vicksburg and shows that leaders must know when and how to take prudent risks.

GRANT'S LINE OF SUPPLY FOR HIS ADVANCE INTO MISSISSIPPI WAS the Mississippi Central Railroad, originating in Grand Junction, Tennessee. Maintaining the railroad sapped the Federal Army of troops both to guard and repair it. In order to get the forces and freedom of maneuver he needed to execute his Vicksburg Campaign, Grant would have to take some risk with his logistics.

As a young quartermaster lieutenant during the Mexican War, Grant had observed General Winfield Scott deal with a similar problem. Scott had begun his campaign with an amphibious landing at Vera Cruz. After the city fell to a siege, he established a supply base there, but this supply line became increasingly costly to maintain. In order to protect his rear from Mexican guerrillas, Scott was forced to leave garrisons at Vera Cruz, Jalapa, and Perote. This requirement, as well as other factors, had reduced his active army at Puebla by 5,820 men, and to regain strength, Scott ordered that all stations between Vera Cruz and Puebla be abandoned. He was effectively cutting his army off from the coast. He would have no supply line, and would live off the land.

Scott's move was bold and audacious. It was also not without its critics. Upon learning of Scott's decision, the Duke of Wellington, who had been closely following the campaign, declared, "Scott is lost! He has been carried

119

away by success! He can't take [Mexico City], and he can't fall back on his base."

Scott, however, would prove the skeptics wrong and developed an effective system of local supply. By ridding himself of the requirement to secure his lines of communication with garrisons, Scott amassed an army of some 14,000 men. Both this greater strength and his freedom from a fixed line of supply allowed him to fight the war of maneuver that he desired.

Scott's lead elements departed Puebla on August 7, 1847 and quickly began to feel the pinch of the reduced logistics. Colonel Ethan Hitchcock lamented, "We have no forage for our horses; our hard bread is getting musty; we have four days' rations for the army and some beef on hoof." Captain Edmund Kirby Smith wrote, "Mexico must fall or we must all find a grave between this and the city." Hitchcock and Smith had accurately described the situation. Scott's bold move of cutting loose from his line of supply required a victory soon in order to reverse the increasingly desperate conditions.

Then at Contreras on August 19 and Churubusco on August 20 Scott got the victories he needed. He had crossed the entire Valley of Mexico and succeeded at what Russell Weigley considers "one of the most daring movements of American military history." Even the Duke of Wellington reversed himself, declaring Scott to be "the greatest living soldier" and urging young English officers to study the campaign as one "unsurpassed in military annals."

Grant's biographer William McFeely describes Grant as "virtually unnoticed himself in the Mexican War," but a man who took the opportunity to "watch his fellow warriors carefully." As a quartermaster, Grant had seen Scott take a logistical risk and reap great dividends. Now no longer a lieutenant in Mexico but a major general commanding the Federal Army approaching Vicksburg, Grant had an opportunity to apply what he had learned.

Grant was reminded of the vulnerability of extended supply lines during his firsts drive on Vicksburg. On December 12, 1862, Pemberton ordered Major General Earl Van Dorn to take command of all the cavalry in the vicinity of Grenada, Mississippi, launch a sweep around Grant's left flank, destroy the Federal depot at Holly Springs, and wreck as much of the Mississippi Central and the parallel Memphis and Charleston Railroad as he could. On December 18, Van Dorn and 3,500 cavalrymen left Grenada, and on December 20 they surprised the Federal force at Holly Springs, capturing or destroying an estimated half million dollars' worth of supplies there. From there, Van Dorn proceeded north, destroying as much of the railroad as he could before returning to Grenada on December 28.

Simultaneously, a twin raid was conducted by Brigadier General Nathan Bedford Forrest against the important rail junction at Jackson, Tennessee on December 20. Forrest rampaged through the area, capturing Union outposts and destroying railroads, bridges, and telegraph lines. The two raids left Grant in serious danger, and he was forced to return to his base near La Grange, Tennessee while Sherman continued unsupported toward his eventual repulse at Chickasaw Bluffs. During his withdrawal, however, Grant found abundant forage in Mississippi to sustain his army. He would file this experience away for future use, resolving not to "starve in the midst of plenty."

Timothy Donovan writes, "To attempt to measure the amount of influence of the two cavalry raids on the subsequent decision by Grant to abandon his overland approach [after the Battle of Port Gibson] can only lead to a subjective estimate at best. . . . [Nonetheless], the raids of Van Dorn and Forrest displayed cavalry in a classic example of the excellent use of a small, highly mobile unit in an economy of force role." Indeed, the Confederate western commander General Joseph Johnston came to place his main effort for defeating Grant on cavalry raids against the vulnerable rail communications in western Tennessee. The Confederate raiders presented Grant with the same problem of a vulnerable line of supply as the Mexican guerrillas had presented Scott, and Grant knew just what to do about it.

On May 3, Grant learned that Major General Nathaniel Banks would be delayed in joining him. In his *Memoirs* Grant writes, "Up to this time my intention had been to secure Grand Gulf, as a base of supplies, detach McClernand's corps to Banks and cooperate with him in the reduction of Port Hudson." With this new development, Grant instead "determined to move independently of Banks, cut loose from my base, destroy the rebel force in rear of Vicksburg or invest or capture the city." In implementing this decision, Grant, who John Keegan describes as having a mind "stocked with an analytic knowledge of past campaigns," drew heavily on his experience in Mexico.

In so doing, Grant demonstrated the correct use of frame of reference. Unlike Pemberton, who inappropriately tried to apply his siege experience from Charleston to the radically different Vicksburg problem, Grant was able to connect two similar experiences and apply what he had learned in the first one to the second. He was not robotically imitating a formula whether the new situation called for it or not. Instead, he was drawing on his frame of reference in Mexico to leverage a skill in a new set of circumstances where it also made sense. Jean Edward Smith explains Grant's frame of reference saying that in Mexico, Grant learned "the intricacies of military logistics from the bottom up. For a man who would go on to command large armies, no training could have been more valuable. During the Civil War, Grant's armies might occasionally have straggled, discipline might sometimes have been lax, but food and ammunition trains were always expertly handled. While Grant's military fame deservedly rests on his battlefield victories, those victories depended on his skill as a quartermaster. Unlike many Union armies, the forces he led never wanted the tools of war."

But there is a huge difference between a risk and a gamble, and Grant certainly overstates the idea that he completely "cut loose" from his supply lines. As he moved east of the Mississippi River, Grant continued to receive a steady stream of supplies carried in wagons from Young's Point to Bower's Landing, where the supplies were loaded on steamboats and carried to Grand Gulf. From Grand Gulf, huge wagon trains, sometimes numbering up to 200 vehicles, then brought the supplies forward. What Grant did not do was occupy and garrison his supply route, and this is where, like Scott, he assumed risk. That risk was mitigated, however, by the logistical infrastructure Grant had carefully put in place before he began his march inland.

While Grant still received supplies by wagons, he was also drawing from the Confederate countryside. Even many of his wagons were brought in by scavenger teams. The result was "an abundant array of farm vehicles, ranging from long-tongued wagons designed for hauling cotton bales, to elegant plantation carriages, upholstered phaetons, and surreys. The vehicles were drawn by an equally odd assortment of horses, mules, and oxen—probably the most unmilitary military train ever assembled." The system worked. One of Grant's privates bragged, "We live fat."

Typical Civil War-era horse and wagon team in Mississippi.
Courtesy of the Library of Congress

LEADERSHIP LESSONS

Grant's decision to "cut loose" from his base exemplifies at least four elements common to all instances in which a leader takes prudent risk. First of all, risk-taking is likely to draw criticism with which the leader must be prepared to deal. Recognizing this, Grant purposely delayed notifying

Ulysses Grant.
Courtesy of the Library of Congress

General-in-Chief Henry Halleck of the decision until it was too late to stop it, because Grant "knew well that Halleck's caution would lead him to disprove of this course." Even Grant's friend Sherman wrote Grant to advise him "of the impossibility of supplying our army over a single road." In spite of less than full support from those above and below him, Grant had the strength of character a leader needs to take risk.

Risk-takers must also take measures to mitigate the risk. This step not only helps create conditions necessary for success, it also prevents disaster if the risk does not fully succeed. Understanding Sherman's concerns, Grant explained, "I do not calculate upon the possibility of supplying the army with full rations from Grand Gulf. I know it will be impossible without constructing additional roads. What I do expect is to get up what rations of hard bread, coffee, and salt we can, and make the country furnish the balance." Grant eventually got an efficient system of wagons rolling, but until then forage would tide his army over. In his *Memoirs*, Grant writes, "We started from Bruinsburg with an average of about two days' rations, and received no more from our supplies for some days; abundance was found in the meantime." Grant mitigated his risk by combining wagons and forage, and also expecting his soldiers to tighten their belts for a few days.

The third element of risk is that it should be designed to be a temporary condition. An organization that is continually at risk is the result of poor planning rather than bold leadership. Risk is taken to meet a specific situation rather than to be a replacement for the long-term need for security. Therefore, Grant knew he had to restore his army to a more stable logistical posture as soon as possible. Time would be of the essence. Grant understood that even with the abundant forage he expected to find, he could not afford any long halts at which local supplies would be exhausted. He would have to keep the army moving. To this end, he wrote Sherman, "It's unnecessary for me to remind you of the overwhelming importance of celerity in your movements."

Finally, leaders take risk in one area to create an opportunity elsewhere. In Grant's situation that opportunity was the ability to fight the war of maneuver upon which his strategy rested. By freeing himself from a static supply system, Grant was able to position his army between Pemberton at Vicksburg and Johnston in Jackson. Through the use of interior lines, Grant now had the opportunity of "threatening both or striking at either." He did so by capturing Jackson on May 14 to block Johnston's reinforcements, and then defeating Pemberton at Champion's Hill on May 16 to force Pemberton to withdraw to a siege situation in Vicksburg.

Takeaways:
- *Leaders must be willing to take risks.*
- *Risk-takers must be prepared for criticism.*
- *There is a difference between a risk and a gamble, and risk-takers must initiate measures to mitigate the risk.*
- *Risk-taking should result in a temporary condition that furthers opportunity elsewhere.*

SIXTEEN

CONFEDERATE CONFUSION
John Pemberton and Frame of Reference

While Grant used his Mexican War background to positively shape his concept for the campaign, Pemberton, a man who was better at handling well-understood sequential tasks than he was ill-defined simultaneous ones, fell back on formative experiences that were less appropriate for the ambiguous situation in which he found himself at Vicksburg.

JOHN PEMBERTON HAD TWO EXPERIENCES THAT ADVERSELY SHAPED his frame of reference for Vicksburg. The first was the inflexible leadership style he had observed in Mexico while serving as an aide to Brigadier General William Jenkins Worth. The second was his experience in Charleston, South Carolina earlier in the Civil War. Both situations left him with a frame of reference that hindered his leadership at Vicksburg.

In August 1846, Zachary Taylor assigned Pemberton, then a lieutenant, to serve as Worth's aide. Worth had a solid military reputation. He had fought in the War of 1812, served as commandant of cadets at West Point, participated in the Black Hawk War, helped suppress Nat Turner's rebellion, been part of the Cherokee Indian removal from Georgia, and commanded in the Seminole War. But Worth also was vain. Observers described him as "rash and impetuous," "intense and narrow," and "self-centered." Even his sympathetic biographer Edward Wallace credits him with "a petulant contumaciousness." Perhaps the best tactical example of Worth's narrowness is his unsophisticated and costly frontal attack at Molino del Rey. In serving so closely with Worth, Pemberton learned nothing of the broad, responsive, flexible, and anticipatory thought needed to operate in an uncertain environment.

Indeed, Pemberton's biographer Michael Ballard concludes that Pemberton and Worth were an unfortunate pairing. He writes, "Pemberton might have been better served for the future if he had been influenced by a different role model. Worth had an inflexible, sometimes abrupt nature. Colleagues would someday describe Confederate General Pemberton as having the same characteristic." This very limited frame of reference would cause Pemberton to respond poorly when Grant began to move against Vicksburg in the spring of 1863.

Strategic leaders must be flexible. They must be able to operate in an environment characterized by volatility, uncertainty, confusion, and ambiguity (VUCA). The leader must be able to sift through the "noise" and "become the master of information and influence." Pemberton lacked such ability. He was a deliberate, inflexible leader who had to understand fully the situation in order to make informed decisions. In the VUCA environment of imperfect intelligence, Pemberton became dysfunctional.

Pemberton's limitations as a leader in the VUCA environment surfaced quickly as Grant began presenting him with multiple threats and diversions. The VUCA environment left Pemberton confused and paralyzed. One example was the cavalry raid led by Colonel Benjamin Grierson out of Tennessee into Mississippi. Pemberton, "who was much better at dealing with the known than with the suspected," focused on Grierson while Grant, the real threat, was sneaking in the back door. In the process, Pemberton inefficiently diverted units from his strategic reserve to chase after Grierson's diversion.

Another part of Pemberton's poor response at Vicksburg can be traced to his frame of reference from his experience in Charleston, where he was posted in November 1861. On January 14, 1862, Pemberton was promoted to major general, and in March he was given command of the Department of South Carolina and Georgia. His principal mission in this capacity was to ensure the defense of Charleston.

As Pemberton surveyed the situation, he became increasingly concerned about his ability to defend the city. South Carolina Governor Francis Pickens, however, stressed to him that "the defence is to be desperate, and if [the Federals] can be repulsed, even with the city in ruins, we should unanimously prefer it." General Robert E. Lee, who President Davis had made responsible for the coasts of South Carolina, Georgia, and north Florida at that time, added that Pemberton must be willing to fight "street by street and house by house as long as we have a foot of ground to stand upon."

Pemberton's stay in Charleston was marked by conflict with Pickens, and on August 28 he was informed that he was being replaced as commander. However, Pemberton took with him from his Charleston experience the lesson that he should focus on terrain rather than the enemy. He had spent his energies on preparing to defend a fixed location rather than maneuver a force in the field. These experiences would negatively shape Pemberton's conduct during the Vicksburg Campaign, where he unimaginatively applied this Charleston formula, even though the two situations were drastically different.

Pemberton also did not anticipate Grant crossing the Mississippi south of Vicksburg. In fact, he believed Grant had abandoned the campaign and withdrawn toward Memphis. Instead, by April 30, the Federal Navy had successfully passed the Confederate positions both at Vicksburg and Grand Gulf, and Grant's army had crossed the Mississippi River unopposed at Bruinsburg. Pemberton seems to have understood intellectually the significance of these developments, writing President Davis on May 1 that the "enemy's success in passing our batteries has completely changed the character of defense." However, James Arnold succinctly concludes, "Whether Pemberton had the mental flexibility to adjust to the new situation was the pressing question. He needed to ask himself what was Vicksburg's value if it could not interdict the river. After Grant crossed the river, he needed to change his focus from holding the city to defeating Grant's army." Pemberton would not adjust.

Instead, he chose to defend Vicksburg by focusing on a piece of terrain as he had done in Charleston rather than focusing on the enemy force. In so doing, he forfeited the initiative and

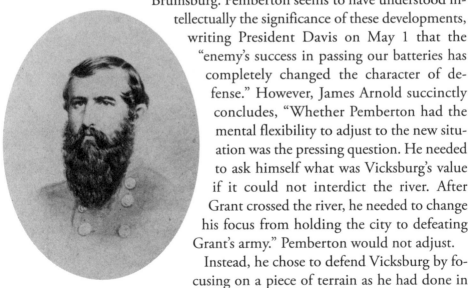

John Pemberton.
Courtesy of the Library of Congress

the advantages of maneuver and the offensive to Grant. By July 4, Pemberton would surrender.

LEADERSHIP LESSONS

Effective leaders build a personal frame of reference from schooling, experience, self-study, and assessment. They reflect on past experience in order to learn from them and to help place the current organization and situation in strategic context. However, the frame of reference is designed to expand, not limit, the leader's horizons. Leaders cannot unimaginatively apply a course of action that worked once to a new situation for which it is inappropriate. They must be mentally agile enough to understand the circumstances around them and adjust. This was Pemberton's failure. He drew on his past experience, but he applied it to an inappropriate situation. His frame of reference inhibited, rather than facilitated, his response to the environment.

Strategic leaders must demonstrate the flexibility needed to handle competing demands. Such prerequisites lay beyond Pemberton's capabilities. Ballard notes that at Vicksburg "much was going on, and Pemberton had lost control of it . . . he had been reduced to a state of total uncertainty." Arnold agrees, writing, "War's uncertainty continued to vex Pemberton. . . . In the absence of certain intelligence and for fear of making a misstep, Pemberton remained passive." Much of this poor response can be explained by Pemberton's misapplication of his frame of reference from Mexico and Charleston.

Takeaways:
- *Leaders build a personal frame of reference that allows them to understand the present situation in a strategic context.*
- *Every situation is different, and the leader uses his frame of reference to tailor his present actions, not robotically repeat his past ones.*
- *Leaders must be agile, imaginative, and flexible.*

The Mississippi River at Vicksburg bustling with activity
in February 1864. *Courtesy of the Library of Congress*

SEVENTEEN

GRANT HEADS NORTHEAST
Ulysses Grant and Clear Communication

While Pemberton struggled to reconcile the confusing situation, Ulysses Grant was issuing clear instructions to his commanders to move. The result was a rapid advance inland.

LEADERS MUST COMMUNICATE THEIR INTENT AND INSTRUCTIONS TO subordinates in an understandable, concise, and effective manner. Grant was an excellent communicator, as a variety of observers have concluded. Edward Bonekemper says, "Grant's orders were lucid and unambiguous— even when issued in the heat of battle." R. Steven Jones adds, "Historians have always regarded Grant's orders as some of the clearest in the war, rarely leaving room for misunderstanding or misinterpretation." William Murray boasts that Grant "could express his thoughts verbally and on paper with a succinctness and eloquence that is remarkable." William McNeely writes, Grant's "crisp, clear orders were almost impossible not to comprehend." This skill allowed Grant to efficiently transmit his intent in a way his subordinates could easily process and act on.

An excellent example of the quality of Grant's orders are those associated with the approach to Raymond. On May 5, 1863, Grant was located at Hankinson's Ferry on the Big Black River about seventeen miles south of Vicksburg. His intention up to this point was to seize a bridgehead across the Big Black and strike directly north toward Vicksburg, but new information caused him to rethink his plan. Major General James McPherson had just returned from a combat patrol toward Vicksburg with news that the terrain in that direction was very restrictive and that the Confederates occupied a fortified line at Redbone Church some nine miles south of the city. To make matters worse, the Confederates that had been forced across the Big Black the previous day had not retreated to Vicksburg as expected, but had instead moved toward the Big Black River Bridge about eleven miles east of Vicksburg. If Grant continued with his plan, these troops might descend on his flank as he engaged the enemy at Redbone Church.

On the other hand, Grant received reports from Major General Peter Osterhaus that the terrain to the northeast opened up beyond Rocky Springs into rolling fields that would allow for both maneuver and effective use of the Federal artillery. To take advantage of these circumstances, Grant decided to change his original plan and instead strike the Confederates at Edwards and Big Black River Bridge. The only problem with this new course was that it would require Grant's army to operate deep in the interior of Mississippi for an extended period of time, dangerously stressing its tenuous supply line. The problem could be partially resolved by foraging, but if Grant advanced in a single column, the lead units might fare well, but those in the rear would find the area depleted of resources by the time they arrived.

To mitigate this problem, Grant decided to advance in three parallel columns with McPherson farthest east, Sherman in the middle, and McClernand to the west. Grant would travel with Sherman in order to give his couriers the shortest distance to travel to the two other columns. The forage problem and the configuration of the road network necessitated there be a fairly wide separation between the columns. The corps commanders would be operating somewhat independently, and Grant's initial orders to them would have to give them sufficient guidance to meet his intent, but also the freedom of action to take the initiative.

McPherson's corps had the farthest distance to cover and Grant's orders to its commander are brilliant in their clarity, completeness, and brevity. On May 11, Grant instructed McPherson,

> Move your command to-night to the next cross-roads if there is water, and to-morrow with all activity into Raymond. At the latter place you will use your utmost exertions to secure all the subsistence stores that may be there, as well as in the vicinity. We must fight the enemy before our rations fail, and we are equally bound to make our rations last as long as possible. Upon one occasion

you made two days' rations last seven. We may have to do the same thing again . . .

McPherson was on the road to Raymond by 3:30 a.m. on May 12. Brigadier General John Gregg's Confederates beat McPherson to Raymond by a few hours, and took up a line along Fourteenmile Creek, about a mile southwest of the town. A confused and piecemealed battle ensued, but in the end, McPherson's greater numbers prevailed. Gregg evacuated Raymond, and McPherson occupied it that night and requested orders from Grant.

News of this development caused Grant to rethink his plan. Gregg's aggressive action seemed to imply that Confederate strength was greater than it really was, and Grant was concerned that a sizeable enemy force was building in Jackson. If he struck Pemberton at Edwards as planned, Grant would be vulnerable to an attack on his rear from Jackson. To neutralize this threat, Grant decided to use his central position to disengage from Pemberton at Edwards and turn his entire Army of the Tennessee east toward Jackson. Success there would isolate Pemberton from outside support, leaving Grant to deal with him on his own terms.

On May 13, Grant ordered McPherson and Sherman to advance to Jackson, with McClernand covering their march from a defense position that ran from Raymond to Clinton. The Federals reached Jackson with little opposition, and on May 14, Grant ordered Sherman "to commence immediately the effectual destruction of the river railroad bridge and the road as far east as practicable, as well as north and south." Sherman's men did their work well, with Sherman reporting destruction of railroads, "4 miles east of Jackson, 3 south, 3 north, and 10 west." He concluded that "Jackson, as a railroad center or Government depot of stores and military factories, can be of little use to the enemy for six months." That was more than enough time for Grant to deal with a now isolated Pemberton.

LEADERSHIP LESSONS

Leadership is about influencing people by providing purpose, direction, and motivation. Communication is obviously an important aspect of a leader's ability to exert influence. A leader's communications to his subordinates must be clear enough to inform the subordinate of the desired outcome, but not so burdensome in detail as to stifle initiative. Grant was a master of such communications.

One reason for the early German success in World War II was its practice of *aufstragstaktik* which General Otto von Moser described as "the leadership action . . . by which the leader does not give his subordinate a binding order, but more an excerpt from his own thought process, through which he demands from [the subordinate] the intellectual cooperation for the accomplishment of the combat mission." *Aufstragstaktik* can be translated as mission-type orders or mission-oriented command and control. Communication in such a system is not the linear type in which the leader provides his subordinate with decisions and instructions. Instead, it is interactive communication that provides the leader's intent and encourages a mindset among the subordinates of free-thinking initiative as to how best to accomplish that intent. Grant's communication to McPherson epitomizes this communication of a leader's intent.

In communicating his intent, the leader tells his subordinate the desired outcome or end state, the key tasks, and the broader purpose of the activity. This information gives the subordinate the freedom to act within certain boundaries to achieve the desired outcome using his initiative. Grant clearly told McPherson the desired outcome, "to secure all the subsistence stores that may be [in Raymond], as well as in the vicinity." He identified two key tasks for McPherson. One was to "move your command to-night to the next cross-roads" as necessary to be able to move to Raymond the next day, and the other was "to make our rations last as long as possible." Finally, Grant also sensitized McPherson to the broader purpose to "fight before our rations fail."

Grant's communication is not exemplary solely for its content, but also for its style. Warren Grabau describes Grant's tone as "fatherly," giving the relatively young McPherson a mix of advice and encouragement. Leaders influence not just by what they say but by how they say it. In reminding McPherson that "upon one occasion you made two days' rations last seven," Grant is telling him it is not unprecedented if "we… have to do the same thing again." Also in using the word "we," Grant is including himself in the challenge, lending to McPherson the moral support of his leader's presence and involvement.

Grant's effective communication was certainly not confined to his dispatch to McPherson. Grant's *Memoirs* is a literary masterpiece that Mark Twain pronounced were "the best [memoirs] of any general's since Caesar." Part of its appeal is certainly the fact that, as Grant's biographer William McFeely observes, its "style [is] unchanged from that of the simple orders he wrote in pencil during the war."

Grant writing his memoirs in 1885.
Courtesy of the Library of Congress

Takeaways:
- *One key way leaders influence subordinates is by communicating.*
- *Communication must be simple.*
- *Communication is a two-way street.*
- *While some communication is intended merely to direct and inform, more often leaders should communicate their broad intent and allow subordinates to use their initiative to reach the desired outcome.*

The Battle of Raymond as depicted in the June 13, 1863 *Harper's Weekly*.

— EIGHTEEN —

THE BATTLE OF RAYMOND
John Gregg and Understanding the Situation

As the three Federal corps converged on Raymond, they were met by a lone Confederate brigade. Not knowing he was so grossly outnumbered, Brigadier General John Gregg attacked, and the Federals scored another victory.

ONE OF THE DANGERS GRANT ACCEPTED WHEN HE CHOSE TO REDUCE his logistical support was that he would need a steady stream of victories to maintain his momentum. Thus, on May 11, 1863 he instructed McPherson, "We must fight the enemy before our rations fail." To this end, Grant pushed his three corps forward with McClernand paralleling the Big Black River, Sherman in the middle, and McPherson on the eastern flank heading toward the crossroads town of Raymond.

The same day that Grant issued his orders, Confederate Brigadier General John Gregg entered Raymond with his brigade. By this point, Grant's effective maneuvering had Pemberton off-balance. Pemberton felt that any Federal advance through Raymond toward Jackson would be merely a feint to divert attention from the main Federal effort toward the Big Black. Thus Pemberton instructed Gregg to retire to Jackson if these circumstances materialized. On the other hand, if Grant turned toward the Big Black, Gregg was to strike the Federal flank and rear. By this point in his career, Pemberton should have known the numerical odds were strongly against Gregg's isolated brigade in such a situation, and Gregg's own aggressiveness did nothing to impose the necessary caution. The result would be a Confederate defeat at Raymond based largely on Gregg's inability to properly assess the situation.

John Gregg, Brigadier General.
Courtesy of the Library of Congress

Early on May 12, Gregg received a report that the Federals were marching on Raymond. Cavalry screened the advance so the size of the force was unknown, but Gregg later received a report estimating the enemy strength at a mere 2,500. Gregg had been forced to surrender his command at Fort Donelson in February 1862, and he now saw an opportunity to exact his revenge. He deployed his 3,000 men overlooking a bridge on Fourteenmile Creek and waited expectantly.

The thick vegetation along the creek under other circumstances may have helped the defense, but in this case it hindered Gregg's view, further preventing him from getting an accurate count of the enemy he faced. Thus, when McPherson's men began reaching the vicinity of the bridge around 10:00 a.m., Gregg still felt he was in good shape. He ordered his three artillery to open fire, and the battle was joined.

Hearing the guns, McPherson rushed to the front of his column and ordered his lead brigade to cross the creek. He also ordered his artillery to return fire. The long-range exchange was not particularly effective, but it did convince Gregg that his artillery was vulnerable and that he better act before his guns were lost. He resolved to attack, planning to use part of his brigade to hold the Federals in place with a frontal attack while the remainder crossed the creek on the right flank and attacked the enemy artillery.

Spurred on by the sword-wielding Gregg, the Confederates crashed into a full division of 6,500 Federals commanded by Brigadier General John Logan. The Federal deployment in the thick terrain had resulted in hastily formed and isolated regiments that initially fared poorly against the Confederate attack. Colonel Hiram Granbury's Seventh Texas, supported on its left by the Third Tennessee, crashed into the Twenty-third Indiana and routed it, also wreaking havoc among the Twentieth Ohio. This early

Confederate success merely reinforced Gregg's assessment that he was facing only a small force. Soon, however, Logan was able to rally his men, even as further units arrived on the field, and the close-in battle raged for two and a half hours.

Still thinking he had the advantage, Gregg was confident his flank attack would be successful. Instead, his men

John Logan and staff in Vicksburg, 1863.
Courtesy of the Library of Congress

quickly realized they were up against a much stronger enemy than expected. Lieutenant Colonel Thomas Beaumont of the Fiftieth Tennessee and Colonel Randall MacGavock of the Tenth and Thirtieth Tennessee Consolidated Infantry halted their attacks.

Pressure soon forced Beaumont to pull his men back which left Mac-Gavock alone on a bare hilltop in the Confederate center where he became the principal target for Federal artillery fire. As Federal infantry began to envelop his isolated position, MacGavock decided he had no choice but to attack, but as he ordered the charge he was killed by a Federal bullet. The Confederates could not sustain their unsupported attack and soon fell back.

Gregg realized he was overwhelmed, and he withdrew his brigade through Raymond to Jackson. He suffered at least 515 casualties. McPherson had exerted no greater control of the battle than Gregg did and piecemealed his attack, but the superior Federal numbers carried the day. McPherson occupied Raymond having suffered 442 losses.

LEADERSHIP LESSONS

The ancient Chinese military theorist Sun Tzu is credited with saying, "If you know the enemy and know yourself, you need not fear the result of a hundred battles. If you know yourself but not the enemy, for every victory gained you will also suffer a defeat." At Raymond, Gregg did not know the enemy. He thought he faced a much smaller force and therefore conducted himself in an inappropriate way.

Leaders first visualize the situation based on their frame of reference. Then they seek to understand the situation by gathering information. However, leaders can quickly become overwhelmed by too much information, so they must carefully prioritize those pieces of information that are critical to their decision-making process. They then assign subordinates to obtain this information. The subordinates must keep in mind that the purpose of their providing information is to facilitate the leader's decision-making, so they must present the information in a manageable way. Even in the best of situations, however, the leader will not have complete information, so he must learn to make decisions based on the knowledge available. At Raymond, Gregg misinterpreted the information he received, in part because he was already predisposed to reach a particular conclusion. The result was that he based his actions on an inaccurate understanding of the situation and suffered defeat.

Takeaways:
- *Leaders must make an assumption based on the available facts, but then they must confirm or deny that assumption by gathering additional information.*
- *Act decisively, but not impulsively.*
- *Maintain situational awareness about the environment, the competition, and yourself.*

NINETEEN

THE BATTLE OF JACKSON
Joseph Johnston and Pessimism

After the Battle of Raymond, Grant changed his plan and headed further east to Jackson to isolate Pemberton from any outside help. However, General Joseph Johnston was in no mood to come to Pemberton's aid.

ON NOVEMBER 24, 1862, CONFEDERATE GENERAL JOSEPH JOHNSTON was made overall commander of the area between the Appalachian Mountains and the Mississippi River. As such he was in charge of departments commanded by Lieutenant General Edmund Kirby Smith, General Braxton Bragg, and Lieutenant General John Pemberton. Johnston's selection for the position was the result of much political jockeying, and certainly did not bode well for hopes of enthusiastic or cooperative action.

Johnston and President Jefferson Davis certainly shared a mutual dislike and distrust that stemmed from the early days of the war. Although Johnston was the highest ranking officer to leave the US Army for the Confederacy, the letter Davis sent to the Senate requesting confirmation of his full generals listed Johnston fourth. Johnston was infuriated by what he interpreted as a slight, and from that day on, he had a difficult and quarrelsome relationship with Davis.

The problems continued when Johnston was in command in Virginia. There Johnston doubted Davis's confidence in him and Davis doubted whether Johnston was up to the tremendous responsibilities he had been assigned. The pair had an uneasy relationship, void of effective communication and plagued with tension. After Johnston was wounded at Seven Pines in May 1862, Davis no doubt felt some relief in being able to replace him with General Robert E. Lee. Perhaps in acknowledgement of his awkward relationship with his commander-in-chief, Johnston himself recognized, "The shot that struck me down is the very best that has been fired in the Southern cause yet." Johnston remained in Richmond, where he recuperated until he was considered fit enough to return to active service, and was given command of the Department of the West in November.

Johnston's new command was confusing both in geographical scope and authority. Geographically, he found that the District of the Gulf, which included parts of Georgia, Alabama, and Mississippi, was under Bragg's departmental jurisdiction even though it was closer to Pemberton. Bragg's and Pemberton's departments were separated by several hundred miles, not to mention Grant's army and the Tennessee River. Any effort to combine forces between Bragg and Pemberton would be at the mercy of the circuitous rail route from Jackson, Mississippi via Mobile, Atlanta, and Chattanooga to Murfreesboro, Tennessee. Johnston estimated it would take a month to shuttle troops along such an unreliable route. His repeated protests to Richmond that he could not possibly control both Bragg and Pemberton were to no avail.

If these geographic problems were not enough, Johnston suffered from ambiguous command authority. Rather than reporting to Johnston, the department commanders continued to report directly to Richmond. Under this arrangement, Johnston was never sure he was completely informed. Although he was empowered to go anywhere in his command where "his presence may, for the time, be necessary," his instructions did not specify if he could give direct orders to field commanders when he was not present with the army. Johnston was theoretically a theater commander who could coordinate affairs among the several departments, but the practical method by which communications passed among headquarters above and below him robbed him of this ability. In fact, Davis routinely sent orders to Pemberton and Bragg garnered from information Johnston had not seen, and in December 1862, Davis completely bypassed Johnston to order reinforcements be sent from Bragg to Pemberton. Feeling increasingly irrelevant, Johnston began to distance himself from responsibility for the situations of his subordinate commanders.

Johnston certainly did not like the predicament in which he found himself. He complained "that my command was a nominal one merely, and useless; because the great distance between the armies of Tennessee and Mississippi, and the fact that they had different objects and adversaries, made it impossible to combine their action; so there was no employment for me unless I should take command of one of the armies in an emergency, which, as each had its own general, was not intended or desirable." As James Arnold aptly summarizes, "Davis chose a general to take command in the decisive theater whom he distrusted and disliked, who returned these feelings in spades, and who forcefully doubted the job could be done." It was not a recipe for success.

Indeed, much of Johnston's post-war writings are spent criticizing both Davis and Pemberton for their handling of Vicksburg. It is true that Johnston was in an awkward command position relative to Pemberton and the Vicksburg situation, but Johnston just as certainly failed to do his part. His attitude throughout the campaign is reminiscent of a hurt child who did not get all what he wanted and then purposefully avoided taking responsibility for what he had been given.

Johnston was obviously deflated when Davis dismissed his initial plans in November and December 1862 aimed at concentrating forces against the Federal armies under Grant and Rosecrans. Upon hearing of Davis's rejection, Johnston commented that the decision had "blown away some tall castles in the air." From that point on, Johnston seems to have passed the initiative for western planning to Davis. On December 25, 1862 and then again on January 6, 1863, Johnston asked to be relieved from what he by now undoubtedly considered a hopeless position. Davis refused, and Johnston was left to a command in which he clearly lacked heart. Along the way, he became despondent

Joseph Johnston.
Courtesy of the Library of Congress

and bitter, and his distrust of the government became almost childish. He began to see himself as being set up to be a martyr in a position of little power and authority but great responsibility.

After the Confederate defeat at Raymond, Davis ordered Johnston to Jackson to salvage the rapidly deteriorating situation. Johnston arrived May 13 and his predetermined pessimism immediately took control. Without any real consideration of an alternative, Johnston wired President Davis saying, "I am too late" and ordered the city evacuated. Had Johnston been of a different mind, he probably could have held Grant at least long enough for Pemberton to move forward and hit Grant's rear. Instead, Johnston withdrew behind a small screen to the north, and the next day, the Federals began their assault on Jackson.

LEADERSHIP LESSONS

Dr. William Cohen is a Professor of Marketing and Leadership at California State University, Los Angeles and a retired major general in the US Air Force Reserve. In his book *The Stuff of Heroes*, Cohen lists eight universal laws of leadership, one of which is to "expect positive results." Johnston, who Michael Ballard notes "usually preferred retreating to fighting," clearly violated this rule.

Cohen is quick to point out that merely expecting positive results will not necessarily ensure their achievement. There may be circumstances beyond the leader's control that prevent a positive outcome in spite of the leader's expectations. However, Cohen is adamant that a leader who does not expect positive results will not get them. "So while expecting positive results may not always lead to success," Cohen explains, "failing to expect positive results will almost always lead to failure."

General Colin Powell agrees, calling optimism "a force multiplier." He considers a leader's positive enthusiasm and confidence to be a factor that multiplies the effectiveness of other capabilities in the organization. When leaders view the situation with hopeful expectation, those around them catch the same positive attitude. On the other hand, Powell considers cynicism, doubt, and negativity to be "force shrinkers." Leaders who view the world negatively are likely to demoralize and reduce the effectiveness of their organization.

If anyone needed a strong dose of optimism from his leader it was

Pemberton at Vicksburg. Instead, he got largely token words from President Davis and defeatism from Johnston. Johnston, in particular, failed to give Pemberton the hope, encouragement, and support he needed. Many times, the way a person sees a problem is the problem. Such was the case for Johnston at Jackson. Himself a pessimist, Johnston was a "force shrinker" when Pemberton needed him to be a "force multiplier."

Takeaways
- *Leaders must rise above personal disappointments for the sake of the organization.*
- *Leaders must be optimistic and expect positive results.*
- *Leader attitudes are infectious.*

TWENTY

THE BATTLE OF CHAMPION HILL
Ulysses Grant and Personal Presence

With Pemberton isolated from Johnston, Grant turned westward, toward Vicksburg. The ensuing Battle of Champion Hill was the decisive battle of the campaign.

IN CONTRAST TO PEMBERTON'S RATHER ALOOF LEADERSHIP STYLE that served to isolate and distance himself from his subordinates, Grant's leadership was characterized by a personal presence that reassured and motivated his men. Examples of Grant's personal presence include after Port Gibson, on the approach to Jackson, and at Champion Hill.

After his May 1, 1863, victory at Port Gibson, Grant made the momentous decision to "cut loose" from his line of supply and head northeast. It was a bold decision, and Grant was personally involved in all aspects of its execution. Jean Edward Smith describes that "For the next four days Grant acted as the quartermaster he had been in the Mexican War, firing off logistical instructions to subordinates, stockpiling ammunition, and dispatching foraging parties into the countryside." This active and hands-on leadership presence did much to ensure the plan's success. Grant demonstrated that he was not just a detached strategic visionary. He was also able by his own energy and action to help will his plan into existence.

Although Grant maintained a personal presence, he did not micromanage his subordinate commanders. According to James Arnold, Grant's leadership style was to allow "his corps commanders to fight their own battles," especially when the subordinate was as trusted and competent as Sherman. Jean Edward Smith argues that "By not specifying movements in detail, [Grant] left his subordinates free to exploit whatever opportunities developed." Thus as the Federal army closed in on Jackson, Grant was with Sherman, not to make Sherman irrelevant, but to multiply Sherman's effect.

One advantage of a leader's personal presence on the scene is that it allows him to see for himself actions as they unfold and to compare his personal observations with information he receives from other sources. Grant had directed Sherman to send a reconnaissance force to the right as far as the Pearl River. When this force did not return, Grant personally rode to the scene and discovered the Confederates had withdrawn from that part of the line. This opening allowed the Federals to advance unmolested, and Grant reports that he "rode immediately to the State House." It was his personal presence at the decisive point that allowed Grant to capitalize on the opportunity.

A leader's presence also is very reassuring to his subordinates. The idea of shared danger, of the leader being intimately aware of the situation, and of the leader providing personal example all have a positive impact on subordinates. As Confederate shells rained down on the Federals, both Grant and Sherman rode among the soldiers, reassuring them and keeping them steady.

Grant's personal presence again had an impact on the morning of the Battle of Champion Hill. Grant positioned himself near Brigadier General Alvin Hovey, where, as he wrote "we were most heavily pressed." Around noon, however, when Major General John Logan began a potentially decisive move to the Confederate rear, Grant, along with part of his staff, moved with Logan. By midafternoon, the Confederates had "fled precipitately," and Grant was in a position to direct the pursuit. He reports riding to a key road junction where he met members of Brigadier General Eugene Carr's division and assessed the situation. Grant knew from his earlier presence with Hovey that his division and Major General James McPherson's two divisions that had been with Hovey, "were not in the best condition to follow the retreating foe." Therefore, Grant sent orders for Brigadier General Peter Osterhaus to chase the fleeing enemy, and he personally explained the situation to Carr, giving him instructions for the pursuit. Again, it was Grant's personal presence that made him aware of the situation concerning both his own forces and the enemy. He made informed decisions based on personal knowledge that allowed him to seize an opportunity.

At Champion Hill, Grant's personal presence also served as a morale boost for his soldiers, many of whom recalled seeing him. At an especially critical point in the battle, Colonel Samuel Holmes led two regiments of his brigade against Brigadier General John Bowen's hard-pressed division. A soldier called out that Grant was watching them and "At once we set up a yell, every man shouting at the top of his voice, and this we kept up." James Arnold concludes, "Grant's prominent presence reassured and inspired. His composure and personal leadership allowed his Army of the Tennessee to triumph in the battle that decided Vicksburg's fate."

LEADERSHIP LESSONS

Leaders, especially leaders of complex organizations, cannot be everywhere at once. They must, however, recognize that their personal presence is a profound force multiplier and make a conscious decision to be where their presence can have the most impact.

At the same time, leaders must remember their role. They cannot become so involved in the action that they cease to maintain the broad perspective necessary to guide the organization. While Grant assumed a hands-on logistical role, he also remained cognizant of the big picture and continued to direct actions necessary for future operations, including ordering "reconnaissances made by McClernand and McPherson, with the view of leading the enemy to believe that we intended to cross the Big Black and attack the city at once." While Grant used his expertise to energize the logistical operation, he never ceased to be the commanding general of his army.

A leader's physical presence influences others' perceptions of the leader. However, the US Army's field manual on leadership notes that "Presence is not just a matter of the leader showing up; it involves the image that the leader projects." Grant's calm demeanor under fire outside Jackson portrayed a confident, determined, and brave attitude that had an infectious effect on his men. Leaders must know that they are always being watched. If they are not on the scene, they cannot use their presence to set an example, and if subordinates look for their leader and do not see him, they are tempted to draw negative conclusions about the validity of their cause. On the other hand, those who see and hear from their leader know they have "an important part to play."

The Army manual also notes that "moving to where duties are performed allows the leader to have firsthand knowledge of real conditions." Many historians consider Champion Hill to be the decisive battle of the Vicksburg Campaign, and Grant's personal presence at critical points allowed him to make timely and informed decisions. Leaders who remain in their offices or otherwise detached from the action must rely on filtered information and cannot use their own senses to determine the situation. Grant's personal presence put him in a position to act immediately when opportunities presented themselves.

Leaders also must recognize that complex operations involve many distinct parts. Some are more important than others and should be allocated additional resources such as more time, money, and people. Another way a leader can contribute to more important tasks is by his personal presence. Grant did this at Champion Hill by locating himself where "we were most heavily pressed."

Takeaways:
- *Leader presence makes a difference.*
- *Being on the scene gives the leader additional information and helps him make timely decisions.*
- *A leader's physical demeanor influences his subordinates' behavior.*
- *When physically on the scene, leaders must not become so involved that they marginalize subordinate leaders or ignore broader leader responsibilities.*

TWENTY-ONE

RETREAT FROM CHAMPION HILL
Lloyd Tilghman and Personal Sacrifice

Climactic Napoleonic victories proved elusive on the Civil War battlefield. Pemberton's army escaped destruction at Champion Hill in part because of the rearguard action of Brigadier General Lloyd Tilghman.

AS THE CONFEDERATE DEFENSE COLLAPSED AROUND CHAMPION Hill, Pemberton ordered a general retreat. By that point, some soldiers had taken matters into their own hands, with many "rushing pell-mell from the scene of action." One colonel who tried to restore order reported bringing his regiment "to the charge bayonets, but even this could not check them in their flight. The colors of three regiments passed through. We collared them, begged them and abused them in vain." As Major General William Loring meandered somewhat aimlessly along a farm road that roughly paralleled the Ratliff Road, he saw "the whole country on both sides of the road covered with the fleeing of our army." With the Federal noose closing in, the Confederates had few options of crossing Baker's Creek to safety. Major General John Logan's division had cut the Jackson Road, leaving the Raymond Road to the south as the only available escape route. Desperate to save his army, Pemberton ordered Brigadier General Lloyd Tilghman "to hold the Raymond road at all hazards." Against two Federal divisions, Tilghman commanded a single brigade, giving the Federals a five to one advantage.

Tilghman had been in desperate straits before. In February 1862, he commanded Fort Henry on the Tennessee River where he had approximately 3,000 to 3,400 poorly armed men. To make matters worse, heavy rains had caused the river to rise, and much of the fort was underwater. On February 6, Brigadier General Ulysses Grant landed a few miles below Fort Henry while Flag Officer Andrew Foote's gunboats steamed upriver to shell the fort. Tilghman realized he did not have a chance and astutely withdrew most of his force to Fort Donelson before the battle. He remained with the ill-fated Fort Henry but there was little he could do against Foote's ironclads. After seventy-five minutes of shelling, Tilghman surrendered. Grant and Foote continued on their rampage, and Fort Donelson, which Tilghman had also previously commanded, surrendered on February 13. Tilghman was imprisoned at Fort Warren in Boston Harbor until he was exchanged. Upon his release he went to Jackson, Mississippi where he began organizing other exchanged prisoners and prepared them to reenter the fighting.

Once friends, by the time of Champion Hill Tilghman and Pemberton had fallen into a tense relationship. In fact, Pemberton had inexplicably relieved Tilghman of command on the eve of the battle, only to revoke the order when William Wing Loring threatened to refuse to fight without Tilghman in command. Nonetheless, Pemberton described Tilghman as "always ready to obey orders," and whatever their difficulties, Tilghman would not fail Pemberton this day. Indeed, James Arnold describes Tilghman as "a pugnacious, fighting officer," which was just what Pemberton needed now.

As always, Tilghman posted himself where the action was hottest. Amidst a hail of bullets, he suggested that a young artillery officer dismount, calmly telling him, "They are shooting pretty close to us, and I do not know if they are shooting at your fine grey horse or my new uniform." Tilghman then sent his seventeen-year-old son with a squad of soldiers to drive the Federal sharpshooters from their covered positions. Tilghman then dismounted and told the artillery officer, "I will take a shot at those fellows myself." He personally sighted a twelve-pound Napoleon in Captain John Cowan's Mississippi battery, gave instructions for cutting the fuse, and then moved to a little knoll a few feet from the gun to observe the shot through his field glasses. Suddenly Tilghman collapsed to the ground. A piece of a Parrott shell had struck him in the stomach, nearly cutting him in two. His men carried him to a shade tree, where he lay for about three hours until he died.

The tenacious and selfless stand of Tilghman and others bought time for Bowen's and Stevenson's divisions to escape across Baker's Creek to Big Black River railroad bridge. There Pemberton had already prepared a 1,800 yard arc of positions extending from the river on the left to Gin Lake on the right in order to defend against an attack from the east. Pemberton directed Bowen to man the bridgehead fortifications while the rest of the army retreated to the west bank of the Big Black.

Pemberton expected Bowen to hold his forward position only until Loring passed through. Loring, however, feared he would be cut off along that route, and had instead moved south and then northeast toward Jackson where he eventually joined Johnston. Unaware of this development, Bowen fruitlessly waited for Loring until the morning of May 17 when Major General John McClernand's corps, leading the Federal pursuit, attacked Bowen.

Confederate artillery fire from well-placed positions on the bluffs on the west side of the river slowed the Federals down long enough for Bowen's men to escape to safety. As they fled, the Confederates burned the railroad bridge and a riverboat, the *Dot*, that had been anchored crosswise in the river as a floating bridge. The Confederates suffered four killed, sixteen wounded, and 1,019 missing compared to thirty-nine killed, 237 wounded, and three missing for the Federals. Pemberton limped back to the defenses of Vicksburg, leaving Grant frustrated that his prey had escaped.

LEADERSHIP LESSONS

In the chaos of Champion Hill, the natural instinct was to flee. Instead, Lloyd Tilghman stood his ground and died helping to hold open the escape route for others. Numerous observers testified to Tilghman's personal sacrifice. Colonel A.F. Reynolds, who succeeded Tilghman upon his death, considered him "always at his post he devoted himself day and night to the interests of his command." In a tribute in the *Confederate Veteran*, L. F. Flatan writes that Tilghman "offered his life in defense of the cause of the South" amid an atmosphere of "self-sacrifice for others." President Jefferson Davis described Tilghman's earlier actions at Fort Henry in terms of "martyrdom."

While few leaders will ever find themselves in a position where they may have to give their lives for their organization, all leaders can benefit from Tilghman's example of servant leadership. In the 1970s, Robert Greenleaf began talking and writing about a type of leadership in which the leader meets the needs of his subordinates. While the traditional authoritarian leader asks, "What can the organization do for me?" the servant leader asks, "What can I do for the organization?" The idea is that if the leader meets his subordinates' needs, they can then concentrate on and are empowered to pursue the organization's needs. While Greenleaf is credited with popularizing this concept more recently, perhaps the most familiar example of servant leadership is the account of Jesus washing the disciples' feet in John 13:14-15. Servant leadership represents the seemingly counterintuitive observation of General Frederick Franks that "To lead is also to serve."

Servant leadership requires attention to the subordinates' situations, humility, and hard work. The servant leader must figure out what his subordinates need, put his own needs aside, and devote time and energy to creating the environment where the subordinates are both cared for and empowered. Many leaders shy away from servant leadership because of its demands, but Major General William Cohen argues, "Many times the dilemma between accomplishing the mission and taking care of the troops is a false one. Many times both objectives can be achieved if the leader is willing to work a little harder himself." Tilghman certainly worked "a little harder himself," giving his life in the process. However, he met the needs of thousands of fellow Confederates who counted on him to hold open their only hope of escape. Loring describes Tilghman's mission as an "important trust," and indeed servant leaders win their subordinates' trust by a record of reliability, care, and service. At Champion Hill, Tilghman modeled this servant leadership.

Takeaways:
- *Leadership is service.*
- *Servant leaders meet their subordinates' needs so the subordinates can concentrate on the organization's mission.*
- *Leadership requires hard work, selflessness, and personal sacrifice.*

— TWENTY-TWO —

ASSAULT ON VICKSBURG
Thomas Higgins and Heroic Leadership

Before commencing siege operations at Vicksburg, Grant attempted two direct assaults. While both failed, individual heroics by soldiers such as Private Thomas Higgins abounded.

THE MEDAL OF HONOR IS THE HIGHEST MEDAL AWARDED TO UNITED States military personnel for bravery in the face of the enemy. Some 121 Medals of Honor were awarded as a result of the Vicksburg Campaign, of which ninety-eight stemmed from the general assault of May 22, 1863. Given these numbers, the criteria for conferring the Medal of Honor during the Civil War obviously were much less restrictive than they are today, but by any standard, the actions that won Thomas Higgins his Medal of Honor comprised an example of heroic leadership.

After the Federal victory at Champion Hill, Pemberton retreated to his defenses around Vicksburg. Hoping to catch the Confederates while they were still disorganized and before they could improve their already formidable defenses, Grant launched two rather impulsive assaults on May 19 and May 22. Both failed.

The only corps Grant had in position for the May 19 assault was that of Sherman on the Graveyard Road northeast of Vicksburg. The focus of the attack was Stockade Redan, a V-shaped fortification open in the rear and protected by a parapet that was seventeen feet high and twenty feet thick. In front of the parapet was a ditch six feet deep and eight feet wide. This formidable position was manned by the reinforced 36th Mississippi Regiment and made even stronger by Green's Lunette, a small outwork about seventy-five yards to the south of the redan, and the 27th Louisiana

Lunette, approximately 150 yards to the west. These lunettes provided excellent enfilading fire in front of the redan.

The main Federal effort against the imposing Confederate position was made by Major General Francis Blair's division of Sherman's XV Corps. The attack was preceded by an artillery preparation that lasted from 9:00 a.m. to 2:00 p.m. Blair's men then attacked in three brigade formations, but they quickly became entangled in abatis, wire, and other obstacles, and were subjected to a murderous fire from front and flank.

Against this hailstorm of fire, only one Federal regiment reached the objective, but even it was unable to breach the parapet and had to withdraw under cover of darkness. Sherman lost 134 killed, 571 wounded, and eight missing in the futile attack.

Undeterred, Grant tried again on May 22 with a more deliberate attack. This time he used his entire army with all three corps attacking along the Confederate line. As on May 19, Sherman was to attack the Stockade Redan, and in the predawn hours of May 22, his sharpshooters worked their way into the ravine in front of the defenses. From these forward positions, they would attempt to suppress the deadly Confederate rifles when the attack began.

At dawn the Federals began an artillery barrage that lasted until 10:00 a.m., when the infantry attacked. In spite of these preparations, the results were no different than on May 19. For the most part, the defenders held their fire until the Federals emerged into an open area some 400 feet to the front. Then the Confederates "rose from their reclining position behind the works, and gave them such a terrible volley of musketry" that the attack was halted in its tracks. Even Sherman recognized the futility, ending the carnage by reportedly ordering, "This is murder. Stop those men." Sherman lost 150 killed, 666 wounded, and 42 missing. All told, 502 of Grant's command were killed, 2,550 were wounded, and 147 were missing.

Amid such carnage, individual acts of courage abound, but those of Private Thomas Higgins deserve special mention. There was nothing about Higgins's prebattle demeanor to indicate he would soon be a hero. He was a quiet man who had been born in Canada and worked as a shoemaker before the war.

Now Higgins belonged to Company D of the 99th Illinois Regiment, and on May 22 he had the honor of carrying the regimental colors. Battle flags and guidons were more than just symbols of unit pride in the Civil War. They played important roles in command and control, providing a visible signal that rose above the noise of the battle to provide direction when voice commands failed. Once the charge was sounded, Higgins's captain had told him not to stop until he planted the colors atop the Confederate works. There it would serve as a rallying point and an encouragement to the entire regiment.

While the Federal attack crumbled in the face of the withering Confederate fire, Higgins obeyed his captain's orders and continued to advance. Battle-hardened Confederate soldiers could not help but be amazed by Higgins's bravery, some even holding their fire and cheering him forward. Once Higgins reached the parapet and planted the colors, he was quickly captured by the Confederates and held prisoner until the garrison's surrender on July 4.

On April 1, 1898, Higgins's bravery was rewarded with the Medal of Honor. His citation reads, "When his regiment fell back in the assault, this soldier continued to advance and planted the flag on the parapet, where he was captured by the enemy."

LEADERSHIP LESSONS

Higgins's citation reads like a synopsis of leadership. Summarizing a leader's duties, Chris Lowney writes, "the leader figures out where we need to go, points us in the right direction, gets us to agree that we need to get there, and rallies us through the inevitable obstacles that separate us from the promised land." Higgins's flag pointed his regiment onward through the Confederate fire to the objective.

Lowney also points out that heroic leadership of the sort Higgins demonstrated under fire comes "not just as a response to crisis but a consciously chosen *approach to life*." Lowney calls this type of leadership *magis*, after the Latin word for "more." Leaders devote themselves to a routine of service, but when the opportunity arises, they must be able to surge to the *magis* level to meet the challenge.

Lowney argues that "*magis*-driven leadership inevitably leads to heroism," which begins with each person considering, internalizing, and shaping his mission until it becomes personal. Higgins reached this *magis* level. His captain had given Higgins a mission, and Higgins then made it his own. Under extraordinary circumstances, Higgins's actions earned him the Medal of Honor. Sometimes leadership takes such dramatic form. More often it is found in the countless small decisions that a leader makes every day to put aside self-interest and do what needs to be done to lead his organization to the objective.

Takeaways:
- *Leaders provide direction by their personal actions.*
- *Leaders must sustain an attitude of routine and regular service but also need to be ready to rise to the occasion in times of extraordinary circumstances.*
- *Individual acts of heroic leadership are the by-products of a broader character.*
- *Leadership entails personal costs.*

TWENTY-THREE

PROBLEM REMOVED
John McClernand and Destructive Ambition

*The failed assault of May 22 had at least one positive result for Grant.
It gave him the opportunity to relieve the troublesome John McClernand from command.*

BEFORE THE CIVIL WAR, JOHN MCCLERNAND WAS A DEMOCRATIC Congressman from southern Illinois, an area well known for its Southern sympathies. His only military service had been as a private in the militia during the Black Hawk War. Nonetheless, McClernand's strong support of Abraham Lincoln, and the President's need to secure the loyalty of southern Illinois helped McClernand gain an appointment as brigadier general of volunteers in May 1861. He commanded a division at Fort Donelson, but had not made a favorable impression on Grant there. A Confederate counterattack had scattered McClernand's division, and Grant found McClernand's men "standing in knots talking in the most excited manner. No officer seemed to be giving any directions. The soldiers had their muskets, but no ammunition, while there were tons of it on hand." Nonetheless, McClernand was promoted to major general in March 1862. He performed better at Shiloh, often working in concert with Major General William Sherman.

In August 1862, McClernand returned to Illinois as part of a recruitment effort. He also made a direct appeal to President Lincoln, bypassing Grant, General-in-Chief Major General Henry Halleck, and Secretary of War Edwin Stanton, to raise a new army which McClernand intended to lead down the Mississippi River to capture Vicksburg. Lincoln, eager to renew activity in the Western Theater, and as of yet unsure of Grant's abilities, authorized McClernand's plans over the objections of Halleck.

McClernand may have thought he scored a political victory in winning Lincoln's approval, but in the process he made many enemies. As Halleck drew up the official orders, he specified that McClernand could move only "when a sufficient force not required by the operations of General Grant's command shall be raised" and even then that McClernand's operation would be "subject to the designation of the general-in-chief." The result was that rather than the independent command McClernand had envisioned, he remained subordinate to Grant.

Even so, Grant was suspicious of McClernand, and he sought to preempt any competition by launching his own drive on Vicksburg while Mc-

John McClernand.
Courtesy of the Library of Congress

Clernand was still in Illinois. As a result, Grant ordered Sherman to embark on his Chickasaw Bayou operation, instructing him to get started at once because Grant "feared that delay might bring McClernand."

Confederate cavalry raids not only prematurely ended Grant's prong of the offensive, they also disrupted telegraph lines to Washington, causing a delay in orders that would have placed McClernand in command over Sherman. As a result, all McClernand could do for the time being was wait impatiently in Illinois. It was not until Sherman returned from his failed attack on the Chickasaw Bluffs that he finally received orders to relinquish command to McClernand, who then left Illinois and assumed command on January 4, 1863.

During the transition, Sherman informed McClernand of a plan he had been considering to attack Fort Hindman (also known as Arkansas Post) on the Arkansas River about 120 miles northwest of Vicksburg. McClernand jumped at the idea and, assisted by Porter's ironclads, captured the fort in an amphibious attack on January 11. This success did little to relieve Grant's misgivings about McClernand, especially after Grant "received messages from both Sherman and Admiral Porter, urging me to come and take command in person, and expressing their distrust of McClernand's ability and fitness for so important and intricate an expedition." Rather than risk further disruption by McClernand, on January 29 Grant travelled from his headquarters at Memphis to Young's Point, Louisiana and assumed command the next day. McClernand was senior to Sherman, James McPherson, and Stephen Hulburt, Grant's other corps commanders, but, to McClernand's chagrin, now Grant was firmly in charge. McClernand protested this turn of events in a way Grant felt was "highly insubordinate," but which Grant "overlooked . . . for the good of the service," owing to McClernand's political clout.

This is not to say Grant's problems with McClernand were over. At Champion Hill, McClernand showed a disturbing lack of initiative, passively waiting for orders on Middle and Raymond Roads while the battle raged all around him. When he finally did attack, he showed such caution as to have little effect. The casualty figures revealed how little action McClernand's men saw. Four regiments outside McClernand's command individually suffered more losses than McClernand's entire corps. Grant again was vexed by McClernand, who, if he had "come up with reasonable promptness," Grant argued, would have made it impossible for "Pemberton [to] have escaped with any organized force."

What finally proved to be McClernand's undoing was the May 22 assault on Vicksburg. While McPherson's attack against the Great Redoubt failed, as did Sherman's on the Stockade Redan, McClernand's attack against the Railroad Redoubt initially experienced fleeting success. McClernand sent Grant an exaggerated report that he had captured portions of the Confederate line and asked for reinforcements and a diversionary attack. Grant was incredulous but nonetheless complied with McClernand's request. However, the additional resources had little effect on Federal progress against the Railroad Redoubt.

After the battle, McClernand issued a congratulatory order to his men in which he implied that the other two corps had left his corps to bear the brunt of the fighting. Sherman and McPherson responded with formal letters of protest to Grant, who investigated and found that McClernand's order was in reality a thinly disguised press release which violated the standing order requiring corps commanders to clear such correspondence through Grant's headquarters. Grant finally had the grounds he needed to relieve McClernand, which he did on June 18. McClernand was ordered back to Illinois and Major General Edward O.C. Ord succeeded him as commander of the XVII Corps.

LEADERSHIP LESSONS

All leaders deal with a mix of subordinates. Servant leadership requires the leader to meet the subordinate's legitimate needs, but if after the appropriate training, counseling, and opportunity, a subordinate continues to fail to perform, he must be removed. Keeping a non-productive or disruptive team member hurts the entire organization.

Patrick Lencioni identifies one of the "five dysfunctions of a team" as the "avoidance of accountability." He writes that many people would rather tolerate poor performance and avoid the interpersonal discomfort of confrontation. He advises leaders to guard against this dysfunction by encouraging team members to hold one another accountable and by clearly publishing guidelines that define expected standards. Grant's saga with McClernand illustrates both of these suggestions.

Lencioni argues that "As politically incorrect as it sounds, the most effective and efficient means of maintaining high standards of performance on a team is peer pressure." When Porter and Sherman requested that Grant personally assume command after the Arkansas Post expedition, they were holding McClernand accountable for his poor performance. Although there is no record of it, one would hope that the pair took their concerns to McClernand before going directly to Grant.

While Grant was exacerbated by McClernand's actions throughout the Vicksburg Campaign, he did not have grounds to relieve him until after the May 22 assault. It was then that McClernand violated a published directive requiring corps commanders to clear press releases with Grant's headquarters. Lencioni writes that "the enemy of accountability is ambiguity," a phenomenon that the military chain of command seemed to understand early on with Halleck's clear definition of McClernand's subordinate relationship to Grant. Grant determined that McClernand's deviation from established standards was detrimental to the organization and required McClernand's removal.

Takeaways:
• *Leaders must hold their subordinates accountable.*
• *When a subordinate's behavior becomes detrimental to the organization, the leader, for the good of the organization, must remove the subordinate.*
• *Clear standards reduce ambiguity and facilitate accountability.*

TWENTY-FOUR

SIEGE WARFARE
Henry Foster and Problem Solving

The siege of Vicksburg involved a variety of engineering activities such as the preparation of Major General John Logan's approach trench to the 3rd Louisiana Redan. Logan's men were subjected to harassing fire from the Confederates, leading Lieutenant Henry Foster to develop an innovative countermeasure.

WITH THE FAILURE OF THE MAY 19 AND 22 ASSAULTS, GRANT RELUC-tantly resorted to siege operations. Faced with a critical shortage of trained engineers, Grant ordered all his West Point officers and others with civil engineering experience to assist chief engineer Captain Frederick Prime with the preparations. Within a few weeks, Grant had ten divisions along the entire seven mile Confederate front, engineer and infantry details were digging thirteen distinct approaches to the Confederate lines, and the beleaguered city was subjected to an incessant bombardment from land artillery and mortars as well as Porter's gunboats.

In addition to Pemberton's army, some 5,000 civilians were trapped inside the city. Although Grant's men targeted military entrenchments and breastworks, many of the shells inevitably landed among the civilian population. Quickly realizing that their homes could offer little protection, many Vicksburg citizens dug caves into the city's hillside. By the end of the siege, some 500 caves formed what the Federals derisively dubbed Vicksburg's "Prairie Dog Village."

While some caves were designed as temporary emergency bomb shelters, others were handsomely equipped with furniture, rugs, private chambers, and doors. In spite of their crudeness, the caves were effective.

Mary Ann Loughborough chronicled the experience in *My Cave Life in Vicksburg*. She described the terror of enduring a shelling from her cave refuge by saying,

> My heart stood still as we would hear the reports from the guns, and the rushing and fearful sound of the shell as it came toward us. As it neared, the noise became deafening; the air was full of the rushing sound; pains darted through my temples; my ears were full of the confusing noise; and, as it exploded, the report flashed through my head like an electric shock, leaving me in a quiet state of terror the most painful I can imagine—cowering in a corner, holding my child to my heart—the only feeling of my life being the choking throbs of my heart, that rendered me almost breathless.

Lacking his own siege guns other than six 32-pounders, Grant turned to the navy to supply him with large caliber guns. Porter's thirteen shore-based naval guns fired 4,500 rounds during the siege, and his mortars added another 7,000 from their river location. Nonetheless, the caves served their purpose well. Loughborough considered it "strange so few casualties occur during these projectile storms." Indeed, fewer than a dozen civilians were reported to have died during the siege, and perhaps three times that number were injured.

While Vicksburg's citizenry suffered inside the city and Confederate soldiers strengthened their defenses, the Federals attempted to tighten their noose and hasten the Confederate surrender. Of the thirteen approaches being dug, the most significant in terms of location and effect was that of Major General John Logan's 3rd Division of McPherson's XVII Corps. Logan's men began digging on May 26 from a location about fifty yards southeast of the Shirley House. The object was the 3rd Louisiana Redan, sometimes referred to in Federal documents as Fort Hill, which lay some four hundred yards away.

Both advancing Federals and defending Confederates were subjected to accurate fire from enemy sharpshooters. Sometimes soldiers would amuse themselves by placing a hat on a stick and raising it a few inches above the parapet to see how long it took for a bullet to strike it. Other times the situation was much more deadly as sharpshooters' bullets found human targets.

Logan's Headquarters at Vicksburg. *Courtesy of the Library of Congress*

In order to protect themselves from this threat, Logan's engineers did their work behind gabions—wicker baskets filled with rocks and dirt. Taking this concept to an even greater level, enterprising soldiers found a railcar, outfitted it with wheels, and loaded it with bales of cotton. They then pushed it along the Jackson Road toward the 3rd Louisiana Redan. Confederate W.H. Tunnard complained that "Protected by this novel, moveable shelter, [the Federals] constructed their works with impunity, and with almost the certainty of eventually reaching our intrenchments." Tunnard declared the device "a perfect annoyance" and reported that several plans to destroy it, including a raid, were considered but determined to be unworkable.

Faced with a seemingly impregnable obstacle, Lieutenant Colonel Samuel Russell of the 3rd Louisiana was forced to be creative. He ordered his men to wrap their musket balls with turpentine-soaked flax or hemp fibers, hoping that when fired into the cotton bales, these modified munitions would cause a fire to ignite. On June 8, 1863, Lieutenant W.M.

Washburn fired one such ball at Tunnard's "hated object." Nothing happened, even after additional balls were fired into the target. The Confederates were just about to declare the experiment a failure when someone exclaimed, "I'll be d——d if that thing isn't on fire!" Twenty bales of smoldering cotton soon burst into flames, and five companies of Confederates rushed to the scene, keeping up a steady fire to dissuade any Federal efforts to extinguish the blaze. Tunnard declared the operation a "complete success" and credited it to "the inventive genius of Lieutenant Washburn."

Washburn had a Federal counterpart with an equally creative approach to problem solving in Lieutenant Henry Foster of the 22nd Indiana, an expert marksman who earned the nickname "Coonskin" for his distinctive non-regulation headgear. Foster would often take his rifle, ammunition, and several days' rations and creep forward at night into the no-man's land between the two lines. There he would build an underground position with a loophole through which he could fire at unsuspecting Confederates.

Foster, however, was plagued by the same problem that hampered the Federal artillery, which could batter the redan and send shells sailing over it, but had difficulty hitting targets within the fort. Foster also had to rely on Confederate soldiers carelessly exposing themselves outside the fort's protective walls. To solve this problem, Foster used railroad ties salvaged from the dismantled Jackson & Vicksburg line to build a tower. Working at night, he laid the ties in log cabin fashion which allowed Federal snipers to fire between the ties while still enjoying sufficient protection. The height of what became known as "Coonskin's Tower" allowed the Federals to fire down on the Confederate position and over its walls. According to Michael Morgan, Foster "became a terror to the Confederates."

LEADERSHIP LESSONS

By all accounts, Foster was a unique individual. From his penchant for operating alone to his nocturnal habits to his coonskin cap, Foster was not the typical military officer. He was also not typical in his ability to meet the challenge Kenneth Blanchard poses in *Leading at a Higher Level* to go beyond "problem spotting" and actually engage in "problem solving." Many Federal soldiers spotted the problem of the Confederate sharpshooters, but Foster was one of the few to try to solve it.

Problem solving requires initiative, creativity, and originality to go beyond the given information. This skill set is often described as "thinking outside the box." Clearly Foster exhibited this ability in constructing his tower.

But such individual initiative would be meaningless in problem solving without leadership that is willing to create "an organizational climate that releases the knowledge, experience, and motivation that reside in people," a process Blanchard refers to as "empowerment." One can only imagine the initial reaction of Foster's superior officer when the coonskin-capped lieutenant first approached him with the idea of building a log cabin tower of railroad ties. Yet Foster was given the opportunity to try his idea, no doubt at some risk to his commander, and absent that empowerment, Federal engineers would have still have been suffering from Confederate fire.

Takeaways:
• *Most anyone can problem-spot. Leaders problem-solve.*
• *Problem solving requires creativity and innovation.*
• *Subordinates must be empowered to use their initiative to solve problems.*
• *Leaders must accept the risk associated with empowerment.*

TWENTY-FIVE

THE FEDERAL MINE
John Logan and Initiative

The work that Foster was protecting was the preparations for a mine to be exploded underneath the Confederate position. While the ensuing attack failed to gain the position, Logan's mine shows an innovative attempt to break the status quo.

MAJOR GENERAL JOHN LOGAN WAS A FORMER ATTORNEY AND CONGRESS-man from Illinois, representing a part of southern Illinois known as "Little Egypt." It was a decidedly Democratic part of the state, but Logan proved to be a strong supporter of the Union. In spite of Logan's political background, Ezra Warner describes him as "perhaps the Union's premier civilian combat general."

Logan certainly looked the part of a general, with a powerful build and a booming voice that could easily rise above the din of the battle. He had shoulder-length black hair and a sweeping mustache which gave him the nickname "Black Jack." He commanded the 3rd Division in Major General James McPherson's corps, launching a powerful counterattack at Fourteen-mile Creek that helped the Federals win a costly victory and compel the Confederates to abandon Raymond. Logan performed even more admirably at Champion Hill, rallying the 34th Indiana on the Federal right flank with personal leadership, a no-nonsense sense of urgency, and, according to one soldier, "the speed of a cyclone." Private soldiers such as Osborn Oldroyd of the 20th Ohio revered Logan, claiming that he "is brave and does not seem to know what defeat means. We feel that he will bring us out of every fight victorious. I want no better or braver officer to fight under." Indeed, John Hubell described Logan as "a soldier's soldier."

Grant also held Logan in high esteem, writing in his *Memoirs* that he "regarded Logan and [Major General Marcellus] Crocker as being as competent division commanders as could be found in or out of the army and both equal to a much higher command." Part of Grant's respect for Logan may have stemmed from what Warner describes as Logan's skill in combining his numerous talents with his "inherent abilities as a leader to produce a record hardly surpassed in the era for its versatility." A man with such energy, motivational ability, and expertise no doubt chafed under the static conditions of a siege, and Logan used his initiative to compel action.

After the failure of the May 19 and 22 attacks, the Federals continued to pressure the Confederates. In several instances, they dug mines underneath the Confederate positions and packed them with explosives in an effort to blast a hole in the defense. One objective for these Federal mining operations was the 3rd Louisiana Redan. There, on May 26, Logan's division began digging an eight-foot-wide and seven-foot-deep zigzag approach trench toward the Confederate position.

Superintending the proceedings was Captain Andrew Hickenlooper, who before the war had been Cincinnati's city surveyor and was now McPherson's chief engineer. Studying the ground, Hickenlooper recognized the way the Confederate positions dominated the field. The only approach was along the ridge bearing the Jackson Road, exposing would-be attackers to fire from both the 3rd Louisiana Redan to the north and the Great Redoubt to the south. Logan had attacked into these twin strongholds on May 22, suffering 359 killed, wounded, or missing. He was not eager to repeat such a bloodletting.

A mine offered an alternative, and Hickenlooper started his digging with 300 men, mostly from Brigadier General Mortimer Leggett's brigade of Logan's division. Under cover of darkness, Hickenlooper spaced his men five feet apart and instructed them to dig until their hole connected to that of the adjacent soldier. At daylight, a new crew reported for duty and expanded the trench to a width of eight feet and a depth of seven. The final result was a sap that zigzagged about 1,500 feet and crossed the Jackson Road five times. As the workers neared Confederate lines, they came under increased enemy fire. Hickenlooper took several precautions, including reducing the size of his work force and constructing artillery batteries from which to deliver harassing fires on the Confederates.

By June 22, the Federals reached the base of the redan. Hickenlooper had collected a force of thirty-six XVII Corps soldiers, many of whom were former lead miners serving in the 45th Illinois of Leggett's brigade. Hickenlooper organized his miners into day and night shifts, each consisting of three squads of six miners. Each squad labored for an hour before the exhausting work necessitated relief. They dug under the redan, and in just three days had excavated a forty-five-foot-long, four-by-five-foot tunnel. The miners then began digging three galleries, each of fifteen feet in length. One extended straight ahead from the tunnel and the other two branched off to the left and right at forty-five degree angles. The navy had provided twenty-five pound bags of black powder, and the miners packed a total of 2,200 pounds into the galleries. Each charge was wired with two strands of fuse in the event one failed to burn. Finally, dirt was tamped against the powder to direct the force of the explosion upward. By June 25, the work was finished.

Depiction of the mine explosion in the July 25, 1863 *Harper's Weekly.*

At 3:30, the Federals began lighting the fuses, and the ensuing explosion was breathtaking. Hickenlooper wrote, "It appeared as though the whole fort and connecting outworks commenced an upward movement, gradually breaking into fragments and growing less bulky in appearance, until it looked like an immense fountain of finely pulverized earth, mingled with flashes of fire and clouds of smoke, through which could occasionally be caught a glimpse of some dark objects, men, gun-carriages, shelters, etc." In spite of the spectacle, initial Confederate casualties were light, in part because the defenders had detected Hickenlooper's work and evacuated the position before the explosion.

The 6th Missouri was positioned in a ravine behind the fort, and the Confederates had built a retrenchment inside the fort's interior as a supplementary line of defense. This barrier survived the explosion, and the Missourians quickly occupied positions behind it. The crater was relatively narrow, allowing only about one hundred men to advance as a front. As the Federal soldiers moved forward, clearing debris as they went, they ran into the stout Confederate defense. The Federals dispatched rotations of several units into the attack throughout the night with little success. The Confederates hurled grenades into the confined space of densely packed troops, inflicting numerous casualties. The Federals responded with 10-pound Parrott shells, but the more dispersed Confederates suffered much less damage.

Fierce fighting raged along the parapet that separated blue and gray, until June 26 when the Federals withdrew to a line of rifle pits they had dug across the center of the crater. Logan had lost 34 killed and 209 wounded, compared to 21 killed and 73 wounded for the Confederates. Undeterred, Logan's men started another mine on June 28 which they detonated on July 1. This second explosion consisted of 1,800 pounds of powder, ripping a twenty-nine foot gap in the interior wall that had stopped the June 25 assault. Federal artillery pounded the breach, but there was no infantry assault. Grant explained that "No attempt to charge was made this time, the experience of the 25th admonishing us."

For the next forty-eight hours, the Federals continued their bombardment, and a general assault was planned for July 6. By then, however, Pemberton and the Confederate defenders had surrendered. In Logan's *The Volunteer Soldier in America*, posthumously published in 1887, Cornelius

Ambrose Logan added the editorial notation that "It was from the front of General Logan's headquarters that the mine was sprung which created such disaster to the enemy on the 25th day of June, and which resulted in a flag of truce on the 3rd of July, followed by the surrender of Vicksburg on the 4th." While such a connection between the mine explosion and the Confederate surrender may be difficult to support, Logan's effort to pressure the Confederates rather than idly letting the siege drag on surely characterizes a leader of initiative and action.

LEADERSHIP LESSONS

Peter Northouse notes that "The overriding function of management is to provide order and consistency to organizations, whereas the primary function of leadership is to produce change and movement. Management is about seeking order and stability, leadership is about seeking adaptive and constructive change." If Logan was solely interested in being a manager, his goal would have been to proceed with the deliberate, orderly conduct of the siege. While time was definitely on the Federals' side, mere preservation of the status quo would not achieve their objective of capturing Vicksburg and opening up the Mississippi River. Instead, Logan was interested in changing the situation. To do so he would have to be a leader, not a manager, and his willingness to use the mine as a means of altering the stalemate to give the advantage to the Federals shows his adaptive, imaginative, and bold leadership.

Northouse notes that leaders "act to expand the available options to long-standing problems" and "change the way people think about what is possible." The assaults of May 19 and 22 had made many Federals believe the Confederate defense was impregnable. By creating a new option, Logan created a new possibility. Counselors often remind their clients that "without change, there will be no change." This advice is appropriate for leaders as well.

> ### *Takeaways:*
> - *Management focuses on order and stability.*
> *Leadership focuses on constructive change.*
> - *Leadership creates new options.*
> - *Leaders must be willing to try new things.*

— TWENTY-SIX —

SURRENDER AND PAROLE
Ulysses Grant and Pragmatism

The surrender of Vicksburg left Grant with the possibility of having to guard and care for 30,000 prisoners until they could be transported north. Rather than assuming this logistical burden at the expense of continued operations, Grant decided to parole the Confederates.

U.S. GRANT HAD EARNED THE NICKNAME "UNCONDITIONAL SURREN-der" based on his refusal to grant terms to the surrendering Confederates at Fort Donelson in February 1862. At Vicksburg, on July 3, 1863, a Confederate delegation led by Brigadier General John Bowen approached the Federal lines under a flag of truce. Having determined further resistance to be futile, Pemberton had sent Bowen forward for the purpose of "arranging terms for the capitulation of Vicksburg." True to his reputation from Fort Donelson, Grant was in no mood to negotiate. Instead, he sent Pemberton a written reply allowing "no other terms" than "the unconditional surrender of the city and garrison." However, in the final agreement, Grant reversed this initial uncompromising position and allowed the Confederates to sign paroles and march out of the Federal lines with various provisions made for side arms, clothing, horses, rations and cooking utensils, wagons, and the sick and wounded. Grant's final decision does not reflect weakness or wavering, but instead it exemplifies the calculating pragmatics that leaders must bear in mind in order to achieve greater goals.

The practice of parole may seem strange to modern sensibilities, but during the Civil War it allowed captured soldiers to give a pledge that they would not again bear arms until being properly exchanged for an enemy soldier who had also been captured. These soldiers were considered "paroled" and were on their honor to abide by the agreement. Paroles occurred early in the war, but the first formal exchange did not take place until February 23, 1862. Until that time, the Federal government had been reluctant to enter into negotiations for fear of giving legitimacy to the Confederacy.

Giving parole released the capturing unit of the responsibility of providing logistical support for the prisoners, and it was often done for tactical reasons. In the case of Vicksburg, Grant explained, "Had I insisted upon unconditional surrender, there would have been over thirty-odd thousand men to transport to Cairo, very much to the inconvenience of the army on the Mississippi; thence the prisoners would have had to be transported by rail to Washington or Baltimore; thence again by steamer to Aiken's—all at very great expense. At Aiken's they would have to be paroled, because the Confederates did not have Union prisoners to give in exchange. Then again Pemberton's army was largely composed of men whose homes were in the south-west; I knew many of them were tired of the war and would get home just as soon as they could."

Pemberton appears to have shared Grant's assessment of the state of his men. When word leaked out that many of the paroled Confederates intended to desert and return to their homes as soon as they passed through Federal lines, Pemberton appealed to Grant to allow for a battalion under arms to march the men to a camp of instruction where they would remain until exchanged. Grant declined to assist Pemberton in this regard and reports that in the final analysis, "Many [Confederates] deserted; fewer of them were ever returned to the ranks to fight again than would have been the case had the surrender been unconditional and the prisoners sent to the James River to be paroled."

Modern research seems to bear out the validity of Grant's reasoning. Terry Whittington has carefully tracked the Vicksburg paroles and while he finds those from Alabama, Tennessee, and Georgia returned to the ranks in considerable numbers, "for the rest of the army—the Mississippi and trans-Mississippi regiments—reorganization fared poorly." As Grant had predicted, Whittington explains, "Vicksburg was vital to the Mississippi and Trans-Mississippi departments, and the outcome of the campaign had disastrous effects on paroles from these areas. As a result, soldiers from

Grant and Pemberton discussing the terms of surrender. *Courtesy Library of Congress*

these regiments expressed overwhelming defeatism, and many deserted."

While paroling Pemberton's army at Vicksburg served Grant's purposes at the time, he applied his pragmatics differently later. When Grant was promoted to lieutenant general and made General-in-Chief of the entire Federal Army, he pursued a strategy of ruthless attrition to leverage the Federal manpower advantage. Pursuant to this end, Grant virtually ended prisoner exchanges, recognizing that the Federals could more easily absorb personnel losses than could the Confederates. Under these conditions, returning soldiers to the Confederate ranks made no sense, and the pragmatic Grant refused to parole captured soldiers as he had done at Vicksburg.

LEADERSHIP LESSONS

Like all good leaders, Grant was able to use different leadership techniques in different situations. At times such as in building unity of effort with Porter, Grant relied on transformational and charismatic leadership to build consensus and tie leader beliefs to follower beliefs. In his decisions about parole, Grant relied much more on pragmatic leadership and its very practical approach to problem-solving that sought to optimize utility. The goal of pragmatic leadership is to maximize benefit, minimize costs, and meet an objective need. The emotional involvement of followers in such a model is of far less importance.

Thus on July 3, Grant convened a meeting of his corps and division commanders that amounted to what he considered "the nearest approach to a 'council of war' I ever held." He informed the assembled group of the status of the negotiations and advised them "that I was ready to hear any suggestion; but would hold the power of deciding entirely in my own hands." At the conclusion of the meeting, Grant decided "against the general, and almost unanimous judgment of the council," and instead to offer Pemberton conditions of surrender that would allow for parole.

This decision went against Grant's precedent at Fort Donelson, his initial inclination at Vicksburg, and the opinion of his subordinates. In a pragmatic leadership situation, such factors carry little weight. In explaining his decision to General-in-Chief Halleck, Grant wrote, "The enemy surrendered this morning. The only terms allowed is their parole as prisoners of war. This I regard as a great advantage to us at the moment. It saves, probably, several days in the capture, and leaves troops and transports ready for immediate service. Sherman with a large force, moves immediately on Johnston, to drive him from the State. I will send troops to the relief of Banks, and return the 9th army corps to Burnside."

Grant's communication clearly spells out the pragmatics of his decision. It was designed to gain "great advantage . . . at the moment." It minimized costs by saving "several days." It maximized opportunities by leaving troops and transports "ready for immediate service" for which Grant had a detailed and specific plan. Any intrinsic rewards such as the sense of complete victory associated with unconditional surrender were subordinated to these larger extrinsic rewards.

Takeaways
- *Leaders need to be able to apply the appropriate leadership model at the appropriate time.*
- *Pragmatic leadership emphasizes immediate utility and is appropriate in situations requiring short term or tactical results.*
- *Pragmatic leadership decisions may be at odds with the preferences of subordinates.*

— TWENTY-SEVEN —

LITTLE HELP FROM ABOVE
Jefferson Davis and Strategic Direction

Although Pemberton bore most of the public criticism for the loss of Vicksburg, in reality there was plenty of blame to go around. Given the complex situation and his limitations as a leader, Pemberton had needed the clear guidance that President Davis and General Johnston had failed to provide.

JEFFERSON DAVIS HAD ALL THE PREREQUISITES TO BE A SUPERIOR commander-in-chief. He had graduated from West Point in 1828, won great fame as a regimental commander in the Mexican War, and been an able Secretary of War under President Franklin Pierce. Herman Hattaway and Archer Jones conclude that "Davis's breadth of background probably better qualified him for high army command than any man in the United States." On top of these qualifications, Davis was a Mississippian. He would seemingly be the ideal leader to provide strategic direction for the defense of Vicksburg. Instead, however, Davis failed to give Pemberton the leadership he needed. Accordingly, Davis serves as a caution to strategic leaders about the importance of communicating clear, actionable, and timely guidance to their subordinates.

Davis took his title as Commander-in-Chief of the Confederate Army quite literally. Although he had six secretaries of war in four years, for all practical purposes, Davis served as his own secretary of war and chief of staff. Clifford Dowdey observes that "as everything about the military fascinated him and he believed only he was capable of running things, the President performed tasks that belonged properly to clerks in the War Office, and even in the Adjutant General's office. Conversely, as he squandered his time and energies in the field of his interests, Davis neglected affairs which properly belonged in the President's office."

The Mexican War and his other military experiences had given Davis such confidence in his own capabilities that he denied himself the advice and counsel of others. Although Davis created the position of general-in-chief in March 1862, he did so not because he thought he needed help, but to put in place some buffer between the War Department and Congress to help prevent Congress from infringing on presidential prerogatives. Davis then named General Robert E. Lee to the post, charging him "under the direction of the President with the conduct of military operations in the armies of the Confederacy."

In Davis's mind, the phrase "under the direction of the President" was key to his concept of Lee's authority. Essentially, Lee was limited to acting as a provider of counsel and information with no authority to initiate or direct any large strategic operations. Lee's biographer Douglas Southall

Freeman calls it "an impossible assignment" and concludes that in Lee's "whole career there was not a period of more thankless service."

Lee vacated the position in June to assume field command of the Army of Northern Virginia, and Davis left the advisor position vacant for approximately twenty months, an indication of how little importance he attached to the office. During that time, he formulated strategy largely without professional military advice. The proximity of Lee to Davis in the Eastern Theater helped facilitate strategic planning there, but operations in the Western Theater suffered greatly. Pemberton was a man who

Jefferson Davis.
Courtesy of the Library of Congress

needed clear direction, but, under these circumstances, he would not get it from Davis.

Pemberton officially took command of the Department of Mississippi and East Louisiana on October 14, 1862. In December, Davis and General Joseph Johnston made an inspection tour of Mississippi and met with Pemberton, but the visit was interrupted by news of Sherman's advance on Walnut Hills. On Christmas Day, Davis departed for Richmond and left Pemberton to tend to what became the Battle of Chickasaw Bayou. There is no indication Davis left Pemberton with any meaningful strategic guidance during the visit.

In fact, Davis and Johnston, the other man to whom Pemberton might expect to look for strategic direction, disagreed over how best to handle the Vicksburg situation. Davis insisted that General Braxton Bragg, commander of the Army of Tennessee, and Pemberton defend their respective departments from stationary locations. If one command or the other needed assistance to meet a threat, troops could be shuttled between them. Johnston disagreed, arguing that distance and an unreliable rail connection precluded such movements. Instead, he urged concentration, with Pemberton and Lieutenant General Theophilus Holmes, commander of the Trans-Mississippi Department, first combining against Grant, and then Pemberton and Bragg uniting to defeat Rosecrans. Davis rejected such an approach, and Johnston was shaken by the decision, thereafter taking an increasingly aloof approach to developments in his command.

On April 28, 1863, Pemberton wired Davis that Grant was conducting a demonstration in force across the Mississippi River at Hard Times, but Pemberton had not yet realized the true nature of the threat. By May 1, Pemberton was much more agitated, notifying Davis that a battle was raging at Port Gibson and requesting reinforcements. In faraway Tullahoma, Tennessee, Johnston knew little of the actual situation, but he advised Pemberton, "If Grant's army lands on this side of the river, the safety of Mississippi depends on beating it. For that object you should unite your whole force." The next day, Johnston reiterated that Pemberton must unite his force against Grant, promising "Success will give back what was abandoned to win it."

At the same time, Lee's success and influence in Virginia worked to the detriment of Pemberton. Lee's great victory at Chancellorsville the first week in May left the Confederate high command with a choice to either approve Lee's plan to invade Pennsylvania or have Lee go on the defensive in order to send reinforcements to Pemberton. Lee's argument to launch a second invasion of Northern territory carried the day, and Pemberton was left to fend for himself.

At first, Pemberton worked to follow Johnston's advice, realizing that without reinforcements he would have to adjust his own priorities. He wrote Davis that he intended to abandon Port Hudson and Grand Gulf to concentrate more troops to meet Grant. Instead, Davis ordered him on May 7 that "To hold Vicksburg and Port Hudson is necessary to a connection with the Trans-Mississippi. You may expect whatever is in my power to do." In spite of this broad promise of support, Davis provided sparse real assistance to Pemberton. Instead of the cavalry that Pemberton requested as being a "positive necessity," Davis sent Pemberton the gratuitous advice to solicit the "good will and support of the people." On May 9, Davis ordered Johnston to go to Mississippi to take command of the deteriorating situation, but this decision was made far too late and predestined to failure by Johnston's pessimism and half-hearted approach to his mission.

Once the situation was reduced to a siege, Davis continued to offer little more than encouraging words and sympathy. He wrote Pemberton, "I made every effort to reinforce you promptly which I am grieved was not successful. Hope that General Johnston will join you with enough force to break up the investment and defeat the enemy. Sympathizing with you for the reverses sustained, I pray God may yet give success to you and the brave troops under your command." Such platitudes ring hollow in contrast to former Army Chief of Staff General Gordon Sullivan's advice to business leaders over a century later that "hope is not a method." For the time being, however, that was all Davis would muster on Pemberton's behalf. It was not enough.

Much of the blame for the Confederate failure at Vicksburg must wrest with Davis. For starters, he did Pemberton no service in assigning him to a post for which he was ill-suited. Having put Pemberton in a position beyond his capabilities, Davis then focused on developments in the Eastern Theater at the time Pemberton found himself in his moment of crisis. The strategic guidance Davis did offer conflicted with what Pemberton had been told by Johnston. Captain Samuel Lockett, Pemberton's chief engineer, explains that the result was that Pemberton then "made the capital mistake of trying to harmonize the instructions from his superiors diametrically opposed to each other, and at the same time bring them into accord with his own judgment, which was adverse to both." Davis realized too late that Pemberton was over his head, and by the time he ordered Johnston to come to his aid, the opportunity was lost. Finally, Davis provided Pemberton little in the way of the tangible resources he had promised him.

LEADERSHIP LESSONS

Strategic leaders must be able to prioritize and allocate finite resources where they are needed. This skill requires timely decision-making based on an ability to see the overall picture. Without a doubt, President Davis had a daunting task in leading the fledgling Confederacy. It was obviously a challenge too great for any one man, even a man of Davis's accomplished background.

Still, Davis refused to apply a delegative approach to his responsibilities. Confident in his own abilities, Davis simply took on too much. As the war became more and more complicated, Davis's ability to control events dwindled. The hands-on leadership style of a regimental commander on a tactical battlefield in Mexico proved ill-suited for the demands of strategic leadership of a nation at war. For whatever his limitations, Pemberton was a man of duty who would do what he was told to the best of his ability, but he needed to be told clearly what to do. Davis failed to provide Pemberton the strategic direction he needed, either personally or through an intermediary commander.

Takeaways
- *Leaders need to prioritize strategic direction to their subordinates in a way that is tailored to the individual subordinate's needs.*
- *Delegation and staff counsel help a strategic leader perform his duties, regardless of his own considerable skills.*
- *Senior leaders must send synchronized and consistent messages to their subordinates.*

TWENTY-EIGHT

A DECISIVE VICTORY
Abraham Lincoln and Admitting When You're Wrong

The capture of Vicksburg opened the Mississippi to Federal transporta-
tion, split the Confederacy in two, and denied the eastern Confederacy
much of the resources of the trans-Mississippi. With the victory com-
plete, President Abraham Lincoln reviewed the campaign and sent
Grant an apology for his earlier doubts.

IN NOVEMBER 1862, PRESIDENT ABRAHAM LINCOLN REPLACED
Major General Benjamin Butler, whose heavy-handed occupation of New
Orleans and other idiosyncrasies had been a source of some controversy,
with Major General Nathaniel Banks as commander of the Federal forces
in southern Louisiana. Banks was a political general who had served as a
member of Congress and governor of Massachusetts. He was part of a team
of Federal generals who had been soundly defeated by Major General
Stonewall Jackson in the Shenandoah Valley earlier in the year. While there
was nothing in Banks's record to indicate he was up for the task, Lincoln
and his general-in-chief Major General Henry Halleck assigned Banks the
mission of moving north from New Orleans to open the Mississippi River.

Banks was senior to Grant, and Halleck advised him that "as the ranking general in the Southwest, you are authorized to assume control of the
military forces from the Upper Mississippi which may come within your
command. The line of division between your department and that of
Major-General Grant is therefore left undecided for the present, and you
will exercise superior authority as far as you may ascend the river." Fur-
thermore, Halleck let Banks know that Lincoln expected this ascension to

occur quickly, telling him, "the President regards the opening of the Mississippi River as the first and most important of all our military and naval operations, and it is hoped that you will not lose a moment in accomplishing it."

Standing in Banks's way was the Confederate strongpoint at Port Hudson, Louisiana, about twenty-five miles north of Baton Rouge and two hundred miles south of Vicksburg. There Major General Franklin Grover commanded some 15,000 Confederates. While Banks built a sizeable Army of the Gulf, Port Hudson first came under fire when Admiral David Farragut steamed past it on March 14, 1863 on his way upriver to Vicksburg.

Banks was a mediocre tactician, and he convinced himself he could not assault Port Hudson without first clearing the west bank of the Mississippi. In April, he launched a campaign designed to destroy a 4,000 man force commanded by Major General Richard Taylor on Bayou Teche, west of New Orleans. Banks concentrated a force of 15,000 men at Brashear (now Morgan City), Louisiana and then advanced in two columns, one up the Bayou Teche and another along a roughly parallel route along the Atchafalaya River. Taylor sensed the trap and was able to slip away after the battles of Irish Bend and Fort Bisland on April 12–14. Taylor continued to retreat to Opelousas, and Banks took Alexandria on May 7 with little opposition.

While Banks was proud of his accomplishment, he seemed to have forgotten all about his instructions from Washington to operate up the Mississippi River. On May 8–10, 1863, Federal gunboats shelled Port Hudson, but the Confederate defenders held on. By this time, Grant had crossed the Mississippi below Vicksburg at Bruinsburg on April 30.

President Lincoln had hoped that once Grant worked his way below Vicksburg, he would continue south and combine forces with Banks. Grant, however, upon learning that Banks would not be able to return to Baton Rouge until May 10 at the earliest, concluded, "I could not lose the time." He decided to "cut loose" from his line of supply and moved north along the route that took him to Jackson before turning west toward Vicksburg. Lincoln considered this move to be a mistake, but he said nothing of it to Grant at the time.

Of course Grant's bold decision shaped the course of the campaign and led to Federal victory. In spite of Lincoln's misgivings at the time,

T. Harry Williams points out how fortunate it was for the Union cause that Grant and Banks did not unite. Recalling that Banks outranked Grant, Williams predicts, "Banks's magnificent incompetency would have nullified the abilities of even Grant."

Grant's decision to move north was not the only time during the campaign that Lincoln found himself concerned with Grant's progress. On March 20, Lincoln confided off the record to a correspondent of the *New York Tribune* that he considered "all these side expeditions through the country dangerous . . . If the rebels can blockade us on the Mississippi, which is a mile wide, they can certainly stop us on the little streams not much wider than our gunboats and shut us up so we can't get back again." Then on April 2, Halleck felt compelled to warn Grant that Lincoln had become "impatient" with all the abortive attempts to approach Vicksburg. By May 26, however, Lincoln had changed his mind. He wrote Isaac Arnold, "Whether Gen. Grant shall or shall not consummate the capture of Vicksburg, his campaign from the beginning of this month up to the twenty second day of it, is one of the most brilliant in the world." When word finally reached Washington of the Federal victory, Lincoln wrote Grant the following letter:

> MY DEAR GENERAL:—I do not remember that you and I ever met personally. I write this now as a grateful acknowledgment for the almost inestimable service you have done the country. I wish to say a word further. When you first reached the vicinity of Vicksburg, I thought you should do what you finally did—march the troops across the neck, run the batteries with the transports, and thus go below; and I never had any faith, except a general hope that you knew better than I, that the Yazoo Pass expedition and the like could succeed. When you got below and took Port Gibson, Grand Gulf, and vicinity, I thought you should go down the river and join General Banks; and when you turned northward, east of the Big Black, I thought it was a mistake. I now wish to make the personal acknowledgment that you were right and I was wrong.

LEADERSHIP LESSONS

Apologies are usually uncomfortable, but when a leader makes a mistake that needs to be acknowledged, the situation is especially delicate. The leader is the one to whom the organization looks to for direction, guidance, and example. If the leader admits to a mistake, his future credibility may be subjected to increased scrutiny. Lincoln was certainly under no obligation to share his confession with Grant, but the fact that he did is a powerful testimony to Lincoln's character as a leader.

The exact appeal of Lincoln's personality is difficult to label, but Richard Current suggests, "Whatever the secret of his leadership, he seems to have had in full measure at least one quality that all the others lacked in some degree. This was not humility or even modesty but a kind of ego perspective, an ability to see himself accurately in relation to people around him. It kept him well away from delusions of grandeur." Current's analysis notwithstanding, Lincoln certainly seemed to meet the definition of humility, as in not thinking less of yourself, but thinking of yourself less.

Lincoln was not alone as a leader who faced the decision of how to respond to a mistake he had made. Public figures often find themselves dealing with situations that have resulted from some inappropriate, unethical, ill-advised, or illegal action. Some take responsibility for the action, both as an individual and as a representative of the organization. Others do not.

In 1977, Chrysler was indicted for testing a small number of cars with the odometer disconnected and then selling them to uninformed customers. The incident caused a lack of consumer confidence that Chrysler CEO Lee Iacocca addressed immediately and directly saying, Chrysler's actions "went beyond dumb and reached all the way to stupid." Iacocca asked, "Did we screw up?," and then answered his own question, "You bet."

Perhaps the most famous and respected example of a corporate apology is the one issued by Johnson & Johnson CEO James Burke in 1982 after seven people died from taking cyanide-laced Tylenol. Even though the crime was beyond Tylenol's control, Burke took responsibility, apologized to consumers, and recalled every Tylenol product immediately, even though capsules were the only form of pill that was associated with the tampering. Burke encouraged customers to return their Tylenol bottles and receive a voucher rather than "risk" injury.

Other corporations and public figures have been less forthcoming in their apologies. Exxon remained silent for six days following the 1989

Valdez oil spill in Alaska. When the company did speak, CEO Lawrence Rawl did not take responsibility and blamed the media for exaggerating the situation. Ten days after the spill, Exxon ran an ad in newspapers in which it apologized for the spill, but did not accept responsibility. For many, Exxon's response to the *Valdez* crisis epitomized corporate arrogance and shirking responsibility. It stood as a stark contrast to the Ashland Oil spill on the Monongahela River a year earlier, which threatened the drinking water supply of thousands of residents in Pittsburgh's suburbs. In that situation, Ashland CEO John Hall apologized for the disaster and pledged to pay for the cleanup. He also personally directed operations from the scene, in contrast to Rawl who had initially sent subordinates to Alaska to deal with the *Valdez* crisis.

More recent public apologies had centered on political figures caught in some moral failing. Men like Bill Clinton, Mark Sanford, and John Edwards have all been criticized for late, weak, insincere, incomplete, and otherwise flawed apologies. Nonetheless, Americans seem to have a resilient ability to forgive their leaders.

Although followers have high expectations of their leaders, subordinates also recognize that leaders are human. Followers do not expect perfection so much as they expect honest effort and sincerity. What they despise more than failure is the arrogant abuse of power that seems to accompany a reluctance to apologize and take responsibility. President Lincoln was seemingly void of ego and personal agenda. He thought in terms of preserving the Union and saw himself as subordinate to that larger cause. His willingness to apologize to Grant is a true demonstration of his noble character and no doubt helped cement the bond the two men would share as Grant assumed duties as commanding general.

Takeaways:
- *Subordinates expect honest mistakes from their leaders and are willing to forgive.*
- *Apologies may be awkward for a leader, but the long-term consequences of not taking responsibility are more damaging to the leader's position*
- *Apologies must be timely, sincere, and complete. Followers can easily see through apologies intended primarily for public relations purposes.*

— TWENTY-NINE —

THE MERIDIAN CAMPAIGN
William Sherman and Creating Opportunity

After the success of the Vicksburg Campaign, and the following Federal victories at Chattanooga and Knoxville in late fall 1863, Major General William Sherman did not want to sit idle waiting for weather sufficient to support the upcoming spring campaign. Instead he executed a masterful raid on Meridian that both included several characteristics of the Vicksburg Campaign and served as a rehearsal for his later "March to the Sea."

MERIDIAN LAY ABOUT 150 MILES DUE WEST FROM VICKSBURG, roughly between the Mississippi capital of Jackson and the cannon foundry and manufacturing center of Selma, Alabama. Like Corinth, which Grant had secured as a prelude to the Vicksburg Campaign, Meridian was a railroad town, with three lines intersecting there. It served as a storage and distribution center for not just the industrial products of Selma but also for grain and cattle from the fertile Black Prairie region just to the north. All of these factors made Meridian a tempting target for a raid.

Sherman figured it would be an easy matter to finish his business in Meridian in time to return to Vicksburg and be ready for future operations; a precondition that Grant had levied upon him. Thus, on February 3, 1864, Sherman began his campaign "to break up the enemy's railroads at and about Meridian, and to do the enemy as much damage as possible in the month of February, and to be prepared by the 1st of March to assist General Banks in a similar dash at the Red River [Louisiana] country . . ."

Sherman's military genius lay more in maneuver and logistics—preserving his own and disrupting his enemy's—than it did in tactics. The

Meridian Campaign was a case study in such methodology, but certainly not one without enormous risk. Sherman would be marching some 150 miles from his base, living off the land, and exposing himself to a potential Confederate concentration from three directions. If the Confederates were able to effect such a concentration, Sherman's entire army faced annihilation. It was an undertaking that caused "much anxiety" in Washington, but Grant was not worried. He knew that any risk was lessened by the fact that Sherman, as a raider, could choose his line of retreat. Grant was confident Sherman would "find an outlet. If in no other way, he will fall back on Pascagoula [on the Gulf], and ship from there under protection of [Admiral David] Farragut's fleet." For historian of Civil War strategy Archer Jones, any threat was alleviated by "the offensive dominance of the raid over a persisting [i.e., territorially-based] defense." Audacious leaders take prudent risks in order to achieve decisive results and dispel uncertainty through action. At Meridian and elsewhere, Sherman epitomized audacity.

Sherman knew that his success depended on speed. He would travel light, ordering, "Not a tent will be carried, from the commander-in-chief down." "The expedition is one of celerity," he explained, "and all things must tend to that." Thus, Sherman began his march in two columns of a corps each in order to facilitate both speed and foraging. As Grant's army had done during parts of the Vicksburg Campaign, Sherman would be living off the land without maintaining a line of supply. This would deny the Confederates resources but would also force Sherman to keep moving in search of more provisions.

Sherman gained surprise from the speed of his advance, but he also followed Grant's Vicksburg example of employing a series of feints and deceptions designed to keep Lieutenant General Leonidas Polk, the Confederate commander at Meridian, guessing. In an effort to maintain flexibility against all possible threats, Polk would never be able to concentrate against Sherman's true attack. To this end, Sherman played on Polk's fear for the safety of Mobile by asking Major General Nathaniel Banks, commander of the Department of the Gulf at New Orleans, to have "boats maneuvering" in the Gulf near Mobile and to "keep up the delusion and prevent the enemy drawing from Mobile a force to strengthen Meridian." Sherman told Banks he would "be obliged" if Banks would "keep up an irritating foraging or other expedition" in the direction of Mobile to help Sherman "keep up the delusion of an attack on Mobile and the Alabama River." As Sherman advanced, he fueled this deception himself. He wrote, "I never had the remotest idea of going to Mobile, but had purposely given out that idea to the people of the country, so as to deceive the enemy and divert their attention."

As another prong of his offensive campaign, Sherman ordered Brigadier General William Sooy Smith, with 8,000 cavalry, to ride south from Memphis, creating havoc through the northern Mississippi farm country, and join him at Meridien by the middle of February. Smith's expedition would have the dual purpose of occupying the attention of the Confederate cavalry general Nathan Bedford Forrest, who, as Sherman explained to Smith, "always attacked with a vehemence for which he must be prepared, and that, after he had repelled the first attack, [Smith] must in turn assume the most determined offensive, overwhelm [Forrest] and utterly destroy his whole force."

By threatening Polk with feints and multiple thrusts, Sherman forced the Confederate department commander to retain forces at Mobile that he could have used against Sherman in Meridian. To further add to Polk's dilemma, Sherman sent gunboats and infantry up the Yazoo River "to reconnoiter and divert attention." The intention was "to make a diversion" and "confuse the enemy." Then when Sherman departed Clinton on February 5, he divided his command, with Major General James McPherson advancing on Jackson from southwest to northeast while Major General Stephen Hurlbut marched due east. Poor Polk had more than he could handle. Convinced Sherman was headed for Mobile, Polk took up a position at Demopolis and waited to strike Sherman's rear. Polk's confusion was compounded by a lack of courage to take the initiative and attack Sherman. Instead, Polk merely kept retreating without making any real attempt to confront the advancing Union force.

Sherman's deception also affected other Confederate commanders. General Joseph Johnston feared Sherman was headed for Johnston's own position at Dalton, Georgia, and, rather than reinforcing Polk, Johnston husbanded his forces for an attack that never came. Throughout the Confederate ranks, inactivity, indecision, and confusion reigned.

Sherman called such a tactic "putting the enemy on the horns of a

William Sherman.
Courtesy of the Library of Congress

dilemma." He had helped Grant do this to Pemberton at Vicksburg, and he would do it later by keeping the Confederates guessing if his objective was Macon or Augusta and then Augusta or Savannah on his March to the Sea. Now Sherman achieved the same effect in the Meridian Campaign. The result of this uncertainty is "enemy paralysis and hesitancy"—objectives of surprise and keys to Sherman's success.

In spite of Sherman's overriding concern for speed, he would not compromise in the size of his force. Sherman's army consisted of four divisions—two from McPherson's corps at Vicksburg and two from Hurlbut's at Memphis—for a total of 20,000 infantry plus some 5,000 attached cavalry and artillery. Sherman's adversary Polk could muster a force just half that size, and these were widely scattered with a division each at Canton and Brandon and cavalry spread between Yazoo City and Jackson.

Sherman devoted his forces to the decisive aim to "do the enemy as much damage as possible." On February 9, his army entered Morton and spent several hours tearing up the railroad track using the usual method of burning crossties to heat the rails and then bending the metal into useless configurations dubbed "Sherman's neckties."

At Lake Station on February 11, Sherman destroyed "the railroad buildings, machine-shops, turning-table, several cars, and one locomotive." But it was after reaching Meridian itself that Sherman unleashed his full fury, making his small foray into total war at Wyatt before the Chickasaw Bayou expedition pale in comparison. For five days, Sherman dispersed detachments in four directions with Hurlbut leading the destruction north and east of Meridian and McPherson focusing on the south and west. For his part, McPherson destroyed 55 miles of railroad, 53 bridges, 6,075 feet of trestle work, 19 locomotives, 28 steam cars, and three steam sawmills.

Hurlbut claimed 60 miles of railroad, one locomotive, and eight bridges. Sherman reported "10,000 men worked hard and with a will in that work of destruction, with axes, crowbars, and with fire, and I have no hesitation in pronouncing the work as well done. Meridian, with its depots, storehouses, arsenal, hospitals, offices, hotels, and cantonments no longer exists." The Confederates were able to repair their railroads within a month, but the weak Confederate industrial base made the loss of locomotives critical.

Sherman lingered at Meridien till the 20th, waiting for the cavalry of Sooy Smith to join him; however, Smith had been intercepted and beaten by Forrest, whose command of some 3,500 Confederate cavalry then chased Smith's force back to Memphis. The rest of his work done, Sherman returned to Vicksburg on February 28, leaving the rest of his command to return "leisurely" after their successful, large-scale raid.

LEADERSHIP LESSONS

Sherman is probably best remembered for his spectacular "March to the Sea" in which he stormed 225 miles through Georgia with no line of communication to make the Confederate population in the Deep South feel the ravages of war. It is hard to imagine that Sherman was not always so daring and independent, but rather is a case study of a general who profoundly grew and developed during the Civil War. The Meridian Campaign was a critical phase of this growth because it was on this raid that Sherman first demonstrated the ability to operate independently deep in enemy territory and far from higher headquarters. It was on this raid that Sherman pioneered the art of destroying Confederate war-making capability.

Like Sherman, all leaders must grow. Chris Lowney describes personal leadership as "a never-ending work in progress that draws on continually maturing self-understanding." Because the external environment evolves and personal circumstances change, leaders must seek opportunities to learn and grow. The goal of the leader should be lifelong learning, which the US Army's leadership manual defines as "the individual lifelong choice to actively and overtly pursue knowledge, the comprehension of ideas, and the expansion of depth in any area in order to progress beyond a known state of development and competency."

Leaders must also ensure their organizations adopt this same attitude by creating a climate that values and supports learning. Techniques that have outlived their purpose should be discarded and replaced by new techniques that experience suggests will get the job done more efficiently or effectively. Opportunities for continued education and training should be given high priority. An organized system of continuous assessment must ensure that the organization is not operating "because we've always done it this way," when superior options are available.

One way leaders can encourage this climate of continuous improvement is through the after action review (AAR). After action reviews are conducted as soon as possible after an event in order to capture lessons learned. The facilitator of the AAR asks the group to answer three questions: What was supposed to happen? What actually happened and why? What can we do to improve what went wrong and sustain what went right? One of the strengths of the AAR is that the group members discover for themselves ways of making themselves and the organization better.

Takeaways:

- *Leaders must grow and create conditions for their organizations to grow as well.*
- *Leadership requires a commitment to lifelong learning.*
- *After action reviews are useful tools to critically assess events and foster continuous improvement.*

THIRTY

A TRAGIC HERO
John Pemberton and Selfless Service

The loss of Vicksburg left John Pemberton not only without a command, but it also left him the object of scorn both within the army and the Confederacy. Unable to obtain another army command, Pemberton requested a reduction to the rank of lieutenant colonel so he could continue to serve.

JOHN PEMBERTON HAS MANY ELEMENTS OF A TRAGIC HERO ABOUT him. He was a competent army officer who simply found himself in a position that far exceeded his capabilities. His Northern birth aroused suspicion and caused some to immediately doubt him. These pressures weighed heavily on Pemberton, and he came to lose confidence in his own abilities. Without a doubt, much about the Confederate loss of Vicksburg can be attributed to Pemberton's personal failure, but he quickly became a lightning rod for the entire Confederate debacle. Even his decision to surrender on the Fourth of July, a national holiday, was seen by many Southerners as an act of cowardice and betrayal.

Pemberton bore the primary responsibility of defending Vicksburg and suffered from the weight. After the surrender, he made his way to Demopolis, Alabama where his family was living. He reached there on July 24, 1863, and his daughter Pattie did not even recognize her father because of the way the ordeal had aged him.

Critics soon began publishing statements blaming Vicksburg's loss on Pemberton, who hoped he would have an opportunity to present his version of the events at a court of inquiry. Instead, the exigencies of war prevented the court from ever meeting, and Pemberton could only attempt

193

to maintain a low public profile to protect himself and his family from the torrent of criticism.

Pemberton's future in the Confederate Army was problematic for President Davis. Pemberton still held the rank of lieutenant general, but the public outcry against him precluded his being assigned to duties commensurate with that rank. In October 1863, Pemberton accompanied Davis on a trip to General Braxton Bragg's headquarters near Chattanooga, in part to explore Davis's idea of giving Pemberton a corps command in the western army. Soldiers quickly let their objection to such a development be known, with many vowing to desert rather than serve under a man they considered to be a traitor.

Thus, Pemberton returned to Virginia where he remained in an exiled state of limbo. On March 9, 1864, when he could stand his "position of inactivity" no longer, he petitioned President Davis for service in the field "or in any capacity in which you think I may be useful." Pemberton explained to Davis, "You are so thoroughly acquainted with the circumstances of my position that I need refer neither to them nor to the causes which have brought them about—but I cannot help thinking that there is much less prejudice against me now, than there was when you offered me a command (conditionally) in Genl. Bragg's Army."

Davis had not lost confidence in Pemberton, but felt that "considerations which I could not control" prevented him from giving Pemberton a new command. On April 19, Pemberton took the initiative and sent General Samuel Cooper, the Confederate Army's Adjutant General, a letter resigning as a lieutenant general and asking to be assigned as an artillery lieutenant colonel. This course was something Pemberton had mentioned to Bragg during Pemberton's visit to the Army of Tennessee the previous October, and Bragg had passed the information on to Davis. Michael Ballard observes that "This humble act, especially humble given the pride of John Pemberton, quieted some of his critics and gave him what he had always preferred: a command in his beloved Virginia."

Pemberton was given command of the Richmond Defense Battery of Artillery, and established battery positions east of Richmond. When anonymous sources criticized his defensive line along Chaffin's Bluff south of Richmond on the James River, Pemberton replied that he had done his best with what he had, and argued that whatever his "defects of skill, I am not liable to the reproach of indolence or neg- lect." Pemberton's response could have just as easily been written about his efforts at Vicksburg. In this case, however, his ar- gument seemingly settled the matter.

In January 1865, Pemberton became the Confederate Army's gen- eral inspector of artillery and ord- nance, travelling to such places as Charleston, which must have evoked certain feelings of nostalgia. In the spring, he went to North Carolina and helped put together artillery batteries to support General Joseph Johnston's doomed defense against the onslaught of Sherman from Georgia. Pemberton's entire artillery was captured near Salisbury by Major Gen- eral George Stoneman, and Pemberton

John Pemberton. *Courtesy of the Library of Congress*

himself barely escaped. He tried to join President Davis's band of refugees that had fled Richmond, reaching Charlotte the day after Davis had left for South Carolina. Unable to catch Davis, Pemberton went to Newton, North Carolina to join his family and wait for the end.

LEADERSHIP LESSONS

General George C. Marshall observed, "There is no limit to the good you can do if you don't care who gets the credit." John Pemberton's request to serve as a lieutenant colonel reflects his sincere desire to serve the Con- federate cause without any quest for personal credit or glory. Granted his contribution as a lieutenant general was flawed, but rather than spend the remainder of the war licking his wounds and engaging in literary defenses of his conduct at Vicksburg, Pemberton found a new way to serve. His assignment as a lieutenant colonel certainly was void of grandeur and was a far cry from his previous position, but Pemberton seemed completely at peace with serving in any capacity. His return to Charleston must have been one of mixed emotions given the conditions under which he had left that command in 1862. Likewise, it would be understandable if in North

Carolina Pemberton felt some discomfort in supporting Johnston, however remotely, after the debacle in Vicksburg had created a rift between the two men. Still, Pemberton selflessly served, providing an excellent example of a leader who put personal pride, position, and status aside for the good of the organization.

> ### *Takeaways:*
> • *Leadership is service.*
> • *Leaders find a way to serve.*
> • *Leaders put the organization before themselves.*
> • *Leaders cannot sulk in the face of setbacks.*
> *They must focus on the future rather than the past.*

Conclusions About Leadership During the Vicksburg Campaign

THE FEDERAL VICTORY AT VICKSBURG WAS FAR FROM PREDESTINED. The two armies were of roughly equal strength at the start, and the Confederacy had the advantages inherent in the defense and in fighting in one's own territory. To be sure, the Federal Navy was a significant force multiplier, but the even more decisive factor was superior Federal leadership.

The Federal generals surpassed their Confederate counterparts in terms of strategy, confidence, unity of effort, frame of reference, situational awareness, and risk taking. This disparity was exacerbated by the Confederate departmental system that placed a premium on the capabilities and weaknesses of individual commanders. Men on both sides exhibited innovative problem-solving, personal bravery, and technical skill. In the final analysis, however, the Federals excelled the Confederates in most aspects of leadership at Vicksburg.

STRATEGY

While Scott's Anaconda Plan was not officially adopted, it did provide a useful framework for Federal strategy, and certainly recognized the importance of the Mississippi River. Within the Western Theater, Grant also understood the "big picture" and was able to create conditions necessary for success and make decisions based on future operations. Confederate strategy was hamstrung by the departmental system, the dominance of the Eastern Theater, President Davis's reluctance to seek strategic advice, and a lack of synchronization between Davis and Johnston. Strategic leaders need to provide a vision, concept, and organization for success. Of particular interest, see "The Mighty Mississippi: Winfield Scott and Strategic Vision," "The Battle of Corinth: Ulysses Grant and Creating Necessary Conditions," "Set Up to Fail: The Confederate Departmental System and Strategic Organization," "Surrender and Parole: Ulysses Grant and Pragmatism," "Little Help from Above: Jefferson Davis and Strategic Direction," and "The Meridian Campaign: William Sherman and Creating Opportunity."

CONFIDENCE

Steven Woodworth notes Grant's advantage in confidence, writing, "Every movement of his army expressed its commander's assurance that he would whip any force that stood in his path. His foes, cut from much flimsier cloth, could not help starting to believe it." Indeed, Pemberton, still stinging from his poor experience in South Carolina, assumed his new position with shaken confidence and quickly became unraveled in the face of the confusing and ambiguous situation at Vicksburg. Likewise, Grant enjoyed the confidence of President Lincoln and was given the freedom to operate without excessive supervision. Leaders are optimistic and infuse that confidence in their subordinates. Of particular interest, see "Wrong Man for the Job: John Pemberton and the Peter Principle," "A Close Call for the Federals: Charles Dana and Dealing with Weakness," "The Battle of Jackson: Joseph Johnston and Pessimism and Responsibility," and "A Decisive Victory: Abraham Lincoln and Admitting When You're Wrong."

UNITY OF EFFORT

The Federals enjoyed remarkable unity of effort thanks in large part to Grant's efforts, especially with Porter. With the exception of McClernand, Grant was blessed with a sound set of subordinates who all worked together well. On the other hand, the departmental system precluded unity of effort for the Confederacy, and several of Pemberton's key subordinates were hostile to him. Leaders must create conditions where cooperation, teamwork, and synergy are the norm. Of particular interest, see "Set Up to Fail: The Confederate Departmental System and Strategic Organization," "The Confederate Conflict: John Pemberton and Poor Relations with Subordinates," "The Federal Team: Ulysses Grant and Positive Relations with

Subordinates," "Running the Gauntlet: Ulysses Grant and David Porter and Unity of Effort," "Helping Run the Gauntlet: William Sherman and Playing a Supporting Role," and "Problem Removed: John McClernand and Selfish Ambition."

FRAME OF REFERENCE

Both Grant and Pemberton drew heavily on the frame of reference provided by past experience. The most noticeable example in Grant's case was his experience with logistical risk in Mexico. Pemberton also drew upon his Mexican War experience, as well as his time in Charleston, but these experiences led him to make inappropriate decisions in the unique situation at Vicksburg. Leaders use their frame of reference not to blindly repeat a past course of action, but to understand present events in a broader context. Of particular interest, see "Cutting Loose: Ulysses Grant and Taking Risk" and "Confederate Confusion: John Pemberton and Frame of Reference."

SITUATIONAL AWARENESS

In terms of situational awareness, Grant created conditions that left Pemberton paralyzed. Steven Woodworth writes, "Grant was far ahead of his opponents in perceiving and assessing the operational situation and determining what to do next—often doing it while his foes were still trying to sort out the results of his previous move, or the one before that." By the time of Champion Hill, Woodworth concludes Grant "had gained complete mental advantage over [Pemberton], winning the battle of minds before the clash of armies had reached its climax. Like a grand master of chess playing an outclassed opponent, Grant left Pemberton dazed and confused, wondering which move had been his great blunder when, in fact, in the face of the master's brilliant play, each of the loser's moves had been a worse blunder than the one before." Leaders must understand their own resources, those of the competition, and the relevant facts of the overall situation. Of particular interest, see "Chickasaw Bayou: William Sherman and Knowing When to Quit," "Confederate Confusion: John Pemberton and Frame of Reference," and "The Battle of Raymond: John Gregg and Understanding the Situation."

RISK-TAKING

The Federals accepted prudent risk in a variety of areas. One significant instance was the risk President Lincoln assumed by leaving Grant in command in the face of mounting suspicion and criticism. Grant personally assumed risk by "cutting loose" from his base of supply after crossing the Mississippi. Both men mitigated their risk, Lincoln by dispatching Dana to check on Grant, and Grant by using the navy, his newly captured position at Grand Gulf, and a steady stream of wagons to augment his forage. Leaders distinguish between prudent risks and careless gambles, and act boldly. Of particular interest, see "A Close Call for the Federals: Charles Dana and Dealing with Weakness," "Cutting Loose: Ulysses Grant and Taking Risk," "Confederate Confusion: John Pemberton and Frame of Reference," and "The Meridian Campaign: William Sherman and Creating Opportunity."

PROBLEM-SOLVING

Both the Federal and Confederate armies are full of examples of individuals who overcame personal situations or tactical challenges by innovative means. As the Confederates tried to hold on against long odds, and the Federals tried to break the status quo, leaders were forced to experiment with new ideas and techniques. Leaders seek constructive change and create options. Of particular interest, see "Other Failed Attempts: Ulysses Grant and Perseverance," "Asymmetric Warfare: Zedekiah McDaniel and Francis Ewing and Innovation," "Siege Warfare: Henry Foster and Problem-solving," and "The Federal Mine: John Logan and Initiative."

PERSONAL BRAVERY

Individual officers and soldiers on both sides demonstrated exceptional valor during the Vicksburg Campaign. By their presence, leaders set the example, even while risking life and limb. Likewise, patriotic and courageous soldiers performed herculean feats for the cause they believed in. Leaders must be able to rise to heroic levels to meet the demands of the given situation. Of particular interest, see "The Battle of Champion Hill: Ulysses Grant and Personal Presence," "Retreat from Champion Hill: Lloyd Tilghman and Personal Sacrifice," "Assault on Vicksburg: Thomas Higgins and Personal Courage," and "A Tragic Hero: John Pemberton and Selfless Service."

TECHNICAL SKILL

By 1863, both Federals and Confederates had been tried by war, and both armies featured talented men who had risen to positions of responsibility. For some, like Forrest, the climb had been steadily upward. For others, like Grant and Van Dorn, it had been one of setbacks and recoveries. Still others like Pemberton found themselves in positions that were poor matches for their skills. Leaders must be personally competent and also place subordinates in situations in which they can succeed. Of particular interest, see "Wrong Man for the Job: John Pemberton and the Peter Principle," "Forrest and Van Dorn: The Self-made Man and the Reinvented Man," "The Battle of Port Gibson: John Bowen and Technical Competence," and "Grant Heads Northeast: Ulysses Grant and Clear Communication."

On the battlefields of the Vicksburg Campaign, this tally sheet of Federal and Confederate leadership abilities shaped the outcome of the contest. In the ranks, Billy Yank and Johnny Reb were a pretty equal match, but the Federal soldier certainly was better led. In 1863, it was this advantage that gave the Federals victory.

Some 150 years later, the situation may be different, but the lessons remain the same. In war, business, politics, communities, families, and schools, leadership is the decisive factor. At Vicksburg, leadership made the difference between two otherwise fairly well matched armies. On today's "battlefields" of all types, it will have the same impact.

Barracks of the 124th Illinois Infantry, Vicksburg.
Courtesy of the Library of Congress

Vicksburg Campaign Order of Battle

(Courtesy of the Vicksburg National Military Park, National Park Service)

ORGANIZATION OF UNION FORCES
ARMY OF THE TENNESSEE
Maj. Gen. Ulysses S. Grant

Escort

Company A, 4th Illinois Cavalry, Capt. Embury D. Osband

Engineers

1st Battalion, Engineer Regiment of the West, Maj. William Tweeddale

XIIIth CORPS

Maj. Gen. John A. McClernand (relieved)

Maj. Gen. Edward O. C. Ord

Escort

Company L, 3d Illinois Cavalry, Capt. David R. Sparks

Pioneers

Independent Company, Kentucky Infantry, Capt. William F. Patterson

NINTH DIVISION

Brig. Gen. Peter Osterhaus (w)

Brig. Gen. Albert L. Lee

Brig. Gen. Peter Osterhaus

1ST BRIGADE
Brig. Gen. Theophilus T. Garrard
Brig. Gen. Albert L. Lee
Col. James Keigwin
118th Illinois, Col. John G. Fonda
49th Indiana, Col. James Keigwin, Maj. Arthur J. Hawhe, Lt. Col.
Joseph H. Thornton
69th Indiana, Col. Thomas W. Bennett, Lt. Col. Oran Perry
7th Kentucky, Maj. H.W. Adams, Lt. Col. John Lucas,
Col. Reuben May
120th Ohio, Col. Marcus M. Spiegel
2D BRIGADE
Col. Lionel A. Sheldon
Col. Daniel Lindsey
54th Indiana, Col. Fielding Mansfield
22d Kentucky, Lt. Col. George W. Monroe
16th Ohio, Capt. Eli W. Botsford, Maj. Milton Mills
42d Ohio, Lt. Col. Don A. Pardee, Maj. William H. Williams,
Col. Lionel Sheldon
114th Ohio, Col. John Cradlebaugh, (w), Lt. Col. John H. Kelly
CAVALRY
2d Illinois (5 Companies), Lt. Col. Daniel B. Bush, Jr.
3d Illinois Cavalry (3 Companies), Col. John L. Campbell
6th Missouri Cavalry (7 Companies), Col. Clark Wright
ARTILLERY
Capt. Jacob T. Foster
7th Michigan Light Artillery, Capt. Charles H. Lanphere
1st Battery, Wisconsin Light Artillery, Lt. Charles B. Kimball,
Lt. Oscar F. Nutting

TENTH DIVISION
Brig. Gen. Andrew J. Smith
Escort
Company C, 4th Indiana Cavalry, Capt. Andrew P. Gallagher
1ST BRIGADE

Brig. Gen. Stephen G. Burbridge
16th Indiana, Col. Thomas J. Lucas, Maj. James H. Redfield
60th Indiana, Col. Richard Owen
67th Indiana, Lt. Col. Theodore E. Buehler
83d Ohio, Col. Frederick W. Moore
96th Ohio, Col. Joseph W. Vance
23d Wisconsin, Col. Joshua J. Guppey, Lt. Col. William F. Vilas
2D BRIGADE
Col. William J. Landrum
77th Illinois, Col. David P. Grier
97th Illinois, Col. Friend S. Rutherford, Lt. Col. Lewis D. Martin
130th Illinois, Col. Nathaniel Niles
19th Kentucky, Lt. Col. John Cowan, Maj. M. V. Evans (k),
Capt. Josiah J. Mann
48th Ohio, Lt. Col. Job R. Parker (w), Col. Peter Sullivan,
Capt. J.W. Lindsey
ARTILLERY
Chicago Merchantile Battery, Illinois Light Artillery, Capt.
Patrick H. White
17th Battery, Ohio Light Artillery, Capt. Ambrose A. Blount,
Capt. Charles S. Rice

TWELFTH DIVISION
Brig. Gen. Alvin P. Hovey
Escort
Company C, 1st Indiana Cavalry, Lt. James L. Carey
1ST BRIGADE
Brig. Gen. George F. McGinnis
Col. William T. Spicely
11th Indiana, Col. Daniel Macauley (w), Lt. Col. William W. Darnell
24th Indiana, Col. William T. Spicely (w), Lt. Col. R.F. Barter
34th Indiana, Col. Robert A. Cameron, Lt. Col. William Swaim (mw),
Maj. Robert A. Jones, Col. Robert A. Cameron
46th Indiana, Col. Thomas H. Bringhurst
29th Wisconsin, Col. Charles R. Gill, Lt. Col. William A. Greene

2D BRIGADE
Col. James R. Slack
87th Illinois, Col. John E. Whiting
47th Indiana, Lt. Col. John A. McLaughlin
24th Iowa, Col. Eber C. Byam, Lt. Col. John Q. Wilds
28th Iowa, Col. John Connell
56th Ohio, Col. William H. Raynor
ARTILLERY
Company A, 1st Missouri Light Artillery, Capt. George W. Schofield
2d Battery, Ohio Light Artillery, Lt. Augustus Beach
16th Battery Ohio Light Artillery, Capt. James A. Mitchell (mw),
Lt. George Murdock, Lt. Russell P. Twist

FOURTEENTH DIVISION
Brig. Gen. Eugene A. Carr
Escort
Company G, 3d Illinois Cavalry, Capt. Enos McPhial (k),
Capt. Samuel S. Marrett
1ST BRIGADE
Brig. Gen. William P. Benton
Col. Henry D. Washburn
Col. David Shunk
33d Illinois, Col. Charles E. Lippincott (w),
99th Illinois, Col. George W.K. Bailey
8th Indiana, Col. David Shunk, Maj. Thomas J. Brady
18th Indiana, Col. Henry D. Washburn, Capt. Jonathan H. Williams
1st U.S. Infantry (Siege Guns), Maj. Maurice Maloney
2D BRIGADE
Col. Charles L. Harris
Col. William M. Stone
Brig. Gen. Michael K. Lawler
21st Iowa Infantry, Col. Samuel Merrill (w),
Lt. Col. Cornelius W. Dunlap (k), Maj. Salue G. Van Anda
22d Iowa, Col. William M. Stone (w), Lt. Col. Harvey Graham
(w and c), Maj. Joseph B. Atherton, Capt. Charles N. Lee

23d Iowa, Col. William H. Kinsoman (k), Col. Samuel L. Glasgow
11th Wisconsin, Lt. Col. Charles A. Wood, Col. Charles L. Harris,
Maj. Arthur Platt
ARTILLERY
Company A, 2d Illinois Light Artillery, Lt. Frank B. Fenton,
Capt. Peter Davidson
1st Battery, Indiana Light Artillery, Capt. Martin Klauss

XVth CORPS
Maj. Gen. William T. Sherman

FIRST DIVISION
Maj. Gen. Frederick Steele
1ST BRIGADE
Col. Francis H. Manter
Col. Bernard G. Farrar
13th Illinois, Col. Adam B. Gorgas
27th Missouri, Col. Thomas Curly
29th Missouri, Col. James Peckham
30th Missouri, Lt. Col. Otto Schadt
31st Missouri, Col. Thomas C. Fletcher, Maj. Frederick Jaensch,
Lt. Col. Samuel P. Simpson
32d Missouri, Maj. Abraham J. Seay
2D BRIGADE
Col. Charles R. Woods
25th Iowa, Col. George A. Stone
31st Iowa, Col. William Smith
3d Missouri, Lt. Col. Theodore M. Meumann
12th Missouri, Col. Hugo Wangelin
17th Missouri, Col. Francis Hassendeubel (mw),
Lt. Col. John F. Cramer
76th Ohio, Lt. Col. William B. Woods
3D BRIGADE
Brig. Gen. John M. Thayer
4th Iowa, Col. James A. Williamson, Lt. Col. George Burton

9th Iowa, Maj. Don A. Carpenter, Capt. Frederick S. Washburn (k),
Col. David Carskaddon
26th Iowa, Col. Milo Smith
30th Iowa, Col. Charles H. Abbott (k), Lt. Col. William M.G. Torrence
CAVALRY
Kane County (Illinois) Company, Lt. Thomas J. Beebe
Company D, 3d Illinois Cavalry, Lt. Jonathan Kershner
ARTILLERY
1st Battery, Iowa Light Artillery, Capt. Henry H. Griffiths
Company F, 2d Missouri Light Artillery, Capt. Clemens Landgraeber
4th Battery, Ohio Light Artillery, Capt. Louis Hoffmann

SECOND DIVISION
Maj. Gen. Frank P. Blair, Jr.
1ST BRIGADE
Col. Giles A. Smith
113th Illinois, Col. George B. Hoge, Lt. Col. John W. Paddock
116th Illinois, Col. Nathan W. Tupper
6th Missouri, Lt. Col. Ira Boutell, Col. James H. Blood
8th Missouri, Lt. Col. David C. Coleman
13th United States, Capt. Edward Washington (mw),
Capt. Charles Ewing, Capt. Charles C. Smith
2D BRIGADE
Col. Thomas Kilby Smith
Brig. Gen. Joseph A.J. Lightburn
55th Illinois, Col. Oscar Malmborg
127th Illinois, Col. Hamilton N. Eldridge
83d Indiana, Col. Benjamin J. Spooner
54th Ohio, Lt. Col. Cyrus W. Fisher
57th Ohio, Col. Americus V. Rice (w), Lt. Col. Samuel R. Mott
3D BRIGADE
Brig. Gen. Hugh Ewing
30th Ohio, Lt. Col. George H. Hildt, Col. Theodore Jones
37th Ohio, Lt. Col. Louis von Blessingh (w), Maj. Charles Hipp,
Col. Edward Siber

47th Ohio, Col. Augustus C. Parry
4th West Virginia, Col. James H. Dayton
CAVALRY
Companies A and B, Thielemann's (Illinois) Battalion,
Capt. Milo Thielemann
Company C, 10th Missouri Cavalry, Capt. Daniel W. Ballou,
Lt. Benjamin Joel
ARTILLERY
Company A, 1st Illinois Light Artillery, Capt. Peter P. Wood
Company B, 1st Illinois Light Artillery, Capt. Samuel E. Barrett,
Lt. Israel P. Rumsey
Company H, 1st Illinois Light Artillery, Capt. Levi W. Hart
8th Battery, Ohio Light Artillery, Capt. James F. Putnam

Cave life in Vicksburg.
Courtesy of the Library of Congress

THIRD DIVISION
Brig. Gen. James M. Tuttle
1ST BRIGADE
Brig. Gen. Ralph P. Buckland
Col. William L. McMillen
114th Illinois, Col. James W. Judy
93d Indiana, Col. De Witt C. Thomas
72d Ohio, Lt. Col. Le Roy Crockett (w), Maj. Charles G. Eaton
95th Ohio, Col. William L. McMillen, Lt. Col. Jefferson Brumback
2D BRIGADE
Brig. Gen. Joseph A. Mower
47th Illinois, Col. John N. Cromwell (k), Lt. Col. Samuel R. Baker
5th Minnesota, Col. Lucius F. Hubbard
11th Missouri, Col. Andrew J. Weber (mw),
Lt. Col. William L. Barnum
8th Wisconsin, Col. George W. Robbins
3D BRIGADE
Brig. Gen. Charles L. Matthies
Col. Joseph J. Woods
8th Iowa, Col. James L. Geddes
12th Iowa, Col. Joseph J. Woods, Lt. Col. Samuel R. Edington
35th Iowa, Col. Sylvester G. Hill
CAVALRY
4th Iowa, Lt. Col. Simeon D. Swan
ARTILLERY
Capt. Nelson T. Spoor
Company E, 1st Illinois Light Artillery, Capt. Allen C. Waterhouse
2d Battery, Iowa Light Artillery, Lt. Joseph R. Reed

XVIIth CORPS
Maj. Gen. James B. McPherson
Escort:
4th Company Ohio Cavalry, Capt. John S. Foster

THIRD DIVISION
Maj. Gen. John A. Logan
Escort:
Company A, 2d Illinois Cavalry, Lt. William B. Cummins
1ST BRIGADE
Brig. Gen. John E. Smith
Brig. Gen. Mortimer D. Leggett
20th Illinois, Lt. Col. Evan Richards (k), Maj. Daniel Bradley
31st Illinois, Col. Edwin S. McCook (w), Lt. Col. John D. Rees (mw),
Maj. Robert N. Pearson
45th Illinois, Col. Jasper A. Maltby
124th Illinois, Col. Thomas J. Sloan
23d Indiana, Lt. Col. William P. Davis
2D BRIGADE
Brig. Gen. Elias S. Dennis
Brig. Gen. Mortimer D. Leggett
Col. Manning F. Force
30th Illinois, Lt. Col. Warren Shedd
20th Ohio, Col. Manning F. Force, Capt. Francis M. Shaklee
68th Ohio, Lt. Col. John S. Snook (k), Col. Robert K. Scott
78th Ohio, Lt. Col. Greenberry F. Wiles
3D BRIGADE
Brig. Gen. John D. Stevenson
8th Illinois, Col. John P. Post, Lt. Col. Robert H. Sturgess
17th Illinois, Lt. Col. Francis M. Smith, Maj. Frank F. Peats
81st Illinois, Col. James J. Dollins (k), Lt. Col. Franklin Campbell
7th Missouri, Maj. Edwin Wakefield, Lt. Col. William S. Oliver (w),
Capt. Robert Buchanan, Capt. William B. Collins
32d Ohio, Col. Benjamin F. Potts
ARTILLERY
Maj. Charles J. Stolbrand
Company D, 1st Illinois Light Artillery, Capt. Henry A. Rogers (k),
Lt. George J. Wood, Capt. Frederick Sparrestrom
Company G, 2d Illinois Light Artillery, Capt. Frederick Sparrestrom,
Lt. John W. Lowell

Company L, 2d Illinois Light Artillery, Capt. William H. Bolton
8th Battery, Michigan Light Artillery, Capt. Samuel De Golyer (mw),
Lt. Theodore W. Lockwood
3d Battery, Ohio Light Artillery, Capt. William S. Williams
Yost's Independent Ohio Battery, Capt. T. Yost

SIXTH DIVISION
Brig. Gen. John McArthur
Escort:
Company G, 1st Illinois Cavalry, Lt. Stephen S. Tripp
2D BRIGADE
Brig. Gen. Thomas E.G. Ransom
11th Illinois, Lt. Col. Garrett Nevins (k), Lt. Col. James H. Coates
72d Illinois, Col. Frederick A. Starring
95th Illinois, Col. Thomas W. Humphrey (w), Lt. Col. Leander Blanden
14th Wisconsin, Col. Lyman M. Ward
17th Wisconsin, Lt. Col. Thomas McMahon, Col. Adam G. Malloy
3D BRIGADE
Col. William Hall
Col. Alexander Chambers
11th Iowa, Lt. Col. John C. Abercrombie, Col. William Hall
13th Iowa, Col. John Shane
15th Iowa, Col. William W. Belknap
16th Iowa, Maj. W. Purcell, Lt. Col. Addison H. Sanders
ARTILLERY
Maj. Thomas D. Maurice
Company F, 2d Illinois Light Artillery, Capt. John W. Powell
1st Battery, Minnesota Light Artillery, Lt. Henry Hunter,
Capt. William Z. Clayton
Company C, 1st Missouri Light Artillery, Capt. Charles Mann
10th Battery, Ohio Light Artillery, Capt. Hamilton B. White,
Lt. William L. Newcomb

SEVENTH DIVISION
Brig. Gen. Marcellus M. Crocker
Brig. Gen. Isaac F. Quinby
Brig. Gen. John E. Smith
Escort:
Company F, 4th Missouri Cavalry, Lt. Alexander Mueller
1ST BRIGADE
Col. John B. Sanborn
48th Indiana, Col. Norman Eddy
59th Indiana, Col. Jesse I. Alexander
4th Minnesota Infantry, Lt. Col. John E. Tourtellotte
18th Wisconsin, Col. Gabriel Bouck
2D BRIGADE
Col. Samuel Holmes
Col. Green B. Raum
56th Illinois, Col. Green B. Raum, Capt. Pickney J. Welsh
17th Iowa, Col. David B. Hillis, Col. Clark R. Weaver,
Maj. John F. Walden
10th Missouri, Lt. Col. Leonidas Horney (k), Maj. Francis C. Deimling
Company E, 24th Missouri, Lt. Daniel Driscoll
80th Ohio, Col. Matthias H. Bartilson, Maj. Prentis Metham
3D BRIGADE
Col. George B. Boomer (k)
Col. Holden Putnam
93d Illinois, Col. Holden Putnam, Lt. Col. Nicholas C. Buswell
5th Iowa, Lt. Col. Ezekial S. Sampson, Col. Jabez Banbury
10th Iowa, Col. William E. Small
26th Missouri, Capt. Benjamin D. Dean
ARTILLERY
Capt. Frank C. Sands
Capt. Henry Dillion
Company M, 1st Missouri Light Artillery, Lt. Junius W. MacMurray
11th Battery, Ohio Light Artillery, Lt. Fletcher E. Armstrong
6th Battery, Wisconsin Light Artillery, Capt. Henry Dillon,
Lt. Samuel F. Clark
12th Battery, Wisconsin Light Artillery, Capt. William Zickerick

IXth CORPS (Detachment)
Maj. Gen. John G. Parke

FIRST DIVISION
Brig. Gen. Thomas Welsh
1ST BRIGADE
Col. Henry Bowman
36th Massachusetts, Lt. Col. John B. Norton
17th Michigan, Lt. Col. Constant Luce
27th Michigan, Col. Dorus M. Fox
45th Pennsylvania, Col. John I. Curtin
3D BRIGADE
Col. Daniel Leasure
2d Michigan, Col. William Humphrey
8th Michigan, Col. Frank Graves
20th Michigan, Lt. Col. W. Huntington Smith
79th New York, Col. David Morrison
100th Pennsylvania, Lt. Col. Mathew M. Dawson
ARTILLERY
Company D, 1st Pennsylvania Light Artillery, Capt. G.W. Durell

SECOND DIVISION
Brig. Gen. Robert B. Potter
1ST BRIGADE
Col. Simon G. Griffin
6th New Hampshire, Lt. Col. Henry H. Pearson
9th New Hampshire, Col. Herbert B. Titus
7th Rhode Island, Col. Zenas R. Bliss
2D BRIGADE
Brig. Gen. Edward Ferrero
35th Massachusetts, Col. Sumner Carruth
11th New Hampshire, Lt. Col. Moses N. Collins
51st New York, Col. Charles W. LeGendre
51st Pennsylvania, Col. John F. Hartranft

3D BRIGADE
Col. Benjamin C. Christ
39th Massachusetts, Lt. Col. Joseph H. Barnes
46th New York, Col. Joseph Gerhardt
50th Pennsylvania, Lt. Col. Thomas S. Brenholtz
ARTILLERY
Company L, 2d New York Light Artillery, Capt. Jacob Roemer
Company E, 2d U.S. Artillery, Lt. Samuel N. Benjamin

XVIth CORPS
Maj. Gen. Cadwallader C. Washburn

FIRST DIVISION
Brig. Gen. William Sooy Smith
Escort:
Company B, 7th Illinois Cavalry, Capt. Henry C. Forbes
1ST BRIGADE
Col. John M. Loomis
26th Illinois, Maj. John B. Harris
90th Illinois, Col. Timothy O'Meara
12th Indiana, Col. Reuben Williams
100th Indiana, Lt. Col. Albert Heath
2D BRIGADE
Col. Stephen G. Hicks
40th Illinois Maj. Hiram W. Hall
103d Illinois, Col. Willard A. Dickerman
15th Michigan, Col. John M. Oliver
46th Ohio, Col. Charles C. Walcutt
3D BRIGADE
Col. Joseph R. Cockerill
97th Indiana, Col. Robert F. Catterson
99th Indiana, Col. Alexander Fowler
53d Ohio, Col. Wells S. Jones
70th Ohio, Maj. William B. Brown

4TH BRIGADE
Col. William W. Sanford
48th Illinois, Lt. Col. Lucien Greathouse
6th Iowa, Col. John M. Corse
ARTILLERY
Capt. William Cogswell
Company F, 1st Illinois Light Artillery, Capt. John T. Cheney
Company I, 1st Illinois Light Artillery, Lt. William N. Lansing
Cogswell's Battery, Illinois Light Artillery, Lt. Henry G. Eddy
6th Battery, Indiana Light Artillery, Capt. Michael Muller

FOURTH DIVISION
Brig. Gen. Jacob Lauman
1ST BRIGADE
Col. Isaac Pugh
41st Illinois, Lt. Col. John H. Nale
53d Illinois, Lt. Col. Seth C. Earl
3d Iowa, Col. Aaron Brown
33d Wisconsin, Col. Jonathan B. Moore
2D BRIGADE
Col. Cyrus Hall
14th Illinois, Lt. Col. William Cairn, Capt. Augustus H. Corman
15th Illinois, Col. George C. Rogers
46th Illinois, Col. Benjamin Dornblaser
76th Illinois, Col. Samuel T. Busey
53d Indiana, Col. Walter Q. Gresham
3D BRIGADE
Col. George E. Bryant
Col. Amory K. Johnson
28th Illinois, Maj. Hinman Rhodes
32d Illinois, Col. John Logan, Lt. Col. William Hunter
12th Wisconsin, Lt. Col. DeWitt C. Poole, Col. George E. Bryant
CAVALRY
Companies F and I, 15th Illinois, Maj. James G. Wilson
ARTILLERY

Capt. George C. Gumbart
Company E, 2d Illinois Light Artillery, Lt. George L. Nispel
Company K, 2d Illinois Light Artillery, Capt. Benjamin F. Rodgers
5th Battery, Ohio Light Artillery, Lt. Anthony Burton
7th Battery, Ohio Light Artillery, Capt. Silas A. Burnap
15th Battery Ohio Light Artillery, Capt. Edward Spear, Jr.

PROVISIONAL DIVISION
Brig. Gen. Nathan Kimball
ENGELMANN'S BRIGADE
Col. Adolph Engelmann
43d Illinois, Lt. Col. Adolph Dengler
61st Illinois, Maj. Simon P. Ohr
106th Illinois, Maj. John M. Hunt
12th Michigan, Col. William H. Graves
RICHMOND'S BRIGADE
Col. Jonathan Richmond
18th Illinois, Col. Daniel H. Brush
54th Illinois, Col. Greenville M. Mitchell
126th Illinois, Maj. William W. Wilshire
22d Ohio, Col. Oliver Wood
MONTGOMERY'S BRIGADE
Col. Milton Montgomery
40th Iowa, Col. John A. Garrett
3d Minnesota, Col. Chauncey W. Griggs
25th Wisconsin, Lt. Col. Samuel J. Nasmith
27th Wisconsin, Col. Conrad Krez

HERRON'S DIVISION
Maj. Gen. Francis J. Herron
1ST BRIGADE
Brig. Gen. William Vandever
37th Illinois, Col. John C. Black
26th Indiana, Col. John G. Clark

20th Iowa, Col. William McE. Dye
34th Iowa, Col. George W. Clark
38th Iowa, Col. Henry Hughes
Company E, 1st Missouri Light Artillery, Capt. Nelson Cole
Company F, 1st Missouri Light Artillery, Capt. Joseph Foust
2D BRIGADE
Brig. Gen. William W. Orme
94th Illinois, Col. John McNulta
19th Iowa, Lt. Col. Daniel Kent
20th Wisconsin, Col. Henry Bertram
Company B, 1st Missouri Light Artillery, Capt. Martin Welfley
UNATTACHED CAVALRY
Col. Cyrus Bussey
5th Illinois Cavalry, Maj. Thomas A. Apperson
3d Iowa Cavalry (six companies), Maj. Oliver H.P. Scott
4th Iowa Cavalry, Lt. Col. Simneon D. Swan
2d Wisconsin Cavalry (seven companies), Col. Thomas Stephens

DISTRICT OF NORTHEAST LOUISIANA
Brig. Gen. Jeremiah C. Sullivan
Brig. Gen. Elias S. Dennis
DETACHED BRIGADE
Col. George W. Neeley
63d Illinois, Col. Joseph B. McCown
108th Illinois, Lt. Col. Charles Turner
120th Illinois, Col. George W. McKeaig
131st Illinois, Col. George W. Neeley, Maj. Joseph L. Purvis
10th Illinois Cavalry (4 companies), Maj. Elvis P. Shaw
AFRICAN BRIGADE
(Post of Milliken's Bend)
Col. Isaac F. Shephard; Col. Hermann Leib
Lt. Col. Charles J. Paine
8th Louisiana (African Descent), Col. Hiram Scofield
9th Louisiana (African Descent), Col. Hermann Lieb,
Maj. Erastus N. Owens, Lt. Col. Charles J. Paine

11th Louisiana (African Descent), Col. Edwin W. Chamberlain,
Lt. Col. Cyrus Sears
13th Louisiana (African Descent), Lt. H. Knoll
1st Mississippi (African Descent), Lt. Col. A. Watson Webber
3d Mississippi (African Descent), Col. Richard H. Ballinger
(Post of Goodrich's Landing)
Col. William F. Wood
1st Arkansas (African Descent), Lt. Col. James W. Campbell
10th Louisiana (African Descent), Lt. Col. Frederick M. Crandall
Post of Lake Providence
(1st Brigade, 6th Division, XVII Corps)
Brig. Gen. Hugh T. Reid
1st Kansas, Col. William Y. Roberts
16th Wisconsin, Col. Benjamin Allen

Chickasaw Bayou.
Courtesy of the Library of Congress

ORGANIZATION OF CONFEDERATE FORCES
ARMY OF VICKSBURG

Lt. Gen. John C. Pemberton

STEVENSON'S DIVISION
Maj. Gen. Carter L. Stevenson
1ST BRIGADE
Brig. Gen. Seth Barton
40th Georgia, Col. Abda Johnson, Lt. Col. Robert M. Young
41st Georgia, Col. William E. Curtiss
42d Georgia, Col. Robert J. Henderson
43d Georgia, Col. Skidmore Harris (k), Capt. Mathadeus M. Grantham
52d Georgia, Col. Charles D. Phillips (m), Maj. John J. Moore
Pettus Flying Artillery, Lt. Milton H. Trantham
Company A, Pointe Coupee Artillery, Lt. John Yoist
Company C, Pointe Coupee Artillery, Capt. Alexander Chust
2D BRIGADE
Brig. Gen. Alfred Cumming
34th Georgia, Col. James A.W. Johnson
36th Georgia, Col. Jesse A. Glenn, Maj. Charles E. Broyles
39th Georgia, Col. Joseph T. McConnel (w), Lt. Col. J.F.B. Jackson
56th Georgia, Col. Elihu P. Watkins (w), Lt. Col. John T. Slaughter
57th Georgia, Lt. Col. Cincinnatus S. Guyton, Col. William Barkuloo
Cherokee Georgia Artillery, Capt. Max Van Den Corput
3D BRIGADE
Brig. Gen. Edward D. Tracy (k)
Col. Isham W. Garrott*
Brig. Gen. Stephen D. Lee
20th Alabama, Col. Isham W. Garrott (k), Col. Edmund W. Pettus
23d Alabama, Col. Franklin K. Beck
30th Alabama, Col. Sharles M. Shelley, Capt. John C. Francis
31st Alabama, Col. Daniel R. Hundley (w),
Lt. Col. Thomas M. Arrington, Maj. George W. Mathieson
46th Alabama, Col. Michael L. Woods (c), Capt. George E. Brewer

Waddell's Alabama Battery, Capt. James F. Waddell
*Garrott was killed on June 7, 1863. His commission as a brigadier general, dated May 28, 1863, arrived after his death.

4TH BRIGADE
Col. Alexander W. Reynolds
3d Tennessee (Provisional Army), Col. Newton J. Lillard
31st Tennessee, Col. William M. Bradford
43d Tennessee, Col. James W. Gillespie
59th Tennessee, Col. William L. Eaken
3d Maryland Battery, Capt. Fred O. Claiborne (k),
Capt. John B. Rowan
Waul's Texas Legion
Col. Thomas N. Waul
1st Infantry Battalion, Maj. Eugene S. Bolling
2d Infantry Battalion, Lt. Col. James Wrigley
Zouave Battalion, Capt. J.B. Fleitas
Cavalry Detachment, Lt. Thomas J. Cleveland
Artillery Company, Capt. J.Q. Waul

ATTACHED
Company C, 1st Tennessee Cavalry, Capt. Richard S. Vandyke
Botetourt Virginia Artillery, Capt. John W. Johnston,
Lt. Francis G. Obenchain
Signal Corps Detachment, Lt. C.H. Barrott

FORNEY'S DIVISION
Maj. Gen. John H. Forney
1ST BRIGADE
Brig. Gen. Louis Hebert
3d Louisiana, Lt. Col. Samuel D. Russell, Maj. David Pierson (w)
21st Louisiana, Col. Isaac W. Patton,
22d Louisiana (detachment), Col. Charles H. Herrick (mw),
Lt. Col. John T. Plattsmier
36th Mississippi, Col. William W. Witherspoon
37th Mississippi, Col. Orlando S. Holland
38th Mississippi, Col. Preston Brent, Capt. Daniel B. Seal

43d Mississippi, Col. Richard Harrison
7th Mississippi Infantry Battalion, Capt. A.M. Dozier
Company C, 2d Alabama Artillery Battalion, Capt. T.K. Emanuel (k),
Lt. John R. Sclater
Appeal Arkansas Artillery, Capt. William N. Hogg, Lt. Christopher C.
Scott, Lt. R.N. Cotten
2D BRIGADE
Brig. Gen. John C. Moore
37th Alabama, Col. James F. Dowdell
40th Alabama, Col. John H. Higley
42d Alabama, Col. John W. Portis, Lt. Col. Thomas C. Lanier
35th Mississippi, Col. William S. Barry, Lt. Col. Charles R. Jordan
40th Mississippi, Col. Wallace B. Colbert
2d Texas, Col. Ashbel Smith
Companies A, C, D, E, G, I, and K, 1st Mississippi Light Artillery,
Col. William T. Withers
Sengstak's Alabama Battery, Capt. Henry H. Sengstak
Company B, Pointe Coupee Artillery, Capt. William A. Davidson

---

SMITH'S DIVISION
Maj. Gen. Martin Luther Smith
BALDWIN'S BRIGADE
Brig. Gen. William E. Baldwin
17th Louisiana, Col. Robert Richardson
31st Louisiana, Lt. Col. Sidney H. Griffin (k),
Lt. Col. James W. Draughon
4th Mississippi, Lt. Col. Thomas N. Adaire (w), Capt. Thomas P. Nelson
46th Mississippi, Col. Claudius W. Sears
Tobin's Tennessee Battery, Capt. Thomas F. Tobin
SHOUP'S BRIGADE
Brig. Gen. Francis A. Shoup
26th Louisiana, Col. Winchester Hall (w), Lt. Col. William C. Crow
27th Louisiana, Col. Leon D. Marks (k), Lt. Col. L.L. McLaurin (k),
Capt. Joseph T. Hatch
29th Louisiana, Col. Allen Thomas

McNally's Arkansas Battery, Capt. Francis McNally
VAUGHN'S BRIGADE
Brig. Gen. John C. Vaughn
60th Tennessee, Capt. J.W. Bachman
61st Tennessee, Lt. Col. James G. Rose
62d Tennessee, Col. John A. Rowan
**MISSISSIPPI STATE TROOPS
Brig. Gen. Jeptha V. Harris
5th Regiment, MST, Col. H.C. Robinson
3d Battalion, MST, Lt. Col. Thomas A. Burgis
**Under General Vaughn's command.
ATTACHED
14th Mississippi Light Artillery Battalion, Maj. Matthew S. Ward
Smyth's Company Mississippi Partisan Rangers, Capt. J.S. Smyth
Signal Corps Detachment, Capt. M.T. Davison

BOWEN'S DIVISION
Maj. Gen. John S. Bowen
1ST (MISSOURI) BRIGADE
Col. Francis M. Cockrell
1st Missouri, Col. Amos C. Riley
2d Missouri, Lt. Col. Pembroke Senteny (k), Maj. Thomas M. Carter
3d Missouri, Lt. Col. Finley L. Hubbard (mw), Col. William L. Gause,
Maj. James K. McDowell
5th Missouri, Lt. Col. Robert S. Bevier, Col. James McCown
6th Missouri, Col. Eugene Erwin (k), Maj. Stephen Cooper
Guibor's Missouri Battery, Capt. Henry Guibor, Lt. William Corkery,
Lt. Cornelius Heffernan
Landis' Missouri Battery, Capt. John C. Landis, Lt. John M. Langan
Wade's Missouri Battery, Lt. Richard C. Walsh
2D BRIGADE
Brig. Gen. Martin E. Green (k)
Col. Thomas P. Dockery
15th Arkansas, Lt. Col. William W. Reynolds, Capt. Caleb Davis
19th Arkansas, Col. Thomas P. Dockery, Capt. James K. Norwood

20th Arkansas, Col. D.W. Jones
21st Arkansas, Col. Jordan E. Cravens, Capt. A. Tyler
1st Arkansas Cavalry Battalion (dismounted), Capt. John J. Clark
12th Arkansas Sharpshooters Battalion, Capt. Griff Bayne,
Lt. John S. Bell
1st Missouri Cavalry (dismounted), Col. Elijah Gates,
Maj. William C. Parker
3d Missouri Cavalry (dismounted), Lt. Col. D. Todd Samuel,
Capt. Felix Lotspeich
3d Missouri Battery, Capt. William E. Dawson
Lowe's Missouri Battery, Capt. Schyler Lowe, Lt. Thomas B. Catron
RIVER DEFENSES
Col. Edward Higgins
1st Louisiana Heavy Artillery, Col. Charles A. Fuller,
Lt. Col. Daniel Beltzhoover
8th Louisiana Hevy Artillery Battalion, Maj. Frederick N. Ogden
22d Louisiana (detachment), Capt. Samuel Jones
1st Tennessee Heavy Artillery, Col. Andrew Jackson, Jr.
***Caruthers' Tennessee Battery, Capt. J.B. Caruthers
***Johnston's Tennessee Battery, Capt. T.N. Johnston
***Lynch's Tennessee Battery, Capt. John P. Lynch
Company L, 1st Mississippi Light Artillery, Capt. Samuel C. Bains
***These three companies were attached to the 1st Tennessee Heavy
ARTILLERY
MISCELLANEOUS
54th Alabama, Lt. Joel P. Abney
6th Mississippi (detachment), Maj. J.R. Stevens
City Guards, Capt. E.B. Martin
Signal Corps Detachment, Capt. C.A. King

ARMY OF RELIEF
Gen. Joseph E. Johnston

BRECKINRIDGE'S DIVISION
Maj. Gen. John C. Breckinridge

ADAM'S BRIGADE
Brig. Gen. Daniel W. Adams
32d Alabama, Lt. Col. Henry Maury
13th and 20th Louisiana (Consolidated), Col. Augustus Reichard
16th and 25th Louisiana (Consolidated), Col. Daniel Gober
19th Louisiana, Col. Wesley P. Winans
14th Louisiana Sharpshooters Battalion, Maj. John E. Austin

HELM'S BRIGADE
Brig. Gen. Benjamin H. Helm
41st Alabama, Col. Martin L. Stansel
2d Kentucky, Lt. Col. James W. Hewitt
4th Kentucky, Col. Joseph P. Nuckols, Lt. Col. John A. Adair
6th Kentucky, Lt. Col. Martin H. Cofer
9th Kentucky, Col. John W. Caldwell

STOVALL'S BRIGADE
Brig. Gen. Marcellus A. Stovall
1st and 3d Florida (Consolidated), Col. William S. Dilworth
4th Florida, Col. Edward Badger
47th Georgia, Col. George W.M. Williams
60th North Carolina, Col. Washington M. Hardy,
Lt. Col. James M. Ray

ARTILLERY
Maj. Rice E. Graves
Johnston (Tennessee) Artillery, Capt. John W. Mebane
Cobb's Kentucky Battery, Capt. Robert Cobb
5th Company, Washington Artillery, Capt. Cuthbert H. Slocomb

FRENCH'S DIVISION
Maj. Gen. Samuel G. French

McNAIR'S BRIGADE
Brig. Gen. Evander McNair
1st Arkansas Mounted Rifles (dismounted), Col. Robert W. Harper,
Lt. Col. Daniel H. Reynolds
2d Arkansas Mounted Rifles (dismounted), Col. J. A. Williamson
4th Arkansas, Col. Henry G. Bunn

25th and 31st Arkansas (Consolidated), Col. Thomas H. McCray
39th North Carolina, Col. David Coleman
MAXEY'S BRIGADE
Brig. Gen. Samuel B. Maxey
4th Louisiana, Lt. Col. William F. Pennington, Col. Samuel E. Hunter
30th Louisiana (battalion), Lt. Col. Thomas Shields
42d Tennessee, Lt. Col. Isaac N. Hulme
46th and 55th Tennessee (Consolidated), Col. Alexander J. Brown,
Lt. Col. Gideon B. Black
48th Tennessee, Col. William M. Voorhees
49th Tennessee, Maj. David A. Lynn
53d Tennessee, Lt. Col. John R. White
1st Texas Sharpshooter Battalion, Maj. James Burnet
EVAN'S BRIGADE
Brig. Gen. Nathan G. Evans
17th South Carolina, Col. Fitz William McMasters
18th South Carolina, Col. William H. Wallace
22d South Carolina, Lt. Col. James O'Connell
23d South Carolina, Col. Henry L. Benbow
26th South Carolina, Col. Alexander D. Smith
Holcombe Legion, Lt. Col. William J.Crawley, Maj. Martin G. Zeigler
ARTILLERY
Fenner's (Louisiana) Battery, Capt. Charles E. Fenner
Macbeth (South Carolina) Artillery, Lt. B.A. Jeter
Culpeper's (South Carolina) Battery, Capt. James F. Culpeper

LORING'S DIVISION
Maj. Gen. William W. Loring
ADAMS' BRIGADE
Brig. Gen. Lloyd Tilghman (k)
Col. Arthur E. Reynolds
Brig. Gen. John Adams
1st Confederate Battalion, Lt. Col. George H. Forney
6th Mississippi, Col. Robert Lowry
14th Mississippi, Lt. Col. Washington L. Doss

15th Mississippi, Col. Michael Farrell
20th Mississippi, Col. Daniel R. Russell, Lt. Col. William N. Brown
23d Mississippi, Col. Joseph M. Wells
26th Mississippi, Col. Arthur E. Reynolds, Maj. Tully F. Parker
Lookout (Tennessee) Artillery, Capt. Robert L. Barry
BUFORD'S BRIGADE
Brig. Gen. Abraham Buford
27th Alabama, Col. James Jackson
35th Alabama, Col. Edward Goodwin
54th Alabama, Col. Alpheus Baker, Maj. T.H. Shackelford
55th Alabama, Col. John Snodgrass
9th Arkansas, Col. Isaac L. Dunlop
3d Kentucky, Col. Albert P. Thompson
7th Kentucky, Col. Edward Crossland
8th Kentucky, Col. Hylan B. Lyon, Lt. Col. A.R. Shacklett
12th Louisiana, Col. Thomas M. Scott
3d Missouri Cavalry (dismounted), Lt. Col. D. Todd Samuels
Company A, Pointe Coupee Artillery, Capt. Alcide Bouanchaud
FEATHERSTON'S BRIGADE
Brig. Gen. Winfield S. Featherston
Col. John A. Orr
3d Mississippi, Col. Thomas A. Mellon, Maj. Samuel A. Dyer
22d Mississippi, Col. Frank S. Schaller, Lt. Col. H.J. Reid
31st Mississippi, Col. John A. Orr, Lt. Col. Marcus D.L. Stephens
33d Mississippi, Col. David W. Hurst
1st Mississippi Sharpshooter Battalion, Maj. William A. Rayburn,
Maj. James M. Stigler
Charpentier's Alabama Battery, Capt. Stephen Charpentier
Company C, 14th Mississippi Artillery Battalion, Capt. J. Culbertson

---

WALKER'S DIVISION
Maj. Gen. William H.T. Walker
ECTOR'S BRIGADE
Brig. Gen. Matthew D. Ector
9th Texas, Lt. Col. Miles A. Dillard

10th Texas Cavalry (dismounted), Lt. Col. C.R. Earp
14th Texas Cavalry (dismounted), Col. John L. Camp
32d Texas Cavalry (dismounted), Col. Julius A. Andrews
Battalion, 43d Mississippi, Capt. M. Pounds
Battalion, 40th Alabama, Maj. Thomas O. Stone
McNally's Arkansas Battery, Lt. F.A. Moore
GREGG'S BRIGADE
Brig. Gen. John Gregg
3d Tennessee, Col. Calvin H. Walker
10th Tennessee, Lt. Col. William Grace
30th Tennessee, Col. Randall MacGavock (k), Lt. Col. James .J. Turner
41st Tennessee, Col. Robert Farquharson
50th Tennessee, Lt. Col. Thomas W. Beaumont (w), Col. Cyrus A. Sugg
1st Tennessee Infantry Battalion, Maj. Stephen H. Colms

7th Texas, Col. Hiram B. Granbury
Bledsoe's Missouri Battery, Capt. Hiram M. Bledsoe
GIST'S BRIGADE
Brig. Gen. Gist
46th Georgia, Col. Peyton H. Colquitt
8th Georgia, Capt. Zachariah L. Watters
16th South Carolina, Col. James McCullough
24th South Carolina, Col. C.H. Stevens
Ferguson's South Carolina Battery, Capt. T.B. Ferguson
WILSON'S BRIGADE
Col. Claudius C. Wilson
25th Georgia, Lt. Col. Andrew J. Williams
29th Georgia, Col. William J. Young
30th Georgia, Col. T.W. Mangham

Big Black River
battlefield,
May 17, 1863.
*Courtesy of the
Library of Congress*

1st Georgia Sharpshooter Battalion, Maj. Arthur Shaaff
4th Louisiana Infantry Battalion, Lt. Col. John McEnery
Martin's Georgia Battery, Lt. Evan P. Howell

CAVALRY DIVISION
Brig. Gen. William H. Jackson
1ST BRIGADE
Brig. Gen. George B. Cosby
1st Mississippi Cavalry, Col. R.A. Pinson
4th Mississippi Cavalry, Col. James Gordon, Maj. J.L. Harris
28th Mississippi Cavalry, Col. Peter B. Starke
Wirt Adams' Mississippi Cavalry, Col. William Wirt Adams
Ballentine's Mississippi Cavalry, Lt. Col. William L. Maxwell
17th Mississippi Cavalry Battalion (State Troops), Maj. Abner C. Steede
Clark's Missouri Battery, Capt. Houston King
2D BRIGADE
Brig. Gen. John W. Whitfield
3d Texas Cavalry, Col. Giles S. Boggess
6th Texas Cavalry, Col. Lawrence S. Ross, Maj. Jack Wharton
9th Texas Cavalry, Col. Dudley W. Jones
27th Texas Cavalry (also called 1st Texas Legion), Lt. Col.
John H. Broocks
Bridge's Arkansas Cavalry Battalion, Maj. H.W. Bridges
ESCORTS AND GUARDS
Company A, 7th Tennessee Cavalry, Capt. W.F. Taylor
Independent Company Louisiana Cavalry, Capt. J.Y. Webb
Provost Guard (Company D 4th Mississippi Cavalry),
Capt. James Ruffin
RESERVE ARTILLERY
Maj. W.C. Preston
Columbus Georgia Battery, Capt. Edward Croft
Durrive's Louisana Battery, Capt. E. Durrive, Jr.
Battery B, Palmetto South Carolina Artillery, Capt. J. Wates

TRANS-MISSISSIPPI DEPARTMENT
Lt. Gen. E. Kirby Smith

DISTRICT OF WESTERN LOUISIANA
Maj. Gen. Richard Taylor

WALKER'S DIVISION
Maj. Gen. John G. Walker
MCCULLOCH'S BRIGADE
Brig. Gen. Henry E. McCulloch
16th Texas, Col. George Flournoy
17th Texas, Col. R.T.P. Allen
19th Texas, Col. Richard Waterhouse
16th Texas Cavalry (dismounted), Lt. Col. E.P. Gregg (w),
Maj. W.W. Diamond (w), Capt. J.D. Woods
Edgar's Battery, Capt. William Edgar
HAWES' BRIGADE
Brig. Gen. James M. Hawes
13th Texas Cavalry (dismounted), Lt. Col. A.F. Crawford
12th Texas, Col. O. Young
18th Texas, Lt. Col. D.B. Culbertson
22d Texas, Col. R. Hubbard
Halderman's Battery, Capt. Horace Halderman
RANDALL'S BRIGADE
Col. Horace Randal
11th Texas, Col. O.M. Roberts
14th Texas, Col. E. Clark
28th Texas Cavalry (dismounted), Col. E.H. Baxter
6th Texas Cavalry Battalion (dismounted), Maj. R.S. Gould
Daniels' Battery, Capt. J.M. Daniels
TAPPAN'S BRIGADE
Brig. Gen. James C. Tappan
27th Arkansas, Col. J.R. Shaler
33d Arkansas, Col. H.L. Grinsted
38th Arkansas, Col. R.G. Shaver

CAVALRY (NOT BRIGADED)
13th Louisiana Cavalry Battalion, Col. Frank A. Bartlett
15th Louisiana Cavalry Battalion, Lt. Col. Isaac F. Harrison
PARSON'S CAVALRY BRIGADE
Col. William H. Parsons
12th Texas Cavalry, Lt. Col. A.B. Burleson
21st Texas Cavalry, Col. B.W. Carter
Pratt's Texas Battery, Capt. J.H. Pratt

Bibliography

Alger, John. *Definitions and Doctrine of the Military Art: Past and Present.* West Point, NY: Department of History, USMA, 1979.

Arnold, James. *Grant Wins the War.* NY: John Wiley & Sons, 1997.

Ballard, Michael. *The Campaign for Vicksburg.* Fort Washington, PA: Eastern National, 1998.

Ballard, Michael. *Civil War Mississippi: A Guide.* Jackson: University Press of Mississippi, 2000.

Ballard, Michael. *Vicksburg: The Campaign that Opened the Mississippi.* Chapel Hill: University of North Carolina Press, 2004.

Ballard, Michael. *Pemberton: The General Who Lost Vicksburg.* Jackson: University Press of Mississippi, 1991.

Baradell, Lang. "Mushroom Cloud at Vicksburg," *Civil War Times,* October 2005: 50–62.

Barrett, John Gilchrist. *Sherman's March Through the Carolinas.* Chapel Hill: University of North Carolina Press, 1956.

Bearss, Margie. *Sherman's Forgotten Campaign: The Meridian Expedition.* Baltimore, MD: Gateway Press, Inc, 1987.

Bearss, Edwin Cole. *Campaign for Vicksburg.* 3 vols. Dayton, OH: Morningside House, 1986.

Bearss, Edwin. *Receding Tide: Vicksburg and Gettysburg, The Campaigns that Changed the Civil War.* Washington, DC: National Geographic, 2010.

Beringer, Richard, et al. *Why the South Lost the Civil War.* Athens: The University of Georgia Press, 1986.

Blanchard, Kenneth. *Leading at a Higher Level.* Upper Saddle River, NJ: FT Press, 2006.

Boatner, Mark. *The Civil War Dictionary.* NY: David McKay Company, Inc, 1959.

Bonekemper, Edward. *Grant and Lee: Victorious American and Vanquished Virginian.* Westport, CN: Praeger, 2008.

Bowman, S. M. and R. B. Irwin. *Sherman and His Campaigns: A Military Biography.* NY: Charles B. Richardson, 1865.

Chaitin, Peter. *The Coastal War.* Alexandria, VA: Time-Life Books, 1984.

Cohen, William. *The Stuff of Heroes.* Marietta, GA: Longstreet, 1998.

Connelly, Thomas. *Autumn of Glory: The Army of Tennessee, 1862–1865.* Baton Rouge: Louisiana State University Press, 1971.

Covey, Stephen. *The 7 Habits of Highly Effective People.* NY: Simon and Schuster, 1989.

Cozzens, Peter. *The Darkest Days of the War: The Battles of Iuka & Corinth.* Chapel Hill: The University of North Carolina Press, 1997.

Cubbison, Douglas. *The Entering Wedge: The Battle of Port Gibson, 1 May

The head of the canal, opposite Vicksburg, now being cut by Command of General Grant. *Courtesy of the Library of Congress*

1863. Danville, VA: McNaughton and Gunn, 2002.

Current, Richard. "The Lincoln Presidents" in *Presidential Studies Quarterly*, Vol. 9, No. 1, The Quality and Character of National Leadership (Winter, 1979): 25–35.

Creech, Bill. *The Five Pillars of TQM*. NY: Truman Talley Books/Plume, 1995.

Czeslik, Knut. "*Aufstragstaktik*: Thoughts of a German Officer," in *Infantry* (January–February 1991): 10–11.

Daniel, Larry. *Days of Glory: The Army of the Cumberland, 1861–1865*. Baton Rouge:Louisiana State University Press, 2004.

Daniel, Larry. *Shiloh: The Battle that Changed the Civil War*. NY: Simon & Schuster, 1997.

Donald, David. *Why the North Won the Civil War*. NY: Collier Books, 1960.

Donovan, Timothy et al. *The American Civil War*. West Point, NY: USMA, 1980.

Dougherty, Kevin et al. *Battles of the Civil War, 1861–1865*. NY: Barnes & Noble, 2007.

Dougherty, Kevin. "Sherman's Meridian Campaign: A Practice Run for the March to the Sea," *Mississippi History Now*, http://mshistory.k12.ms.us/articles/2/shermans-meridian-campaign-a-practice-run-for-the-march-to-the-sea.

Dougherty, Kevin. *Weapons of Mississippi*. Jackson: University Press of Mississippi, 2010.

Doughty, Robert. *American Military History and the Evolution of Western Warfare*. Lexington, MA: D. C. Heath and Company, 1996.

Dowdey, Clifford. *The Land They Fought For*. Garden City, NY: Doubleday and Company, 1955.

Eisenhower, John S. D. *Agent of Destiny: The Life and Times of General Winfield Scott*. NY: The Free Press, 1997.

Eisenhower, John S. D. *So Far From God: The U. S. War with Mexico, 1846–1848*. NY: Random House, 1989.

Flanagan, E. M. "Hands-On Leadership," in *Army* (April 1992): 5455.

Flood, Charles Bracelen. *Grant and Sherman: The Friendship that Won the Civil War*. NY: Farrar, Straus, and Giroux, 2005.

FM 3-0, *Operations*. Washington, DC: Headquarters, Department of the Army, 2001.

FM 6-22, *Army Leadership*. Washington, DC: Headquarters, Department of the Army, 2006.

Foote, Shelby. *The Civil War: A Narrative: Fredericksburg to Meridian*. Vol 2. NY: Random House, 1963.

Foster, Buck. *Sherman's Mississippi Campaign*. Tuscaloosa: University of Alabama Press, 2006.

Franks, Frederick and Tom Clancy. *Into the Storm: A Study in Command*. Itasca: Putman Publishing Group, 1997.

Freeman, Douglas Southall. *Lee's Lieutenants: A Study in Command*. 3 vols. NY: Charles Scribner's Sons, 1942–1944.

Freeman, Douglas Southall. *R. E. Lee: A Biography,* 4 vols. NY: Charles Scribner's Sons, 1934.

Fuller, J. F. C. *The Generalship of Ulysses S. Grant*. Bloomington: Indiana University Press, 1958.

Gabel, Christopher, "Battle Command Incompetencies: John C. Pemberton in the Vicksburg Campaign," in *Studies in Battle Command*, ed by Faculty Combat Studies Institute, Fort Leavenworth, KS: US Army Command and General Staff College: 43–49.

Grant's transports running the batteries.
Courtesy of the Library of Congress

The surrender at Vicksburg, July 4, 1863.
Courtesy of the Library of Congress

Gabel, Christopher. *Railroad Generalship: Foundations of Civil War Strategy.* Fort Leavenworth, KS: Combat Studies Institute, 1997.

Gabel, Christopher. *Staff Ride Handbook for The Vicksburg Campaign, December 1862–July 1863.* Fort Leavenworth, KS: Combat Studies Institute, 2001.

Grabau, Walter. *Confusion Compounded: The Pivotal Battle of Raymond, 12 May 1863.*

Danville, VA: McNaughton and Gunn, 2001.

Grant, Ulysses. *Personal Memoirs of U. S. Grant.* NY: Da Capo Press, Inc, 1982.

Grant, Ulysses, "The Vicksburg Campaign," In *Battles and Leaders*, vol III, Edison, NJ:

Castle, 1995, 493–539.

Greenleaf, Robert. *Servant Leadership.* Mahwah, NJ: Paulist Press, 2002

Groom, Winston. *Vicksburg, 1863.* NY: Vintage Books, 2009.

Harari, Oren. *The Leadership Secrets of Colin Powell.* NY: McGraw-Hill, 2002.

Hart, B. H. Liddell. *Strategy.* NY: New American Library, 1974.

Hartje, Robert. *Van Dorn: The Life and Times of a Confederate General.* Nashville, TN: Vanderbilt University Press, 2007.

Hattaway, Herman and Archer Jones. *How the North Won: A Military History of the Civil War.* Chicago: University of Illinois Press, 1983.

Johnston, Joseph. "Jefferson Davis and the Mississippi Campaign." In *Battles and Leaders*, vol III, Edison, NJ: Castle, 1995, 472–482.

Joint Pub 3-0, *Operations*. Washington, DC: Joint Chiefs of Staff, 17 Sept 2006.

Joint Pub 5-0, *Joint Operational Planning*. Washington, DC: Joint Chiefs of Staff, 26 Dec 2006.

Jomini, Baron Antoine Henri de. *The Art of War*. London: Greenhill Books, 1996.

Jones, Archer. *Civil War Command & Strategy: The Process of Victory and Defeat*. NY: The Free Press, 1992.

Jones, Archer. *Confederate Strategy from Shiloh to Vicksburg*, Baton Rouge: Louisiana State University Press, 1961.

Keegan, John. *The Mask of Command*. NY: Viking Penguin, 1997.

Korn, Jerry. *War on the Mississippi: Grant's Vicksburg Campaign*. Alexandria, VA: Time-Life Books, 1985.

Lencioni, Patrick. *The Five Dysfunctions of a Team*. San Francisco, CA: Jossey-Bass, 2002.

Logan, John. *The Volunteer Soldier in America*, 1887, rpt, Whitefish, MT: Kessinger Publishing, LLC, 2008.

Loughborough, Mary. *My Cave Life in Vicksburg*. Wilmington, N.C.: Broadfoot, 1989.

Lowney, Chris. *Heroic Leadership*. Chicago, IL: Loyola Press, 2003.

Macartney, Clarence. *Mr. Lincoln's Admirals*. NY: Funk & Wagnalls Co, 1956.

Marszalek, John. *Sherman: A Soldier's Quest for Order*. NY: The Free Press, 1993.

Maxwell, John. *The 17 Indisputable Laws of Teamwork*. Nashville, TN: Thomas Nelson, Inc, 2001.

McFeely, William. *Grant: A Biography*. NY: W. W. Norton & Company, 1982.

Millett, Allan and Peter Maslowski. *For the Common Defense: A Military History of the United States of America*. NY: The Free Press, 1984.

Morgan, Michael. "Digging to Victory at Vicksburg," in *America's Civil War*. July 2003.

Musicant, Ivan. *Divided Waters: The Naval History of the Civil War*. Edison, NJ: Castle Books, 1995.

Nevin, David. *The Road to Shiloh.* Alexandria, VA: Time-Life Books, 1983.

"News of the Day: The Operations Against Vicksburgh," *New York Times,* January 12, 1863, 4.

Northouse, Peter. *Leadership Theory and Practice.* Thousand Oaks, CA: Sage Publications, 2003.

Oldroyd, Osborn. *A Soldier's Story of the Siege of Vicksburg. From the Diary of Osborn H. Oldroyd.* Springfield, IL: self-published, 1885.

Peter, Laurence. *The Peter Principle: Why Things Always Go Wrong.* NY: HarperBusiness, 2009.

Reaves, George. "Corinth." In *The Civil War Battlefield Guide.* Ed. Frances Kennedy. Boston, MA: Houghton Mifflin, 1990, 87–90.

Reed, Rowena. *Combined Operations in the Civil War.* Annapolis, MD: Naval Institute Press, 1978.

Rosecrans, William. "The Battle of Corinth," In *Battles and Leaders of the Civil War,* vol II. Edison, NJ: Castle Books, nd, 737–757.

Sears, Stephen. *To the Gates of Richmond: The Peninsular Campaign.* NY: Ticknor and Fields, 1992.

Shea, William and Terry Winschel. *Vicksburg Is the Key: The Struggle for the Mississippi River.* Lincoln: University of Nebraska Press, 2003.

Sherman, William. *Memoirs of General William T. Sherman.* NY: The Library of America, 1990.

Smith, Jean Edward. *Grant.* NY: Simon & Schuster, 2002.

"Strategic Leadership Primer." Carlisle Barracks, PA: United States Army War College, 1998.

Stuckey, Scott. "Joint Operations in the Civil War," in *Joint Forces Quarterly,* (Autumn/Winter 94–95): 92–105.

Thomas, Emory. *Robert E. Lee.* NY: W. W. Norton, 1997.

United States War Department. *War of the Rebellion: A Compilation of the Official Records of the Union and Confederate Armies.* Vol XXXII. Washington, DC: Government Printing Office, 1880–1900.

Wallace, Edward. *General William Jenkins Worth: Monterey's Forgotten Hero.* Dallas, TX: Southern Methodist University Press, 1953.

Weigley, Russell. *The History of the United States Army.* NY: MacMillan Publishing Company, Inc, 1967.

Williams, T. Harry. *The History of American Wars.* NY: Alfred A. Knopf, 1981.

Winschel, Terrence. "Chickasaw Bayou: A Battlefield Guide." Np:nd.

Woodworth, Steven. *Nothing but Victory: The Army of the Tennessee 1861–1865*. NY: Alfred A. Knopf, 2005.

Woodworth, Steven. *Grant's Lieutenants: From Cairo to Vicksburg*. Lawrence: University Press of Kansas, 2001.

Wyeth, John Allan. *That Devil Forrest*. Baton Rouge: Louisiana State University Press, 1989.